RESTRUCTURING
AMERICAN
EDUCATION

RESTRUCTURING
AMERICAN
EDUCATION

INNOVATIONS AND ALTERNATIVES

Edited by
RAY C. RIST

Transaction Books
New Brunswick, New Jersey
Distributed by E. P. Dutton & Co., Inc.

FOR PAUL
With the hope that his experience in schools
may be liberating rather than destructive

Contents

Introduction

RAY C. RIST

Americans have always been interested in education, but the decade of the 1960s witnessed an unprecedented output of writing on the condition of the nation's public schools. Central concepts, such as "crisis," "demise," "collapse" or "failure," underlie the message: the public schools have not lived up to our expectations. Dissatisfaction with the way we educate our citizens has been compounded by disillusionment. The educational establishment in this country has until very recently received larger amounts of financial support every year, but this has not measurably improved the educational process. Nor is it that schools have failed due to lack of participation in their programs. Schooling in the United States is compulsory and students are essentially a captive audience. Whatever innovations schools have wanted to attempt, subjects have been available for the experiment. What then has gone wrong? Why the crisis of confidence in America's "secular religion"? The answers can be found by exam-

1

ining the expectations held for public education and the structures created to fulfill those expectations.

Historically, the public schools in the United States have been justified by the twin beliefs that an enlightened citizenry is necessary to preserve democratic institutions and that schooling enhances opportunities for social and economic mobility. These two assumptions have complemented the emphasis upon individuality and competition prevalent in the American ethos. Schools were to enhance in each individual a critical spirit, the desire to question and to reject dictates given without explanation. Schools also were to serve as the means whereby those of low social origin but significant intellectual ability and determination could achieve mobility. Higher social and economic positions were assumed to be open to those who took advantage of their opportunities. Schooling would allow a "filtering to the top," contributing to the development of a meritocracy in which social class origin was of small concern.

Objectively, one could conclude that the schools have fulfilled neither of these expectations. There is little indication that individuality and independence of thought have been fostered and encouraged in the schools. Such critics as Charles Silberman and Jules Henry have convincingly argued that schools destroy creativity in children and instead reinforce docility, passivity and conformity to institutional values and rules. Children assume the role of a client, accommodating to the moral order as interpreted by the schools. Failure to conform earns the student the label of "disruptive," "unsocialized," "rude," "delinquent" or perhaps "uneducable." There is also strong evidence that schools do *not* serve as vehicles for mobility, but reinforce the current social, political and economic distinctions that crisscross this society. What mobility does occur often results when an individual sheds a cultural background that is at odds with the school and assumes the values of the school. Schools develop ways of "cooling out" those who cannot make this transition, through tracking systems, denial of rewards in the schooling system and reinforcement of negative self-concepts. Essentially, the student leaves the public schools in much the same societal position that he had when he entered. In his major study for the United States Office of Education, *Equality of Educational Opportunity,* James Coleman noted:

> One implication stands out above all: That schools bring little influence to bear on a child's achievement that is independent of his background and general social context; and that this very lack of independent effect means that the inequalities imposed on children by their home, neighborhood and peer environment are carried along to become the inequalities with which they confront adult life at the end of school. For equality of educational opportunity through the schools must imply a strong effect of schools that is independent of the child's immediate social environment, and that strong independent effect is not present in American schools.

THE FAILURE OF CURRENT REFORM EFFORTS

In large measure, then, the public schools have not met the expectations set for them. Under what conditions could present bureaucratic and institutional structures be altered to meet those expectations, and yet retain their current power, authority and decision-making positions? I suggest that there are no such conditions. The way the educational bureaucracy is organized and the values it espouses are nearly antithetical to the goals of free inquiry and social mobility. But schools by themselves cannot achieve a radical restructuring of the political, economic and social institutions in American society. Reversing the decline of democracy in the United States and increasing avenues for mobility can occur only through fundamental reform in the entire society. Yet the schools' complicity in maintaining the status quo makes imperative that they be included in any such restructuring.

Schools have done both themselves and the society a disservice by continuing to maintain, or by refusing to deny, that they could in fact meet public expectations with more funding, larger facilities and the implementation of modest reforms. The schools' sometimes frantic attempts to enhance individuality and encourage mobility have had results that were anything but desirable. When the schools were confronted with public awareness that large numbers of poor white and black children were not performing at the pedagogical levels established for middle-class students, a frontal assault was directed upon the cultural values and behavioral patterns of those who did not fit the accepted norms. This assault was defended as an attempt to eradicate "cultural deprivation." Another way that schools planned to improve their performance was by introducing technological gadgets and gimmicks. Any number of devices ranging from "talking" typewriters to "responsive" tape recorders to "individualized" audio-visual kits were employed to deal with such disparate problems as reading difficulties and "unmotivated" students. Superficially, significant changes resulted from the flurry of activity in the schools, particularly during the 1960s. But things are not always as they appear. The bureaucratic structure, the normative system and the configurations of power remain essentially untouched. The illusion has been movement; the reality has been preservation of the status quo.

Recent attempts at educational reform in the United States have failed for several reasons. First, much reform dialogue has occurred among those who are already convinced that some type of change is necessary. As a consequence, the reformers have appeared to avoid confronting those in decision-making positions as well as parents and school staff. Much discussion on school reform has occurred in a vacuum, away from those who will ultimately have to evaluate and decide upon the merits and opportunities available in different reform proposals. The lack of dialogue has led to situations in which reforms have been initiated, but thwarted or not supported due to absence of information.

A second reason for the failure of reform efforts has been the inability to spell out the costs and benefits that might accrue from a particular reform attempt. The costs and benefits should have been articulated along several dimensions—the economic, the pedagogical and the political. There is often the implicit notion that those who would be directly affected by the effort must take a "leap of faith" and that undue attention to cost-benefit analysis would stifle the creative thrust. Parents, administrators and teachers have often, with good reason, refused to take such leaps.

Concurrent with the failure to articulate specific costs and benefits of educational reform has been the failure to examine the inherent contradictions and conflicts within the reform movement. Perhaps the clearest example of this confusion has surrounded the notion of "community control." On the one hand, reformers have moved toward what Michael Katz terms "democratic localism," in which the emphasis is upon local control of the school—its activities, its curriculum and its staff—by members of the immediate district surrounding the school. There is talk of redistributing power away from the centralized bureaucracy which governs the schools to the neighborhood. The call for community control has most often emerged from poor and black communities and has found strong support among leftist and radical proponents of educational change. What has not been as extensively debated and elaborated upon are some of the by-products of community control which are not congruent with democratic theory. For example, in the Ocean Hill-Brownsville attempt at community control, the bylaws of the local governing board established that they possessed the absolute right to control all activities within the school. The dilemmas for a civil libertarian who, in advocating the decentralization of control to the community would be allowing the substitution of one form of absolute authority for another, need to be articulated.

Another example of the conflicts inherent in the community control approach can be observed in the debate over integrating schools by race and social class. Integration in schools would appear to vary in inverse proportion to the degree of autonomy of the neighborhood school. If urban schools come under the control of local neighborhoods which are themselves segregated by race and class, how is integration to be achieved?

In the cities, neighborhood schools have usually meant segregated schools. To break down such segregation barriers, Thomas Pettigrew, among others, has suggested the formation of large educational parks that would draw students from diverse social and racial areas of the city. Yet strong central authority would be essential to create such a park and to have the authority to bring together the various groups of students. In short, the opposite of integrated schools would be small, flexible, local units controlled by the community. I offer these examples not to belittle or degrade community control efforts, for I am sympathetic to this approach, especially in its attempts to debureaucratize education. But if the current reform failures in this area are to be reversed, there must be a conceptual clarity about the fundamental assumptions.

Educational reform in the United States has also been thwarted by inaccurate perception of the genesis of the problems which the schools face. In the numerous "horror story" descriptions of urban schools, for example, the cause of the crisis is attributed to such diverse circumstances as the flight of whites to the suburbs, the deterioration of housing in the central city, the over-crowding of urban classrooms, the decline of the city tax base, and the lack of two-parent families among the poor. A common theme among these explanations is that the problems which schools face are overwhelmingly outside the schools and their bureaucratic structures. An "external social forces" model is suggested. By blaming the children's failure to learn (by literally any measure of learning one would care to use) on forces outside the schools, the present administration and organization is assumed to be viable and adequate to facilitate the children's learning. Only because of any number of dysfunctional forces outside the domain and influence of the schools, but which directly impinge upon its activities, are the schools handicapped and unable to operate in a manner they would desire. Being powerless to effect change in these external social forces, the schools must "merely do the best they can" in the face of adversity. As the problems continue to manifest themselves, the schools can only respond with such ameliorative steps as more blackboards, more social workers, smaller classrooms and more testing. Under such circumstances, learning is possible, but certainly not probable.

Given the framework in which this model locates the problems of American urban education, the solution is seen in terms of finding the correct "mix" of therapeutic remedies to alleviate the manifested ills. For example, one may add more paraprofessionals while subtracting some grading practices. Whatever the mix ultimately turns out to be, it is always "safe." It does not question the basic premises of the institution of schooling—its long and compulsory attendance, age-sex segregation, peer competitiveness and inherent boredom. The dilemmas of the schools are conventionally seen to require programmatic response rather than problematic analysis.

The position that the source of the crisis in American

education lies outside the structure of the schools themselves contains several implicit assumptions. First and most
important is that "problems" *do* exist. Second, these
problems are such that they are of concern to the
community, the school administration and the teaching
staff. These assumptions legitimate the school's intervention in whatever ways it may deem effective. Social
workers, psychologists, school juvenile officials, counselors
and even police are defined as having an appropriate role in
the functioning of the school.

By establishing that the schools' problems originate
outside of the schools themselves, any analysis of the
structure and practices of the schools is itself blunted. The
political ramifications of this deflection of the analysis are
crucial; the established positions of authority and
decision-making within the educational establishment remain unthreatened. The disenfranchised parents are sent
scurrying about to mend their family patterns, provide
quiet places for the children to study and demonstrate
concern for their child's education by attending meetings
of the Parent-Teachers Association. Thus the educational
bureaucracy transforms political situations into administrative ones, thereby legitimating administrative decision-
making. Attempts to establish "community control" in
any number of school districts provide examples of the
depoliticalization of educational issues.

The assumption that one can blame the schools' failure
to meet societal expectations to any number of causes
outside the structure of the educational system is incorrect
both in its assessment of cause and its prescription for
cure. A crucial reason schools fail is that they neither
recognize nor come to grips with the essential political
nature of schooling in American society. Ignoring the
political dimension of education and educational systems
has placed an undue and misguided emphasis upon
ameliorative approaches which assume that somehow the

problems are external to the schools themselves. The parameters which define the schooling experience in this country are in large measure the result of various political decisions, from compulsory attendance to state certification of teachers and the curriculum they teach, to modes of citizen taxation and the location of the school buildings themselves. To assume that schooling is a consequence of a series of apolitical administrative decisions necessarily results in large and vital gaps in the analysis of the role and function of schools as an institution in American society.

It does not take great insight to predict that attempts to alleviate the problems of schools based on the apolitical model outlined above would not provide the desired results. The institutional arrangements by which schools operate are not based solely on apolitical administrative procedures. Rather, as Charles Silberman has noted:

... education is becoming the gateway to the middle and upper reaches of society, which means that the schools and colleges thereby become the gatekeepers of the society. And this transforms the nature of educational institutions. They are inevitably politicized, for whoever controls the gateways to affluence and social position exercises political power, whether he likes it or not, and whether he is conscious of the fact or not.

It would appear that with regards to education in this country the decision-making process has been able to proceed on the basis of an apolitical model because there has been no other power base to challenge the decisions of the administrative policymakers. In short, decisions became apolitical due to lack of opposition and the resultant one-sidedness of the power distribution. With community control, the formation of groups who disputed the decisions and policies of the school administrators resulted in the politicalization of educational decision-making. This attempt to rebalance the policy-making process is being undertaken by parents and community groups as well as teachers, all of whom have organized in recognition of the political ramifications inherent in educational systems.

ALTERNATIVES TO FAILURE

Having suggested some of the reasons for the current crisis in American education, it is only proper to ask, "What is to be done?" As noted, fundamental change in the current institutional practices of this nation's educational bureaucracy implies the necessity of fundamental social reform. But one cannot merely sit and wait for that reform somehow miraculously to happen. Alternative means for educating children must be developed, debated and where there is promise, attempted. Reform cannot, however, lose sight of the basic issues involved. The current educational system is such that to be transformed is, in some instances, to be discarded. The sporadic tinkering with the schools that has dominated previous attempts at reform will no longer suffice in the present.

And what are the needs of children? First and foremost, children should be able to learn about themselves and their world in humane and supportive surroundings. Silberman states:

> Schools can be humane and still educate well. They can be genuinely concerned with gaiety and joy and individual growth and fulfillment without sacrificing concern for intellectual discipline and development. They can be simultaneously child-centered and subject or knowledge centered. They can stress esthetic and moral education without weakening the three R's.

Silberman notes what can be, not what is. The present institutional arrangements in schools have relegated children, metaphorically, to the equivalent of a warehouse commodity supervised by teachers relegated to the role of custodians. Neither children nor teachers seem to like school very much. They are both unhappy; they suffer from pervasive boredom, lack of individual autonomy and respect and perhaps most fundamentally, lack of freedom.

The issue of freedom—or lack of it—in American schools is at the very heart of the thrust towards alternative milieus in which children may learn. American schools do not permit one to choose whether or not to attend. Teachers and students alike meet in an institutional setting where the element of coercion may be hidden but is never absent. It is a setting dominated by a series of normative mandates that lock its participants into roles that inhibit dialogue, maintain patterns of social distance and legitimate gross disparities in influence over the decision-making process of how and what is to be learned.

C. Wright Mills has suggested:

> Freedom is not merely the chance to do as one pleases; neither is it merely the opportunity to choose among set alternatives. Freedom is first of all, the chance to formulate the available choices, to argue over them—and then, the opportunity to choose.

Without succumbing to the temptation of reification, American schools represent nearly the antithesis of what Mills articulates as the conditions of freedom. Students and teachers alike are bound in a system that does not allow freedom of exploration, freedom to question or freedom to formulate alternative choices as to how they might educate and be educated. And where students *are* allowed the freedom to formulate such alternatives, what opportunities do they have to choose among them? The thrust of American educational reform in the past has been to provide new but nonetheless "set" alternatives from which choices can be made. Those most centrally concerned—teachers, students and parents—have not been in a position to articulate alternatives to the options provided. Learning how to exercise one's freedom is not synonymous with learning how to be schooled.

SOME POLICY IMPLICATIONS

If new structures and milieus for children are to be created, a number of current institutional constraints upon policy options will have to be overcome. They are size, conditions surrounding attendance, age segregation and control of the institution and its activities.

Those who advocate new learning milieus for children make a conscious attempt to limit size by avoiding unnecessary bureaucratization, institutional regimentation and large numbers, for all three are highly correlated in the present school systems. The alternative forms stress simply organized learning situations in which teachers and children alike are free to explore, to move about and share with one another in small groups. Michael Katz suggests:

It is difficult to see the functional relationships between large size, economies of scale, bureaucratic organization, and so on, on the one hand, and learning to read, write, and do math on the other. Unless the effectiveness of electronic computers proves revolutionary at these tasks (which I doubt), it is hard to see why the business of learning these things cannot be managed more simply, directly, and informally by skilled teachers working with small groups of children wherever they find some space.

Yet these goals of small, humane and happy learning situations for children do not appear to be feasible given the present structural configuration of American public education. One of the main obstacles is that too many cities and towns have invested tens of millions of dollars in physical plants built to hold hundreds of students at one time. The taxpayers and administrators who have such a heavy investment in large educational facilities are not likely to suggest that alternative ways of bringing teachers and children together—which might forego use of the large buildings—should be high on the agenda of educational experimentation. The resistance to seeking smaller alternative locations for the learning milieu is compounded by the fact that school buildings are good for very little but schooling. There are few other, if any, institutional arrangements which require that groups of people be isolated in rooms of the same size, shape and architectural starkness. Lacking any other organization to whom school buildings might be transferred without loss of investment to the citizens, educational systems will probably continue to make heavy use of the present facilities. Those who desire alternative settings which emphasize small and informal learning situations, such as a store-front school, can expect little in the way of assistance from current public school systems.

A second constraint on policy options concerns the compulsory nature of schooling in the United States. Children have no real choice as to whether or not they wish to go to school. Likewise, parents have no real choice but to send their children to school, and those who wish to teach children must become teachers inside the schools. As a consequence, the element of compulsion has created a situation where learning is supposed to be accomplished with a captive audience. In many respects, one can say that schools resemble "total institutions" such as mental institutions, hospitals, prisons and the armed forces. Phillip Jackson suggests a denominator common to all of them:

> One subgroup of their clientele [here students] are involuntarily committed to the institution, whereas another subgroup [the administrators and teachers] has greater freedom of movement, and most important, has the ultimate freedom to leave the institution entirely. Under these circumstances it is common for the more privileged group to guard the exits, either figuratively or literally.

A key factor which does not allow unreserved acceptance of the analogy of schools as total institutions is that children are permitted to leave the institution for significant periods of time. Whereas in prisons or mental institutions the client population is allowed no exit, the schools are such that the students, staff and administrators all sever ties at regulated times and for defined intervals. While children may possess some degree of autonomy outside the domain of the schools, there is little doubt as to whom the schools themselves belong. Children are by far the largest single group of participants in the schooling process, but they remain only clients and not coproprietors in the institution. As Goffman has noted about staff-client relations in total institutions:

> Two different social and cultural worlds develop, jogging alongside each other with points of official contact, but little mutual penetration. Significantly, the institutional plant and name come to be identified by both staff and inmates as somehow belonging to the staff, so that when either group refers to the views or interests of "the institution," by implication, they are referring . . . to the views and interests of the staff.

In response to the compulsory and institutional nature of the milieu in which they are to learn, the children's chief task becomes knowing how to make it in such a setting—in short, how to survive. As with prisons and hospitals, one needs to know the rules, both implicit and explicit, to get through with a minimum of disruption and attention. Students as well as inmates learn how to do time "standing on one's head." The role of student is expected to be one who knows his place, is docile, and does not disturb the smooth functioning of his own confinement.

Serious pitfalls exist, however, if one attempts to make learning a voluntary activity without also recognizing the necessity of fundamental restructuring in other major social institutions, particularly those involved in economic and political activity. Katz avers to some of the dangers inherent in such a position:

Parents might pressure children to leave school early
in order to go to work; employers would exploit
juvenile labor. We offer at present little worthwhile
work to a young person uninterested in formal
schooling, and most important of all, we do not offer
alternative ways of becoming educated or easy access
back into schooling. ... Abolishing compulsory
education could work against the interests of all
children, especially the poor if it were not
accompanied by provisions to enable them to find
worthwhile work and to resume education with
financial support whenever they want to do so. The
connection between level of schooling and
employment opportunity will have to be broken as
well, as it should be.

Though the policy option of noncompulsory education in
the United States appears virtually nil at present, it is
nevertheless a vital issue that cannot be avoided if one is
serious about transforming the learning situation from
coercion to choice.

As suggested previously, the majority of schools in the
United States are segregated by class and race. Yet another
form of segregation that schools participate in is age
segregation. Children have little or no contact with any
adults while in school other than those directly responsible
for their supervision—the staff. Children learn of various
roles available to them in adulthood by reading a
textbook, not from direct observation, for schools do not
take children out into the world to observe how adults
spend their time during the day. Concurrent with the lack
of movement of children out of the schools is the lack of
movement of non-staff adults into the schools. There is
virtual isolation of experience from the activities of the
"outside" world. A key policy goal in changing this
situation would be to formulate the means by which
mobility would become the norm. The time spent inside
the classroom where children are cut off and absent from

the movement of society around them must be justified, not the time spent outside the classroom. The major factor working against such a transformation of the learning milieu is resistance to the decentralization of schooling. This relates to the point noted earlier that the presence of expensive and large educational facilities stands as a major obstacle to certain kinds of learning reforms.

A fourth constraint on the policy options available to those who would restructure American education relates to the issue of control. On a superficial level, one could argue that any form of control over the institution and its activities other than that currently operational is desirable, given that high school graduates in many schools cannot read eighth grade reading materials, that children are regarded as subhuman, and that learning is secondary in importance to conformity. But if the learning situation for children is to become a creative experience, then it is imperative that new forms of control over the process of schooling be devised. If it is desirable that children learn how to exercise their freedom through the articulation and formulation of options, the current structural constraints on such exploration will have to be avoided. For children as well as their parents and teachers to have the opportunity to create such learning experiences, the power and decision-making authority inherent in the educational bureaucracy will have to be decentralized. This would occur only with great reluctance and hesitation, I suspect, for it strikes at the very core of the myth of the apolitical schoolhouse. But if such decentralization cannot be achieved, one should expect the exodus from the public schools continually to increase. (In the movement away from the public school systems, the issue of authority and control is somewhat different for there is from the beginning the absence of a centralized authority.) In any event, what must be avoided is the transfer from one type of absolute authority to another. Under any form of absolute control, formulation of alternatives is hindered and the ennui of the bureaucratic ethos emerges in its place. For the transfer of authority to improve the circumstances in which children are able to learn, there must be liberation for children as well as for parents and teachers.

POSTSCRIPT: ON THE CONTRIBUTIONS TO THIS BOOK

There are presently about 45 million students in the elementary and secondary schools of the United States taught by slightly more than 2.1 million instructors. Consequently, when one speaks of educational innovation and reform in the creation of alternative learning centers for children, the very magnitude of the educational establishment and the number of participants makes nonsensical suggestions that fundamental change is quick and easy. This is not to suggest that the learning milieus of children cannot be reconstructed on a mass scale or that one must wait an indefinite period of time for the reform mysteriously to appear. However, pragmatic policy decisions will have to be made as to what facets of the learning process deserve immediate attention and what aspects can be postponed or incorporated into long-range structural change.

The selections in this book attempt to speak to both of these views. The first portion of the book outlines a variety of policy decisions that could be implemented very quickly to bring about immediate changes in the schools. In a sense, these proposals represent a reformist thrust suggesting that temporary patching and mending of the educational structure can provide some semblance of a humane and stimulating learning atmosphere. The second section of the book suggests that there has to be something beyond an unending series of short-term reform measures; the very structure of American education must be transformed. These articles are nearly unanimous in suggesting that those who seek alternative forms for the learning milieu of children must go outside the present structure of public education. They call into question the very legitimacy of the current establishment and seek to provide a number of radical alternatives.

But rather than presenting the two sections as representing "either-or" decisions, the first may well serve as the immediate response while the latter provides guidelines for long-range and fundamental change in the structure of American education. Both are applicable and current, for while fundamental change is not going to come about overnight, there is still a responsibility to those children presently in schools. And I am sure that those authors in the first section would not suggest that changes in the structure of schools stop with their proposals for reform. The efforts they outline are necessary, but admittedly not sufficient.

In one manner or another, all of the selections in this volume address themselves to two crucial policy concerns. The first concern revolves around issues of pedagogical methods which are destructive to children and their learning. The dominant motif in American schools is a rather benign form of "mindlessness" in which learning happens only sporadically, and often in spite of the schooling rather than because of it. For schools to accomplish even the most basic tasks of teaching reading, writing and arithmetic, there will have to be incisive changes in present classroom procedures and practices. To stumble on and on with the "tried and true" is to wander in confusion and uncertainty. Children deserve more than such blindness. A second concern is the educational establishment's bureaucratic structures, which have developed an administrative ethos that inhibits change, is conducive to stagnation and sees learning as only a byproduct to schooling. As C. Wright Mills might suggest, the bureaucracies of schools are strong on rationality, but weak in reason and thus devoid of freedom. It is not the system that need endure, but rather the integrity of the child; not the administrative positions, but the concern of parents and teachers in the learning experience of each child; and not the need to learn institutional survival, but how to gain and sustain individual freedom. Such must be the goals of those who would offer alternatives to the present victimization of children. No longer can this society expect children to be passive participants in their own destruction. I should like to think that the time is now at hand when new learning forms will be sought and explored—for to do less is to give silent consent to the present assault on children.

PART I

INNOVATIONS
WITHIN
THE PRESENT
EDUCATIONAL SYSTEM

Children and Their Caretakers

NORMAN K. DENZIN

Schools are held together by intersecting moral, political and social orders. What occurs inside their walls must be viewed as a product of what the participants in this arena bring to it, be they children, parents, instructors, administrators, psychologists, social workers, counselors or politicians. A tangled web of interactions—based on competing ideologies, rhetorics, intents and purposes—characterizes everyday life in the school. Cliques, factions, pressure groups and circles of enemies daily compete for power and fate in these social worlds.

Children and their caretakers are not passive organisms. Their conduct reflects more than responses to the pressures of social systems, roles, value structures or political ideologies. Nor is their behavior the sole product of internal needs, drives, impulses or wishes. The human actively constructs lines of conduct in the face of these

Reprinted with the permission of **Society** magazine (formerly *trans*action), Vol. 8 No. 9-10, July/August 1971. Copyright © Transaction, Inc.

forces and as such stands over and against the external world. The human is self-conscious. Such variables as role prescription, value configurations or hierarchies of needs have relevance only when they are acted on by the human. Observers of human behavior are obliged to enter the subject's world and grasp the shifting definitions that give rise to orderly social behavior. Failing to do so justifies the fallacy of objectivism: the imputing of motive from observer to subject. Too many architects of schools and education programs have stood outside the interactional worlds of children and adults and attempted to legislate their interpretation of right and proper conduct.

Such objectivistic stances have given schools a basic characteristic that constitutes a major theme of this essay. Schools are presently organized so as to effectively remove fate control from those persons whose fate is at issue, that is, students. This loss of fate control, coupled with a conception of the child which is based on the "under-estimation fallacy" gives rise to an ideology that judges the child as incompetent and places in the hands of the adult primary responsibility for child-caretaking.

SCHOOLS AS MORAL AGENCIES

Schools are best seen, not as educational settings, but as places where fate, morality and personal careers are created and shaped. Schools are moral institutions. They have assumed the responsibility of shaping children, of whatever race or income level, into right and proper participants in American society, pursuing with equal vigor the abstract goals of that society.

At one level schools function, as Willard Waller argued in 1937, to Americanize the young. At the everyday level, however, abstract goals disappear, whether they be beliefs in democracy and equal opportunity or myths concerning the value of education for upward mobility. In their place appears a massive normative order that judges the child's development along such dimensions as poise, character, integrity, politeness, deference, demeanor, emotional control, respect for authority and serious commitment to classroom protocol. Good students are those who reaffirm through their daily actions the moral order of home, school and community.

To the extent that schools assume moral responsibility for producing social beings, they can be seen as agencies of fate or career control. In a variety of ways schools remind students who they are and where they stand in the school's hierarchy. The school institutionalizes ritual turning points to fill this function: graduations, promotions, tests, meetings with parents, open-houses, rallies and sessions with counselors. These significant encounters serve to keep students in place. Schools function to sort and filter social selves and to set these selves on the proper moral track, which may include recycling to a lower grade, busing to an integrated school or informing a student that he has no chance to pursue a college preparatory program. In many respects schools give students their major sense of moral worth—they shape vocabularies, images of self, reward certain actions and not others, set the stage for students to be thrown together as friends or enemies.

Any institution that assumes control over the fate of others might be expected to be accountable for its actions toward those who are shaped and manipulated. Within the cultures of fate-controlling institutions, however, there appears a vocabulary, a rhetoric, a set of workable excuses and a division of labor to remove and reassign responsibility. For example, we might expect that the division of labor typically parallels the moral hierarchy of the people within the institution, that is, the people assigned the greatest moral worth are ultimately most blameworthy, or most accountable. Usually, however, moral responsibility is reversed. When a teacher in a Head Start program fails to raise the verbal skills of her class to the appropriate level she and the project director might blame each other. But it is more likely that the children, the families of the children or the culture from which the children come will be held responsible. Such is the typical rhetorical device employed in compensatory education programs where the low performances of black children on white middle-class tests is explained by assigning blame to black family culture and family arrangements. Research on the alleged genetic deficiencies of black and brown children is another example of this strategy. Here the scientist acts as a moral entrepreneur, presenting his findings under the guise of objectivity.

WHAT IS A CHILD?

Any analysis of the education and socialization process must begin with the basic question, "What is a child?" My focus is on the contemporary meanings assigned children, especially as these meanings are revealed in preschool and compensatory education programs.

In addressing this question it must be recognized that social objects (such as children) carry no intrinsic meaning. Rather, meaning is conferred by processes of social interaction—by people.

Such is the case with children. Each generation, each social group, every family and each individual develops different interpretations of what a child is. Children find themselves defined in shifting, often contradictory ways. But as a sense of self is acquired, the child learns to transport from situation to situation a relatively stable set of definitions concerning his personal and social identity. Indeed most of the struggles he will encounter in the educational arena fundamentally derive from conflicting definitions of selfhood and childhood.

The movement of an infant to the status of child is a

socially constructed event that for most middle-class Americans is seen as desirable, inevitable, irreversible, permanent, long term in effect and accomplished in the presence of "experts" and significant others such as teachers, parents, peers and siblings.

For the white middle income American the child is seen as an extension of the adult's self, usually the family's collective self. Parents are continually reminded that the way their child turns out is a direct reflection on their competence as socializing agents. These reminders have been made for some time; consider this exhortation of 1849:

> Yes, mothers, in a certain sense, the destiny of a redeemed world is put into your hands; it is for you to say whether your children shall be respectable and happy here, and prepared for a glorious immortality, or whether they shall dishonor you, and perhaps bring you grey hairs in sorrow to the grave, and sink down themselves at last to eternal despair!

If the child's conduct reflects upon the parent's moral worth, new parents are told by Benjamin Spock that this job of producing a child is hard work, a serious enterprise. He remarks in *Baby and Child Care:*

> There is an enormous amount of hard work in child care—preparing the proper diet, washing diapers and clothes, cleaning up messes that an infant makes with his food . . . stopping fights and drying tears, listening to stories that are hard to understand, joining in games and reading stories that aren't very exciting to an adult, trudging around zoos and museums and carnivals . . . being slowed down in housework. . . . Children keep parents from parties, trips, theaters, meetings, games, friends. . . . Of course, parents don't have children because they want to be martyrs, or at least they shouldn't. They have them because they love children and want some of their very own. . . .

Taking care of their children, seeing them grow and develop into fine people, gives most parents—despite the hard work—their greatest satisfaction in life. This is creation. This is our visible immortality. Pride in other worldly accomplishments is usually weak in comparison.

Spock's account of the parent-child relationship reveals several interrelated definitions that together serve to set off the contemporary view of children. The child is a possession of the adult, an extension of self, an incompetent object that must be cared for at great cost and is a necessary obligation one must incur if he or she desires visible immortality.

These several definitions of childhood are obviously at work in current educational programs. More importantly, they are grounded in a theory of development and learning that reinforces the view that children are incompetent selves. Like Spock's theory of growth, which is not unlike the earlier proposals of Gesell, contemporary psychological theories see the child in organic terms. The child grows like a stalk of corn. The strength of the stalk is a function of its environment. If that environment is healthy, if the plant is properly cared for, a suitable product will be produced. This is a "container" theory of development: "What you put in determines what comes out." At the same time, however, conventional wisdom holds that the child is an unreliable product. It cannot be trusted with its own moral development. Nor can parents. This business of producing a child is serious and it must be placed in the hands of experts who are skilled in child production. Mortal mothers and fathers lack these skills. Pressures are quickly set in force to move the child out of the family into a more "professional" setting—the preschool, the Head Start program.

Preschools, whether based on "free school" principles, the Montessori theory, or modern findings in child development, display one basic feature. They are moral caretaking agencies that undertake the fine task of shaping social beings.

Recently, after the enormous publicity attendant to the Head Start program for the poor, middle income Americans have been aroused to the importance of preschool education for their children. "Discovery Centers" are appearing in various sections of the country and several competing national franchises have been established. Given names such as We Sit Better, Mary Moppit, Pied Piper Schools, Les Petites Academies, Kinder Care Nursery and American Child Centers, these schools remind parents (as did the Universal Education Corporation in the *New York Times*) that:

> Evaluating children in the 43 basic skills is part of what the Discovery Center can do for your child. The 43 skills embrace all the hundreds of things your child has to learn before he reaches school age. Fortunately preschoolers have a special genius for learning. But it disappears at the age of seven. During the short-lived period of genius, the Discovery Center helps your child develop his skills to the Advanced Level.

Caretaking for the middle classes is a moral test. The parent's self is judged by the quality of the product. If the product is faulty, the producer is judged inadequate, also faulty. This feature of the socialization process best explains why middle class parents are so concerned about the moral, spiritual, psychological and social development of their children. It also explains (if only partially) why schools have assumed so much fate control over children; educators are the socially defined experts on children.

The children of lower income families are often assumed to be deprived, depressed and emotionally handicapped. To offset these effects, current theory holds that the child must be "educated and treated" before entrance into kindergarten. If middle income groups have the luxury of withholding preschool from their children, low income, third-world parents are quickly learning they have no such right. Whether they like it or not, their children are going to be educated. When formal education begins, the culturally deprived child will be ready to compete with his white peers.

The term "culturally deprived" is still the catchall phrase which at once explains and describes the inability (failure, refusal) of the child in question to display appropriate conduct on I.Q. tests, street corners, playgrounds and classrooms. There are a number of problems with the formulation. The first is conceptual and involves the meanings one gives to the terms *culture* and *deprived*. Contemporary politicians and educators have ignored the controversy surrounding what the word *culture* means and have apparently assumed that everyone knows what a culture is. Be that as it may, the critical empirical indicator seems to be contained in the term *deprived*. People who are deprived, that is, people who fail to act like white, middle income groups, belong to a culture characterized by such features as divorce, deviance, premarital pregnancies, extended families, drug addiction and alcoholism. Such persons are easily identified: they tend to live in ghettos or public housing units, and they tend to occupy the lower rungs of the occupation ladder. They are there because they are deprived. Their culture keeps them deprived. It is difficult to tell whether these theorists feel that deprivation precedes or follows being in a deprived culture. The causal links are neither logically nor empirically analyzed.

The second problem with this formulation is moral and ideological. The children and adults who are labeled culturally deprived are those people in American society who embarrass and cause trouble for middle income moralists, scientists, teachers, politicians and social workers. They fail to display proper social behavior. The fact that people in low income groups are under continual surveillance by police and social workers seems to go unnoticed. The result is that members of the middle class keep their indelicacies behind closed doors, inside the private worlds of home, office, club and neighborhood. Low income people lack such privileges. Their misconduct is everybody's business.

The notion of cultural deprivation is class based. Its recurrent invocation, and its contemporary institutionalization in compensatory education programs reveals an inability or refusal to look seriously at the problems of the middle and upper classes, and it directs attention away from schools which are at the heart of the problem.

Herbert Gans has noted another flaw in these programs. This is the failure of social scientists to take seriously the fact that many lower income people simply do not share the same aspirations as the middle class. Despite this fact antipoverty programs and experiments in compensatory education proceed as if such were the case.

Schools are morally bounded units of social organization. Within and from them students, parents, teachers and administrators derive their fundamental sense of self. Any career through a school is necessarily moral; one's self-image is continually being evaluated, shaped and molded. These careers are interactionally interdependent. What a teacher does affects what a child does and vice versa. To the extent that schools have become the dominant socializing institution in Western society it can be argued that experiences in them furnish everyday interactants with their basic vocabularies for evaluating self and others. Persons can mask, hide or fabricate their educational biography, but at some point they will be obliged to paint a picture of how well educated they are. They will also be obliged to explain why they are not better educated (or why they are too well educated), and why their present circumstances do not better reflect their capabilities (e.g., unemployed space engineers). One's educational experiences furnish the rhetorical devices necessary to get off the hook and supply the basic clues that will shore up a sad or happy tale.

THE SCHOOL'S FUNCTIONS

I have already noted two broad functions served by the schools: they Americanize students, and they sort, filter and accredit social selves. To these basic functions must be added the following. Ostensibly, instruction or teaching should take precedence over political socialization. And indeed teaching becomes the dominant activity through which the school is presented to the child. But if schools function to instruct, they also function to entertain and divert students into "worthwhile" ends. Trips to zoos, beaches, operas, neighboring towns, ice cream parlors and athletic fields reveal an attempt on the part of the school to teach the child what range of entertaining activities he or she can engage in. Moreover, these trips place the school directly in the public's eye and at least on these excursions teachers are truly held accountable for their class's conduct.

Caretaking and babysitting constitute another basic function of schools. This babysitting function is quite evident in church oriented summer programs where pre-schools and day-care centers are explicitly oriented so as to sell themselves as competent babysitters. Such schools compete for scarce resources (parents who can afford their services), and the federal government has elaborated this service through grants-in-aid to low income children.

Formal instruction in the classroom is filtered through a series of interconnected acts that involve teacher and student presenting different social selves to one another. Instruction cannot be separated from social interaction, and teachers spend a large amount of time teaching students how to be proper social participants. Coaching in the rules and rituals of polite etiquette thus constitutes another basic function of the school. Students must be taught how to take turns, how to drink out of cups and clean up messes, how to say please and thank you, how to take leave of a teacher's presence, how to handle mood, how to dress for appropriate occasions, how to be rude, polite, attentive, evasive, docile, aggressive, deceitful; in short, they must learn to act like adults. Teachers share this responsibility with parents, often having to take over where parents fail or abdicate, though, again, parents are held accountable for not producing polite children. Because a child's progress through the school's social structure is contingent on how his or her self is formally defined, parents stand to lose much if their children do not conform to the school's version of good conduct. When teachers and parents both fail, an explanation will be sought to relieve each party of responsibility. The child may be diagnosed as hyperactive, or his culture may have been so repressive in its effects that nothing better can be accomplished. Career tracks for these students often lead to the trade school or the reformatory.

Another function of the schools is socialization into age-sex roles. Girls must be taught how to be girls and boys must learn what a boy is. In preschool and day-care centers this is often difficult to accomplish because bathrooms are not sex segregated. But while they are open territories, many preschools make an effort to hire at least one male instructor who can serve as male caretaker and entertainer of boys. He handles their toilet problems among other things. Preschool instructors can often be observed to reinterpret stories to fit their conception of the male or female role, usually attempting to place the female on an equal footing with the male. In these ways the sexual component of self-identity is transmitted and presented to the young child. Problem children become those who switch sex roles or accentuate to an unacceptable degree maleness or femaleness.

Age-grading is accomplished through the organization of classes on a biological age basis. Three-year-olds quickly learn that they cannot do the same things as four-year-olds do, and so on. High schools are deliberately organized so as to convey to freshmen and sophomores how important it is to be a junior or senior. Homecoming queens, student body presidents and athletic leaders come from the two top classes. The message is direct: work hard, be a good student and you too can be a leader and enjoy the fruits of age.

It has been suggested by many that most schools centrally function to socialize children into racial roles, stressing skin color as the dominant variable in social relationships. Depictions of American history and favored symbolic leaders stress the three variables of age, sex and race. The favored role model becomes the 20- to 25-year-old, white, university-educated male who has had an outstanding career in athletics. Implicitly and explicitly students are taught that Western culture is a male-oriented, white-based enterprise.

Shifting from the school as a collectivity to the classroom, we find that teachers attempt to construct their own versions of appropriate conduct. Students are likely to find great discrepancies between a school's formal codes of conduct and the specific rules they encounter in each of their courses and classes. They will find some teachers who are openly critical of the school's formal policies, while at the same time they are forced to interact with teachers who take harsh lines toward misconduct. They will encounter some teachers who enforce dress standards and some who do not. Some teachers use first names, others do not, and so on. The variations are endless.

The importance of these variations for the student's

career and self-concept should be clear. It is difficult managing self in a social world that continually changes its demands, rewards and rules of conduct. But students are obliged to do just that. Consequently the self-concept of the student emerges as a complex and variegated object. He or she is tied into competing and complementary worlds of influence and experience. Depending on where students stand with respect to the school's dominant moral order, they will find their self-concept complemented or derogated and sometimes both. But for the most part schools are organized so as to complement the self-concept of the child most like the teacher and to derogate those must unlike him or her. And, needless to say, the moral career of the nonwhite, low income student is quite different from the career of his white peer.

I have spelled out the dimensions around which a student comes to evaluate himself in school. Classrooms, however, are the most vivid stage on which students confront the school, and it is here that the teacher at some level must emerge as a negative or positive force on his career. While the underlife of schools reflects attempts to "beat" or "make-out" in the school, in large degree the student learns to submit to the system. The ultimate fact of life is that unless he gets through school with some diploma he is doomed to failure. Not only is he doomed to failure, but he is socially defined as a failure. His career opportunities and self-conceptions are immediately tied to his success in school.

Schools, then, inevitably turn some amount of their attention to the problem of socializing students for failure. Indeed, the school's success as a socializing agent in part depends on its ability to teach students to accept failure. A complex rhetoric and set of beliefs must be instilled in the students. Children must come to see themselves as the school defines them. They are taught that certain classes of selves do better than other classes, but the classes referred to are not sociological but moral. A variation of the Protestant ethic is communicated and the fiction of equality in education and politics is stressed. Students must grasp the fact that all that separates them from a classmate who goes to Harvard (when they are admitted to a junior college) are grades and hard work, not class, race, money or prestige. Schools, then, function as complex, cooling out agencies.

Two problems are created. School officials must communicate their judgments, usually cast as diagnoses, prescriptions, treatments and prognoses, to students and parents. And second, they must establish social arrangements that maximize the likelihood that their judgments will be accepted, that is, submission to fate control is maximized, and scenes between parents and students are minimized.

The most obvious cooling out agents in schools are teachers and counselors. It is they who administer and evaluate tests. It is they who see the student most frequently. In concert these two classes of functionaries fulfill the schools' functions of sorting out and cooling out children. Their basic assignment is to take imperfect selves and fit those selves to the best possible moral career. They are, then, moral entrepreneurs. They design career programs and define the basic contours around which a student's self will be shaped.

A basic strategy of the moral entrepreneur in schools is co-optation. He attempts to win a child's peers and parents over to his side. If this can be accomplished, the job is relatively easy. For now everyone significant in the child's world agrees that he is a failure or a partial success. They agree that a trade school or a junior college is the best career track to be followed.

Another strategy is to select exemplary students who epitomize the various tracks open to a student. Former graduates may be brought back and asked to reflect on their careers. In selecting types of students to follow these various paths, schools conduct talent searches and develop operating perspectives that classify good and bad prospects. Like the academic theorist of social stratification, these officials work with an implicit image of qualified beings. They know that students from middle and upper income groups perform better than those from lesser backgrounds. They know that students who have college educated parents do better than those whose parents dropped out of high school. They learn to mistrust nonwhites. In these respects schools differ only slightly from medical practitioners, especially the psychiatrist who has learned that his trade works best on persons like him in background. Teachers too perpetuate the system of stratification found in the outside world.

STUDENT TYPES

Schools can cool out the failures in their midst. They have more difficulty with another type of student, the troublemakers or militants. Troublemakers, as would be predicted, typically come from low income white and nonwhite ethnic groups. Forced to process these children, school systems developed their own system of stratification, making low-status schools teach troublemakers. This has become the fate of the trade school or the continuation high school. Here those who have high truancy or arrest records, are pregnant, hyperactive or on probation are thrown together. And here they are presented with white middle-class curricula.

Militants and troublemakers refuse to accept the school's operating perspective. To the extent that they can band together and form a common world view, they challenge the school's legitimacy as a socializing agent. They make trouble. They represent, from the middle-class point of view, failures of the socializing system.

In response to this, schools tend to adopt a strategy of denial. Denial can take several forms, each revealing a separate attempt to avoid accountability. Denial of responsibility takes the form of a claim that "we recognize your problem, but the solution is outside our province." The need for alternative educational arrangements is recognized, but denied because of reasons beyond control. Private and public guilt is neutralized by denying responsibility and placing blame on some external force or variable such as the state of the economy.

When some resource is denied to a social group, explanations will be developed to justify that denial. My earlier discussion has suggested that one explanation places blame on the shoulders of the denied victim. Thus the theory of cultural deprivation removes blame, by blaming the victim. Scientific theory thus operates as one paradigm of responsibility.

Another form of the strategy is to deny the challengers' essential moral worth. Here the victim is shown to be socially unworthy and thereby not deserving of special attention. This has been the classic argument for segregation in the South, but it works only so long as the victim can be kept in place, which has lately in that part of the world involved insuring that the challenger or victim is not presented with alternative self-models. Shipping black instructors out of the South into northern urban ghettos represents an attempt to remove alternative self-models for the southern black child.

Insofar as they can organize themselves socially, victims and challengers may assume one of three interrelated stances. They may condemn the condemner, make appeals to higher authorities or deny the perspective that has brought injury. In so doing they will seek and develop alternative scientific doctrines that support their stance.

Condemning the condemner reverses the condemner's denial of moral worth. Here the school or political and economic system is judged hypocritical, corrupt, stupid, brutal and racist. These evaulations attempt to reveal the underlying moral vulnerability of the institution in question. The victim and his cohort reverse the victimizer's vocabulary and hold him accountable for the failures they were originally charged with (for example, poor grades or attendance records).

These condemnations reveal a basic commitment to the present system. They are claims for a just place. They are a petition to higher authority. Democratic ideology is proclaimed as a worthy pursuit. The school is charged with failure to offer proper and acceptable means to reach those goals. Here the victims' perspective corresponds with dominant cultural ideologies.

Denial of perspective is another stance. Best seen in the Nation of Islam schools, the victim now states that he wants nothing the larger system can offer. He leaves the system and constructs his own educational arrangements. He develops his own standards of evaluation. He paints his own version of right and proper conduct. (Private educational academies in the South, partly a function of the Nixon administration, serve a similar function for whites.)

Denials of perspective thus lead to the substitution of a new point of view. If successfully executed, as in the case of the Nation of Islam, the victims build their own walls of protection and shut off the outside world. In such a setting, one's self-concept is neither daily denied nor derided. It is affirmed and defined in positive terms.

Lower self-concepts would be predicted in those settings where the black or brown child is taught to normalize his deficiencies and to compensate for them. This is the setting offered by Head Start and Follow-Through. The victim accepts the victimizers' judgments and attempts to compensate for socially defined flaws.

Americans of all income levels and from all racial groups, including white, are troubled over the current educational system. They are demanding a greater say in the social organization of schools; they are challenging the tenure system now given teachers; they feel that schools should accept greater responsibilities for the failures of the system. (A Gallup Poll in late 1970 showed that 67 percent of those surveyed favor holding teachers and administrators more accountable for the progress of students.) Accordingly it is necessary to consider a series of proposals that would bring education more in line with cultural and social expectations.

From this perspective education must be grounded in principles that recognize the role of the self in everyday conduct. The child possesses multiple selves, each grounded in special situations and special circles of significant others. Possessing a self, the child is an active organism, not a passive object into which learning can be poured.

Conventional theories of learning define the child as a passive organism. An alternative view of the social act of learning must be developed. George Herbert Mead's analysis provides a good beginning. Creativity or learning occurred, Mead argued, when the individual was forced to act in a situation where conventional lines of conduct were no longer relevant. Following Dewey's discussion of the blocked act, Mead contended that schools and curricula must be organized in ways that challenge the child's view of the world. Standard curricula are based on an opposite view of the human. Redundancy, constant rewards and punishments, piecemeal presentation of materials, and defining the child as incompetent or unable to provoke his own acts best characterize these programs. Course work is planned carefully in advance and study programs are assidously followed. The teacher, not the child, is defined as the ultimate educational resource. Parents and local community groups, because they tend to challenge the school's operating perspective, are treated only ritualistically at P.T.A. meetings, open houses, school plays, athletic contests. Their point of view, like the child's, is seldom taken seriously. They are too incompetent. Taking them seriously would force a shift in existing power arrangements in the school.

Mead's perspective proposes just the opposite view of parents, children and education. Education, he argued, is an unfolding social process wherein the child comes to see himself in increasingly more complex ways. Education leads to self-understanding and to the acquisition of the basic skills. This principle suggests that schools must be socially relevant. They must incorporate the social world of child and community into curriculum arrangements. Cultural diversity must be stressed. Alternative symbolic leaders must be presented, and these must come from realistic worlds of experience. (Setting an astronaut as a preferred "self model" for seven-year-old males as a present textbook does, can hardly be defined as realistic.) Problematic situations from the child's everyday world must be brought into the classroom. Mead, for example, proposed as early as 1908 that schools teach sex education to children.

Children and parents, then, must be seen as resources around which education is developed and presented. They must be taken seriously. This presupposes a close working relationship between home and school. Parents must take responsibility for their children's education. They can no longer afford to shift accountability to the schools. This simple principle suggests that ethnic studies programs should have been central features of schools at least 50 years ago. Schools exist to serve their surrounding communities, not bend those communities to their perspective.

REDEFINING SCHOOLS

If this reciprocal service function is stressed, an important implication follows. Schools should educate children in ways that permit them to be contributing members in their chosen worlds. Such basics as reading, writing and counting will never be avoided. But their instruction can be made relevant within the worlds the child most directly experiences. This suggests, initially at least, that black and brown children be taught to respect their separate cultural heritages. Second, it suggests that they will probably learn best with materials drawn from those cultures. Third, it suggests that they must be presented with self models who know, respect and come from those cultures—black teachers must not be removed from southern schools.

To the extent that schools and teachers serve as referent points for the child's self-concept it can be argued that it is not the minority student who must change. But instead it is the white middle class child who must be exposed to alternative cultural perspectives. Minority teachers must be made integral components of all phases of the educational act.

Mead's perspective suggests, as I have attempted to elaborate, that the classroom is an interactive world. Research by Roger G. Barker and Paul V. Gump on big schools and little schools supports this position and their findings suggest an additional set of proposals. Briefly, they learned that as class and school size increases student satisfaction decreases. Teaching becomes more mechanized, students become more irrelevant and activities not related to learning attain greater importance, social clubs, for example. In short, in big schools students are redundant.

Classroom size and school size must be evaluated from this perspective. If schools exist to serve children and their parents, then large schools are dysfunctional. They are knowledge factories, not places of learning or self-development. Culturally heterogeneous, small-sized classes must be experimented with. Students must have opportunities to know their teachers in personal, not institutional terms.

Students must be taught to take one another seriously, not competitively. Small, ecologically intimate surroundings have a greater likelihood of promoting these arrangements than do large-scale, bureaucratically organized classes.

At present, standardized, state and nationally certified tests are given students to assess their psychological, emotional, intellectual and social development. Two problems restrict the effectiveness of these methods, however. With few exceptions they have been standardized on white middle class populations. Second, they are the only measurement techniques routinely employed.

A number of proposals follow from these problems. First, open-ended tests which permit the child to express his or her perspective must be developed. These tests, such as the "Who Am I?" question, would be given to students to determine the major contours of their self-concepts. With this information in hand teachers would be in a better position to tailor teaching programs to a child's specific needs, definitions, intentions and goals.

Second, tests such as "Who is Important to You?" could be given students on a regular basis to determine who their significant others are. It is near axiomatic that derogation of the people most important to one leads to alienation from the setting and spokesman doing the derogation. Teachers must learn to respect and present in respectful terms those persons most important to the child.

A third methodological proposal directs observers to link a student's utterances, wishes and self-images to his or her day-to-day conduct. Written test scores often fail to reflect what persons really take into account and value. In many social settings verbal ability, athletic skill, hustling aptitudes, money and even physical attractiveness serve as significant status locators. I.Q. tests often do not. Furthermore, a person's score on a test may not accurately reflect his ability to handle problematic situations, which is surely a goal of education. Observations of conduct (behavior) in concrete settings can provide the needed leads in this direction.

METHODOLOGICAL IMPLICATIONS

A critic of these proposals might remark that such measures are not standardized, that their validity is questionable, that they cannot be administered nationally, and that they have questionable degrees of reliability. In response I would cite the ability of Roger Barker and colleagues to execute such observations over time with high reliability (.80-.98 for many measures). But more to the point I would argue that conventional tests are simply not working and it is time to experiment with alternative techniques, perspectives and theories.

This defense suggests that schools of education must begin to consider teaching their students the methodologies of participant observation, unobtrusive analysis and life history construction. These softer methods have been the traditional province of sociologists and anthropologists. Members of these disciplines must consider offering cross-disciplinary courses in methodology, especially aimed for everyday practitioners in school settings. Graduate requirements for teaching credentials must also be reexamined and greater efforts must be made to recruit and train minority students in these different approaches.

These proposals reflect a basic commitment. Schools should be organized so as to maximize a child's self-development and they should permit maximum child-parent participation. It is evident that my discussion has not been limited to an analysis of compensatory education programs. This has been deliberate. It is my conviction that education, wherever it occurs, involves interactions between social selves. Taking the self as a point of departure I have attempted to show that what happens to a preschool child is not unlike the moral experiences of a black or brown 17-year-old senior. But most importantly, both should find themselves in schools that take them seriously and treat them with respect. Schools exist to serve children and the public. This charge must be also taken seriously.

Participation, Decentralization, Community Control and Quality Education

MARIO D. FANTINI

Those who, like myself, view emerging community participation patterns with more hope than despair hypothesize that school governance—the politics of urban education—is instrumentally related to the form, shape and direction of educational institutions and, therefore, to their quality and relevance. Participation by the clients of the city public schools—students, parents, community residents—represents the emergence of important publics wielding an enormous amount of energy. These publics can combine their energies with those of the professionals to bring about fundamental reforms or they can level their energies against the officials of city schools. A collision course can only be avoided if basic changes are made in urban schooling, changes which—ironically—are not likely without these publics' support. The schools do not now have

Reprinted from "Participation, Decentralization, Community Control and Quality Education" by Mario D. Fantini, *Teachers College Record*, Vol. 71, No. 1, September 1969.

the capacity to respond to the multiple new demands being made upon them. Rooted in nineteenth-century concepts, the educational system simply cannot be expected to solve twentieth and twenty-first century problems; and the consequences are loss of confidence, frustration, disconnection, alienation and retaliation by the new publics.

The problem is not, therefore, with any particular group. It is with the form and shape of the institution in which administrators, teachers, supervisors, students, parents, communities et al function, with the institutional environment and its effects on the parties concerned. In brief, the problem is with the "system," not the people. The parties of interest all want to see the schools updated and made relevant; but they have been tragically sidetracked into conflict. This is a fantastic waste of energy which can be mobilized to generate the power necessary for school reform. It will be my purpose, therefore, to provide a rationale in defense of the emerging participatory movement and relate them to educational development.

JUSTIFYING COMMUNITY PARTICIPATION

There are at least three levels of justification for the community-centered participatory approaches now being advanced as alternatives for urban educational reform. The first is the *conceptual* level, i.e., the *theoretical* assumptions on which the community participation plans are based. The second is at the educational *input* level; the third, the *output* level. Before moving into these three levels of analysis, which will hopefully provide an overall framework for reviewing the school participation movement, let me provide a few direct answers to the questions most often posed by the critics.

Is there any evidence that neighborhood control of

urban schools improves student achievement? The answer is that, if there is no evidence, it is because there are really no community-controlled urban public schools. There are several experiments underway in New York City, Washington, D.C. and Chicago, for example; but these have been in existence only for a couple of years—years mainly consumed by community struggles to wrest some element of control from a usually unsympathetic centralized structure. Moreover, these communities inherit a failing situation. We do have ample evidence of the massive failure that the standard (centrally controlled) urban school has produced. It is ironic, therefore, that those in control of a failing system should demand results of people who are offering constructive, democratically oriented alternatives before they have had a chance to implement them.

The second objection usually pooh-poohs community participation as a political gimmick without relation to quality education: Transferring control isn't the real answer; more money to urban schools is. There is logic to this. For, if all that occurs through participation and decentralization is merely a shift of authority, if all that happens is a transfer of control as an end in itself and not as a means to reform, the cycle of educational decline will not likely be reversed. The problem is still with the outdatedness of the educational system, regardless of who is in control. However, parents, community residents and students who are seeking an increased voice in decision making have moved to this stage of activity as a result of the failure of the existing educational system. In a sense, their involvement platform has been to change the present system, not to accept it through control.

The answer continues, more money for what? In New York City, for example, the school system doubled its budget in the last decade from $508,622,151 in 1959 to $1,251,153,235 in 1968. The per pupil expenditures rose to the $1000 per pupil level above most other cities and even some suburban school districts. Medium elementary-school class size was reduced by 8 percent and classroom teaching staff increased by 37.6 percent—with no results. Special compensatory programs which increase per pupil expenditure also fail to show increase in student performance. The point is that more of the same approach has limited payoff, and most of the money being requested is for more of the same.

OUTDATED MODELS

There are also some real questions concerning universally accepted "inputs" said to be central to quality education. For example, many argue that class size is crucial to quality, then point to the lowering of pupil-teacher ratios as a prime indicator of quality. There is little evidence, however, to suggest any actual relationship between lowered class size from 35 to 30 or from 30 to 25 and student performance. Moreover, the cost of lowering class size in urban school systems is staggering. A reduction of class size for a teacher in a self-contained classroom, age-graded, egg-crated school with irrelevant curricula, and so forth will have a minimal effect because the total institution is dysfunctional. If the educational system is outdated so is its conception of education. Hence trying to improve one "piece" of the system, for example, class size, is like trying to improve an old car by putting a new carburetor in it. Instead of pouring money into an outdated model of education, we need to build a new model. A key question becomes: What is the process by which a major social institution like the schools is reformed in an open society? In our society, building a new model of education requires direct participation by parents, students and other citizens. Basic educational reform is not exclusively a professional undertaking; it cannot or should not be in an open society.

The other dominant question concerns desegregation: Don't these types of local efforts hinder desegregation? The responses vary but they usually start with the observation that since 1954 there has actually been more segregation rather than less. Moreover, there is a distinction between desegregation and integration. Desegregation refers to the physical mixing of black and white students; integration refers to humans connecting as equals. Agreeing on the goal of integration, one could argue that it is necessary for black and other minority groups to have a sense of cohesion and identity. This can in part be achieved through the control of their own institutions. Once blacks attain a status of potency, they will be in a better position to connect up with white society as equals rather than as "junior" members. Therefore, such participatory efforts as decentralization and community control can be viewed as necessary steps toward a further stage of integration.

Under the present concept of desegregation, blacks are moved to white areas and a kind of dependency relationship develops in which improvement is dependent on the presence of a majority of whites. For many, this is another indication of a superior-inferior relationship, communicating once again, albeit subtly, another form of discrimination. Nevertheless, most argue that the goal of desegregation stimulated by the civil rights movement is quality education. That goal remains, as does the option of school desegregation, having been opened to many who had been denied this path to equality. Yet, desegregation moved slowly at best; other options to greater education were needed. Enter the greater local control alternative.

This participation made a great deal of sense, given the present reality. If the schools are still largely segregated and an inferior quality of education is continued, the natural approach seems to be for the community to take a hand in reshaping the institution toward quality education.

Many of those favoring greater local control claim that those who are now talking about desegregation and integration are using this as an excuse for not allowing communities to pursue the option of community participation and increased involvement in decision making.

The clients of our city schools are demanding a voice in updating and thereby raising certain philosophical and theoretical arguments which take us to the conceptual level of justification.

ACCOUNTABILITY AND CONTROL

The first concept concerns public accountability and control of education. In our society, public schools belong to the public. It is the public that decides on policies and objectives for the school; it is the public that delegates to the professional the role of implementor and reserves for itself the role of accountant. The people are the trustees of the schools. They have a right to ask why Johnny can't read. Moreover, if 85 percent of the Johnnies can't read, as is the case in most of our so-called inner city schools, then the public has the right and responsibility, as trustee, to supervise or monitor the needed changes—changes aimed at reducing the discrepancy between policy and implementation.

This process has in essence been in effect; black parents and community residents have been asking why so many black children are failing. The usual answer is that the children are "culturally deprived" or "disadvantaged," that they are failing because there is something wrong with *them*. This verdict has increasingly been rejected, and in the absence of improvement in the performance of the children, the public—in the form of certain communities— has begun to exercise its role as both accountant and trustee. Those in the forefront of this urban movement poignantly ask: What would happen in Scarsdale or Grosse

Pointe if 85 percent of the children in these schools were academically retarded and if 1 percent went to college? What would be the reaction of the parents and the community?

Many black parents who had patiently waited for improvement through such efforts as compensatory education and desegregation have begun to turn away from these efforts. Increasingly, communities are rendering the diagnosis that the problem is not with the learner: the problem is with the system, with the institution. The cry now is: "We need a new system, one that is responsive to our kids and to us. It is up to us to build this new and relevant system."

Sincere schoolmen have been aware of the crises for some time, but they have been victimized by the constraints of an outdated system. Often the professionals have become defensive in the belief that the public expects the school and the schoolmen to solve all the ills of society. Many have attempted to respond with programs of remediation on the one hand and token desegregation on the other. Both approaches, although stimulated by federal legislation, have been less than successful. Some educators attribute the failures to the underlying assumption that the problem was with the learner and not with the institution. Certainly it is difficult, if not impossible, for those trying to keep the present system running to serve also as the major agents of institutional change. Other legitimate parties are needed. And surely the parents and students constitute legitimate parties of the public school.

But even if school people were able, by themselves, to bring about radical institutional changes, they would thereby be denying opportunities for parents and students to learn and grow through the process of involvement and participation. Through involvement, parents and students can learn more about the complexities of teaching and learning and relate this learning to their own roles of parents as teachers or students as teachers. Through involvement, parents and students can be more attuned to the role of the schoolman as an individual in a setting which places severe constraints on him; have a better view of program options; be more cognizant of the need for increased funds for education. Even more important, perhaps, is the realization that if the professional tries to go it alone, this could lead to a professional monopoly.

THE IMPORTANCE OF PROCESS

The second major principle emerging from the new participatory movement concerns the importance of process. Communities no longer accept the process of something being done for or to them—even if the product is desirable. Increasingly, the acceptance process is with or by the community, and this includes students as well. This principle is intrinsically tied to the broader self-determination movement embraced by many blacks and other minority groupings. The reasons for this shift are not difficult to understand. Generally, they are a reaction to the bitter realization that whites cannot solve black problems. Accompanying this are the distrust and alienation that come from the feeling of powerlessness.

By emphasizing the process of participation in decision making, communities are employing the basic tools of democracy itself—tools which increase people's sense of potency. Professionals, including researchers, are increasingly referring to the drive for self-determination as the "fate control" variable. The preliminary findings indicate that fate control fundamentally affects human motivation essential to achievement in all areas.

It is during this process that student participants, for example, can begin to translate their concern for relevance into policy. Students can begin to legitimize educational objectives that deal with individual and group identity, potency and disconnection, in short, with humanistic concerns. They are concerned with legitimizing affective educational objectives in order to restore a needed balance with the present cognitively oriented school. They can contribute to making the educational process more experiential and reality-oriented with instrumental links to the major societal roles, e.g., worker, citizen, parent and community residents can add support for more diversity in school staffing. Talents can be tapped from various sources, including the immediate community. This would lead to the valuing of performance over credentials as the major personnel criterion. Included in performance is how human (sensitive, authentic, emphatic, trustworthy) the person is.

EXPECTANCY AND SOCIALIZATION

Two other key principles have their roots in social-psychological theories. The first has to do with expectancy. The concept that it is the system, rather than the child, that has failed is a hopeful concept for black parents and communities. The transition from blaming the client to doing something about institutional renewal is illustrated by perceptions of schoolmen—largely white—who possess attitudes which brand black children as inferior. "After all," say black parents, "they call our kids 'culturally deprived' and 'disadvantaged,' don't they?" The argument continues: "The white professionals expect black children to fail, and so do Negro professionals who have been taught the ways of the system. These attitudes are, at best, colonial behaviors that have a negative effect on the motivation and learning for black children. Our children *can* learn and indeed they *will* learn!"

Attempting to reverse the psychology of institutional expectations is difficult indeed; but it is crucial. We are all familiar with the self-fulfilling prophecy—the apparent relationship between expectation and performance. We all seem to agree that a school is better when positive instead of negative self-fulfilling prophecies are made. When parents, students and communities participate in reform, we can assume that the chances for developing a climate of high rather than low expectations will be significantly increased. Parents have an intrinsic interest in the maximum growth and development of the children. Couple this intrinsic tie with the choice to break the shackles of inferiority, and the opportunities of generating a new climate of "making it" are enhanced considerably.

The other theoretical principle deals with socialization, that is, the broader processes of growth, development and cultural transmission. We have known for some time now that the major agents of socialization for the young child are his family, his peer group and his school. We seem to know, also, that growth and development are significantly affected, positively or negatively, depending on the relationship that exists among these major socializing agents. When there exist disconnection and discontinuity between or among them, the child's potential can be affected adversely.

Such is the case now in most urban schools; the family is disconnected from the school. Moreover, the culture of the family is often different from the culture of the school, and frequently the child is asked to make a choice between them. The result is deep internal conflict. Add to this the fact that the peer group is at odds with both the family and the schools, and we get a picture of a disjointed socialization process. Achieving continuity in socialization seems to depend on the ability of these three agents to become joined. This connection can emerge through the process of participation and involvement. When parents, students and professionals join together in the common pursuit of reform, the process itself serves to cement new relationships among them. Too, each has a stake in what has developed jointly.

Another principle emanating from the community participation movement has to do with respect for the preservation of diversity. When black communities participate in the process of educational decision making, they will most likely favor programs that emphasize black culture: language, dress, food, music, art, history and so on. The basic point is that to be black is to belong to a rich cultural identity—an identity largely dissipated and relinquished as blacks attempted to adjust to the demands of white cultural social institutions of which the school is the most prominent. In this adjustment process, blacks were—and still are—made to feel that their own values and culture are nonexistent or at best inferior to the acceptable cultural standard. This left many blacks with an "identity" problem, a problem induced by the dilemma of accepting the culture of white society—a culture which has discriminated against them and is, by its own admission, racist. To adjust, therefore, is to accept the very environment that they were struggling to change.

Other cultural groups were beginning to come to this same conclusion. Spanish-speaking populations, for example, are beginning to demand bilingual programs—programs which would maintain the legitimacy of Spanish, the language of the home and the culture. The issue raised by this emphasis on cultural differences is quite fundamental: diversity is not just a reality to be tolerated; it is a value to be nurtured. Cultural diversity is important to the individual cultural group; it is equally important to the vitality and renewal of society itself. To be assimilated or homogenized into some colossal mainstream culture has a stultifying effect on both the individual and society. Growth and development of individuals and society feed on a diet of pluralism. Diversity is essential to human and social renewal.

Another concept deals with the institutional change.

Fundamental change leading to a new and more relevant educational institution cannot really happen unless three major pillars of the present educational system are altered.

1. Governance—The realignment of the parties involved in the process of educational decision making. A shift toward giving parents, community residents and students an increased voice in policy. The *politics* of education.

2. Substance—The objectives to be achieved and the content to be learned. The search for relevance toward more humanistically oriented curricula dealing with individual and group problems, e.g., identity, disconnection, powerlessness, or a more functional emphasis, e.g., preparation for major societal roles such as worker, citizen, parent.

3. Personnel—The people who will be responsible for implementation. Opening the educational system to a far broader base of talent than the conventionally prepared career educator; training through the reality of community needs and expressions.

These are the pillars which are being altered at the several community-oriented experiments in New York, Washington, D.C. and Boston. The experiments in increased participation have first altered the governance pattern, which in turn has triggered change in the other basic pillars. The direction of the change appears to be as follows:[1]

	Traditional	Reformed
Center of Control	Professional dominance	The public, the community as partners
Role of parent organizations	To interpret the school to the community, for public relations	To participate as active agents in matters substantive to the educational process
Bureaucracy	Centralized authority, limiting flexibility and initiative	Decentralized decision making allowing for maximum local

	to the professional at the individual school level	lay and professional initiative and flexibility, with central authority concentrating on technical assistance, long-range planning and system-wide coordination
Educational Objectives	Emphasis on grade level performance, basic skills, cognitive (intellectual) achievement	Emphasis on both *cognitive* and *affective* (feeling) development. Humanistically oriented objectives, e.g., identity, connectedness, powerlessness
Tests of professional efficiency and promotion	Emphasis on credentials and systemized advancement through the system	Emphasis on performance with students and with parent-community participants
Instructional philosophy	Negative self-fulfilling prophecy, student failure blamed on learner and his background	Positive self-fulfilling prophecy —no student failures, only program failures—accountable to learner and community
Basic learning unit	Classroom, credentialized teacher, school building	The community, various agents as teachers, including other students and paraprofessionals

PARTICIPATORY VEHICLES

The final set of concepts deals with the participatory vehicles for implementation. It is necessary to examine the different patterns and schemes that are intended to search out improved education. The vehicles are all manifestations of a basic participation movement. The differences among them are largely the result of how much of a voice in school governance is sought.

The first of the patterns is decentralization. Participation under this form comes through, in part, as shared decision making: The clients—in this case, the parents and community residents—have anywhere from an advisory to an equal voice with those who are operating the existing educational system. The difference between administrative decentralization, which is established practice in many large school districts, and political decentralization (governance) is that the latter creates a new public relationship between communities and their public schools—a relationship in which there is a basic redistribution of authority and responsibility. Under political decentralization in big-city systems, for example, parents and community residents share certain decisions and not others with a central school board. The same is true with the superintendent of schools, teachers and/or supervisors' association and so on.

An illustration may be helpful. If, under decentralization, a local school board elected by the community demands the right to select a district superintendent, various shared decision-making plans can be advanced. The superintendent may indicate that the local board can submit to him the names of three candidates from which he would make the final selection. The supervisors' association may demand that the three names submitted be from the top three on a qualified list. The central board would then approve or reject the final candidate. Another procedure could be that the superintendent present the names of three candidates whom he has checked with the supervisory group. The local board then makes its choice for district superintendent and submits it to the central board for final approval.

If the local board wished to select candidates from outside the established city-wide personnel policies, it could have serious problems attempting to do so. The local board would have to initiate a new personnel policy with the other parties. If agreement were not reached, the local board could appeal to the state department of education, but this would begin to lead to controversy and conflict unless the appeal to the state were done with the cooperation and support of all the parties in question.

Decentralization is a federation of local school boards,

each with limited authority over a portion of the total school system. Under this scheme, there would be a city-wide school system with a central school authority which may have final veto power over most decisions which local boards could make or which can impose sanctions on local districts through appeals to the state. Procedures governing recruitment, selection, transfer and tenure of personnel, budget, maintenance and curriculum must be worked out together. Usually each group must compromise to achieve a consensus. These consensus procedures become the new ground rules for making decentralization work.

Community control, in its purest form, shifts to a local school board the bulk of the authority necessary for governing schools. Under maximum community control, a locality does not share decision making with a central school board; the local board is independent of the central board and assumes the same status as any other school district in the state. Since education is a state function, the local district shares authority with the state and is subjected to state regulation. There is, therefore, no absolute total control as such. However, under community control, sections of city schools—usually in the heart of the city—secede from the larger school system to become an independent school district. As an independent district the community is free to recruit, hire, transfer and release personnel—the same as, for example, a Scarsdale or a Newton. Harlem CORE has developed a plan for an Independent Harlem School District which it hopes will be considered by the New York State Legislature.

Communities which reach an advanced stage of frustration and concern over the failure to supply quality education for their children tend to assume an increasingly stronger stance of reform, sometimes called "militancy." They begin to demand that basic and fundamental changes be made. They are demanding a relevant educational system: one that works, one that has payoff for the children. In other words, the community is sanctioning change.

INPUT QUALITY

The second level of justification concerns the quality of the inputs in the community-oriented school experiments; inputs of the programs developed to achieve educational objectives. Since standard school programs are not working, there is a need for innovation measures. There is a problem of determining the general worth of any innovation. Usually educators legitimize innovations through the medium of professional journals. A review of the professional literature would indicate that the following innovations are among those most frequently mentioned as holding considerable promise:

1. Individualized learning
2. Continuous progress
3. Ungraded schools
4. Cooperative teaching
5. On-the-job staff development
6. Preschool education
7. Community involvement
8. Paraprofessional development
9. Bilingual teaching

These are the very programs being utilized in community-oriented subdistricts. For example, in the Ocean Hill-Brownsville demonstration district in New York City, there are two quite different early childhood programs in operation—Montessori and Bereiter-Englemann, with still a third model—Leicestershire integrated infant school—being introduced. Moreover, in the Ocean Hill community-centered district, an individualized, nongraded elementary school utilizing programmed reading curricula is in operation. In the same district (at P.S. 155) a bilingual program is attempting to reach Spanish-speaking children in their native language during the early phases of schooling. Of course, bilingual programs are not uncommon but there is a qualitative dimension which sometimes is captured by the clinical judgment of experts such as Vera John and Vivian Horner who surveyed existing bilingual programs in the United States:

> The work as P.S. 155 is unique. To begin with, it is the first program in a major U.S. city in which the members of the Spanish-speaking community have been given an opportunity *de facto* to cooperate actively in an innovative program. One might describe the program as refreshingly audacious . . . bilingual program is not a copy of anything—it is a truly innovative approach and has drawn attention to itself among bilingual educators at the national level. . . .

In the Ocean Hill district each school has a full-time teacher-trainer. The trainer is responsible for developing an on-the-job staff development program. Working with teachers individually and in groups, the teacher-trainer tries to deal with the developmental instructional problems in each school.

The Adams-Morgan Community School in Washington, D.C. utilizes a nongraded cooperative teaching format. Under this arrangement, teams of teachers and paraprofessional community interns (four teachers, two community interns) work with a family of children (approximately 100). Each of the team teachers selects one area of specialization in order to maximize individual talents and interests.

Personnel utilization and staffing patterns are also important "input" areas. The staffs of the community-centered schools vary along a wide horizontal spectrum from the professional to the lay, the latter including parents, community residents and students themselves.

They vary vertically as well to include not only professional educators with administrative and supervisory credentials but specialists from other fields and disciplines.

The chief education officer in the I.S. 201 experimental district in New York City, for example, is foremost a public administrator. The administrator of the Adams-Morgan Community School in Washington, D.C. is a social worker. Community districts such as Ocean Hill have made wide use of lawyers, engineers and others outside professional education. The recruiting pattern of regular teachers has broken with tradition in the New York City experiment by fanning out beyond the city limits for personnel. Further, the subdistricts have a high proportion of new teachers who are graduates from top-ranking liberal arts colleges and former Peace Corpsmen and VISTA Volunteers. [2] The principals appointed in the Ocean Hill demonstration also depart from convention. The first male black principal of a secondary school, the first Puerto Rican principal and the first Chinese-American principal in the history of New York City are found there.

IMPROVED OUTPUTS

The third level of justification concerns outputs, that is, the results, especially on student achievement. Because all of the community-controlled experiments have been in existence for only a short period (no more than two years), reporting at this level is limited. However, despite both the developmental problems confronted by each experiment, together with their short existence span, there are more signs of hope than despair. [3]

Most of these signs come from observations, judgments and testimony of various visitors to and workers in these community schools, but more objective data are being reported. They range from a report on improved school climate to reading gains reported from standardized tests.

For example, a teacher who has worked in one of the Ocean Hill schools for three years was quoted as saying:

> You get a really positive feeling when you go into the school. The children give those teachers a tremendous amount of respect. There have always been discipline problems, but now there aren't as many as before.

Another teacher in I.S. 201 describes what it means for her to teach in a community-controlled school:

> Being a teacher at I.S. 201 is a way of life. It makes teaching more than a job. Teaching is a career at 201. If you ever come to visit 201, and just about everyone does eventually, in the principal's office there is a slogan that sums up the goals and ambitions of the professional staff: Parent Power + Teacher Power = Powerful Children.

Other results are more invisible as one of the Ocean Hill principals reported. He explained that the custom before the community experiment was for the staff to leave shortly after the 3:00 p.m. dismissal so that by 3:15 p.m. the chains were fastened on the school gates. The custom began to change when members of his staff began to be locked in for staying until 5:00 p.m.

NEW EDUCATIONAL PROCESSES

However, skeptics will also call for "hard data." For example, are the students reading at grade level? There are several points to be made here. First, the experiments in community participation, in addition to consuming most of their energies in a struggle for survival, in addition to starting from a position with the schools which they have inherited, are also in the process of developing a new educational process. What is therefore being evaluated is the process of development and not the results of a developed program.

Second, the experiments are attempting to implement

new pedagogic concepts and are after new educational objectives. These new arrangements do not lend themselves to "objectives measures" especially if those measures are ones associated with conventional education. The newer educational objectives are more process-oriented objectives dealing with rather intangible forces: quality of "human interaction," empathy, feelings, awareness, style and the like.

Nonetheless, more objective indices are being reported. In the Adams-Morgan experiment, for example:

1. *Suspensions.* There were *no* suspensions or expulsions of students since the project's inception (1967)—an obvious improvement from the pre-experiment period.

2. *Vandalism.* The superintendent of schools in Washington, D.C. reported a 70 percent decrease in vandalism since the experiment.

3. *Reading.* During the 1967-68 school year, of the 176 elementary schools in Washington, D.C., Adams-Morgan was among only six schools in which reading scores had improved. Standardized tests now being analyzed (STEP) are expected to show similar gains for the 1968-69 school year.

At the Ocean Hill Demonstration District in New York City, Rhody McCoy, Unit Administrator, reported the following:[4]

1. *Suspensions.* During the period since the beginning of the community experiment (less than two years) there were fewer than 30 suspensions for the eight-school complex. In a similar period immediately prior to the experiment 628 suspensions were reported for the same eight schools.

2. *Vandalism.* Acts of vandalism were practically non-existent in the district in the past year—two cases for the year. In the year prior to the establishment of the district at least two per week were reported for the year.

3. *Attendance.* The average pupil attendance for the

elementary schools in the district is now 90 percent. The average pupil attendance before was between 70 percent and 75 percent.

4. *Daily Teacher Absences.* The daily absence rate among teachers prior to the experiment was 15 percent. The present rate is closer to 2 percent.

5. *Teacher Turnover.* Teacher turnover before Ocean Hill was between 20 and 25 percent. Presently the rate of turnover is 3 percent.

6. *Teacher Vacancies.* At the time of the formation of the Ocean Hill District there were 78 vacancies and no waiting list. Presently there are no vacancies and a waiting list of 130 persons.

7. *Community Participation.* Each school has parent associations which reported "handful" attendance prior to the experiment. During the past year the attendance averaged closer to 100 per meeting. At every open meeting of the Ocean Hill Governing Board there was an average attendance of 250 persons. In over half of these meetings the attendance was reported to be closer to 500.

8. *Reading.* Utilizing standardized tests (Metropolitan Reading Test) nearly 98 percent of the children in the seven elementary schools in the district showed growth in reading with an average gain of one and one-half years.

Also one might be tempted to add the numerous testimony from thousands of visitors from all parts of the United States and the world who visit these community schools.

In conclusion it is important to emphasize that to achieve quality education for urban schools we will need to develop an entirely new conception of education housed in an updated educational institution. Today, certain communities—especially black and other minority —are deciding on a new, more human education system. In one way, the new lay participatory movement appears to be ushering in the second progressive period of education.

The first, a short-lived attempt by a key group of professionals, faltered earlier in this century and ended with the second world war. Hence the new participatory movement seems to be exactly what professional reformers have been waiting for these many years. The participants carry with them the seeds to a new humanistically oriented educational process which they themselves legitimize. Lest we forget, when professionals attempted to impose a type of progressive education on to a community which was not receptive, the results were a defeat for both the professional and the concept of education. The professional has to provide the public with educational options that maximize growth for students. These options must be presented in as vivid a manner as possible, but in the last analysis, it is the public which must decide. The future of our civilization may well rest on how well this is achieved.

NOTES

1. Taken from papers prepared for Brookings Conference (December 12, 1968) on community schools.

2. See, for example, "Teachers Who Give a Damn," October 4, 1968 ed. of *Time* Education Section; and "With Love . . . ," *Newsweek*, October 7, 1968.

3. See, for example, *New York Times*, Sunday, March 16, 1969.

4. Reported by Mr. McCoy in a testimony before the California Senate Education Committee, May 26, 1969.

Educational Vouchers:
A Proposal for
Diversity and Choice

JUDITH AREEN and CHRISTOPHER JENCKS

Ever since Adam Smith first proposed that the government finance education by giving parents money to hire teachers, the idea has enjoyed recurrent popularity. Smith's ideal of consumer sovereignty is built into a number of government programs for financing higher education, notably the GI Bill and the various state scholarship programs. Similarly a number of foreign countries have recognized the principle that parents who are dissatisfied with their local public school should be given money to establish alternatives.[1] In America, however, public financing for elementary and secondary education has been largely confined to publicly managed schools. Parents who preferred a private alternative have had to pay the full cost out of their own pockets. As a result, we have almost no evidence on which to judge the merit of Smith's basic

Reprinted from "Education Vouchers: A Proposal for Diversity and Choice" by J. Areen and C. Jencks, *Teachers College Record,* Vol. 92, No. 3, February 1971.

principle, namely, that if all parents are given the chance, they will look after their children's interests more effectively than will the state.

During the late 1960s, a series of developments in both public and nonpublic education led to a revival of interest in this approach to financing education. In December 1969, the United States Office of Economic Opportunity made a grant to the Center for the Study of Public Policy to support a detailed study of "education vouchers." This article will summarize the major findings of that report and outline briefly the voucher plan proposed by the Center.[2]

THE CASE FOR CHOICE

Conservatives, liberals and radicals all have complained at one time or another that the political mechanisms which supposedly make public schools accountable to their clients work clumsily and ineffectively.[3] Parents who think their children are getting inferior schooling can, it is true, take their grievances to the local school board or state legislature. If legislators and school boards are unresponsive to the complaints of enough citizens, they may eventually be unseated. But mounting an effective campaign to change local public schools takes an enormous investment of time, energy and money. Dissatisfied though they may be, few parents have the political skill or commitment to solve their problems this way. As a result, effective control over the character of the public schools is largely vested in legislators, school boards and educators— not parents.[4]

If parents are to take genuine responsibility for their children's education, they cannot rely exclusively on political processes. They must also be able to take individual action on behalf of their own children. At present, only relatively affluent parents retain any effective control over the education of their children. Only they are free to move to areas with "good" public schools, where housing is usually expensive (and often unavailable to black families at any price). Only they can afford nonsectarian, private schooling. The average parent has no alternative to his local public school unless he happens to belong to one of the few denominations that maintain low-tuition schools.

Not only does today's public school have a captive clientele, but it in turn has become the captive of a political process designed to protect the interests of its clientele. Because attendance at a local public school is nearly compulsory, its activities have been subjected to extremely close political control. The state, the local board and the school administration have established regulations to ensure that no school will do anything to offend anyone of political consequence. Virtually everything of consequence is either forbidden or compulsory. By trying to please everyone, however, the schools have often ended up pleasing no one.

A voucher system seeks to free schools from the restrictions which inevitably accompany their present monopolistic privileges. The idea of the system is relatively simple. A publicly accountable agency would issue a voucher to parents. The parents could take this voucher to any school which agreed to abide by the rules of the voucher system. Each school would turn its vouchers in for cash. Thus parents would no longer be forced to send their children to the school around the corner simply because it was around the corner.

Even if no new schools were established under a voucher system, the responsiveness of existing public schools would probably increase. We believe that one of the most important advantages of a voucher system is that it would encourage diversity and choice within the public system. Indeed, if the public system were to begin matching students and schools on the basis of interest, rather than residence, one of the major objectives of a voucher system would be met without even involving the private sector. Popular public schools would get more applicants, and they would also have incentives to accommodate them, since extra students would bring extra funds. Unpopular schools would have few students, and would either have to change their ways or close up and reopen under new management.

As this last possibility suggests, however, there are great advantages to involving the private sector in a voucher system if it is properly regulated. Only in this way is the overall system likely to make room for fundamentally new initiatives that come from the bottom instead of the top. And only if private initiative is possible will the public sector feel real pressure to make room for kinds of education that are politically awkward but have a substantial constituency. If the private sector is involved, for example, parents can get together to create schools reflecting their special perspectives or their children's special needs. This should mean that the public schools will be more willing to do the same thing—though they will never be willing or able to accommodate *all* parental preferences. Similarly if the private sector is involved, educators with new ideas—or old ideas that are now out of fashion in the public schools—would also be able to set up their own schools. Entrepreneurs who thought they could teach children better and more inexpensively than the public schools would have an opportunity to do so. None of this ensures that every child would get the education he needs, but it would make such a result somewhat more likely than at present.

Beyond this, however, differences of opinion begin. Who would be eligible for vouchers? How would their value be determined? Would parents be allowed to supplement the vouchers from their own funds? What requirements would schools have to meet before cashing vouchers? What arrangements would be made for the children whom no school wanted to educate? Would church schools be eligible? Would schools promoting unorthodox political views be eligible? Once the advocates of vouchers begin to answer such questions, it becomes clear that the catch phrase around which they have united stands not for a single panacea, but for a multitude of controversial programs, many of which have little in common.

REVISED VOCABULARY

To understand the voucher plan recommended by the Center, it is useful to begin by reconsidering traditional notions about "public" and "private" education. Since the nineteenth century, we have classified schools as public if they were owned and operated by a governmental body. We go right on calling colleges public, even when they charge tuition that many people cannot afford. We also call academically exclusive high schools public, even if they have admissions requirements that only a handful of students can meet. We call neighborhood schools public, despite the fact that nobody outside the neighborhood can attend them, and nobody can move into the neighborhood unless he has white skin and a down payment on a $30,000 home. And we call whole school systems public, even though they refuse to give anyone information about what they are doing, how well they are doing it, and whether children are getting what their parents want. Conversely, we have always called schools "private" if they were owned and operated by private organizations. We have gone on calling these schools private, even when, as sometimes happens, they are open to every applicant on a nondiscriminatory basis, charge no tuition, and make whatever information they have about themselves available to anyone who asks.

Definitions of this kind conceal as much as they reveal, for they classify schools entirely in terms of *who* runs them, not *how* they are run. If we want to describe what is really going on in education, there is much to be said for reversing this emphasis. We would then call a school public if it were open to everyone on a nondiscriminatory basis, if it charged no tuition, and if it provided full information about itself to anyone interested. Conversely, we would call any school private if it excluded applicants in a discriminatory way, charged tuition, or withheld information about itself. Admittedly, the question of who governs a school cannot be ignored entirely when categorizing the school, but it seems considerably less important than the question of how the school is governed.

Adopting this revised vocabulary, we propose a regulatory system with two underlying principles:

1. No public money should be used to support private schools.
2. Any group that operates a public school should be eligible for public subsidies.

THE PROPOSAL

Specifically, the Center has proposed an education voucher system (for *elementary* education) which would work in the following manner:

1. An Educational Voucher Agency (EVA) would be established to administer the vouchers. Its governing board might be elected or appointed, but in either case it should be structured so as to represent minority as well as majority interests. The EVA might be an existing local board of education, or it might be an agency with a larger or smaller geographic jurisdic-

tion. The EVA would receive all federal, state and local education funds for which children in its area were eligible. It would pay this money to schools only in return for vouchers. (In addition, it would pay parents for children's transportation costs to the school of their choice.)

2. The EVA would issue a voucher to every family in its district with children of elementary school age. The value of the basic voucher would initially equal the per pupil expenditure of the public schools in the area. Schools which took children from families with below-average incomes would receive additional incentive payments. These "compensatory payments" might, for example, make the maximum payment for the poorest child worth double the basic voucher.

3. To become an "approved voucher school," eligible to cash vouchers, a school would have to:

—accept each voucher as full payment for a child's education, charging no additional tuition.

—accept any applicant so long as it had vacant places.

—if it had more applicants than places, fill at least half these places by picking applicants randomly, and fill the other half in such a way as not to discriminate against ethnic minorities.

—accept uniform standards established by the EVA regarding suspension and expulsion of students.

—agree to make a wide variety of information about its facilities, teachers, program and students available to the EVA and to the public.

—maintain accounts of money received and disbursed in a form that would allow both parents and the EVA to determine where the money was going. Thus a school operated by the local board of education (a "public" school) would have to show how much of the money to which it was entitled on the basis of its vouchers was actually spent in that school. A school operated by a profit-making corporation would have to show how much of its income was going to the stockholders.

—meet existing state requirements for *private* schools regarding curriculum, staffing and the like.

Control over policy in an approved voucher school might be vested in an existing local school board, a PTA, or any private group. Hopefully, no government restrictions would be placed on curriculum, staffing and the like, except those already established for all private schools in a state.

4. Just as at present, the local board of education (which might or might not be the EVA) would be responsible for ensuring that there were enough places in publicly managed schools to accommodate every elementary school age child who did not want to attend a privately managed school. If a shortage of places developed for some reason, the board of education would have to open new schools or create more places in existing schools. (Alternatively, it might find ways to encourage privately managed schools to expand, presumably by getting the EVA to raise the value of the voucher.)

5. Every spring each family would submit to the EVA the name of the school to which it wanted to send each of its elementary school age children next fall. Any children already enrolled in a voucher school would be guaranteed a place, as would any sibling of a child enrolled in a voucher school. So long as it had room, a voucher school would be required to admit all students who listed it as a first choice. If it did not have room for all applicants, a school could fill half its places in whatever way it wanted, choosing among those who listed it as a first choice. It could not, however, select these applicants in such a way as to discriminate against racial minorities. It would then

have to fill its remaining places by a lottery among the remaining applicants. All schools with unfilled places would report these to the EVA. All families whose children had not been admitted to their first-choice school would then choose an alternative school which still had vacancies. Vacancies would then be filled in the same manner as in the first round. This procedure would continue until every child had been admitted to a school.

6. Having enrolled their children in a school, parents would give their vouchers to the school. The school would send the vouchers to the EVA and would receive a check in return.

SOME CAVEATS

The voucher system outlined above is quite different from other systems now being advocated; it contains far more safeguards for the interests of disadvantaged children. A voucher system which does not include these or equally effective safeguards would be worse than no voucher system at all. Indeed, an unregulated voucher system could be the most serious setback for the education of disadvantaged children in the history of the United States. A properly regulated system, on the other hand, may have the potential to inaugurate a new era of innovation and reform in American schools.

One common objection to a voucher system of this kind is that many parents are too ignorant to make intelligent choices among schools. Giving parents a choice will, according to this argument, simply set in motion an educational equivalent of Gresham's Law, in which hucksterism and mediocre schooling drive out high-quality institutions. This argument seems especially plausible to those who envisage the entry of large numbers of profit-oriented firms into the educational marketplace. The argument is not, however, supported by much evidence. Existing private schools are sometimes mere diploma mills, but on the average their claims about themselves seem no more misleading, and the quality of the services they offer no lower, than in the public schools. And while some private schools are run by hucksters interested only in profit, this is the exception rather than the rule. There is no obvious reason to suppose that vouchers would change all this.

A second common objection to vouchers is that they would "destroy the public schools." Again, this seems far-fetched. If you look at the educational choices made by wealthy parents who can already afford whatever schooling they want for their children, you find that most still prefer their local public schools if these are at all adequate. Furthermore, most of those who now leave the public system do so in order to attend high-cost, exclusive private schools. While some wealthy parents would doubtless continue to patronize such schools, they would receive no subsidy under the proposed system.

Nonetheless, if you are willing to call every school public that is ultimately responsible to a public board of education, then there is little doubt that a voucher system would result in some shrinkage of the public sector and some growth of the private sector. If, on the other hand, you confine the label public to schools which are equally open to everyone within commuting distance, you discover that the so-called public sector includes relatively few public schools. Instead, racially exclusive suburbs and economically exclusive neighborhoods serve to ration access to good public schools in precisely the same way that admissions committees and tuition charges ration access to good private schools. If you begin to look at the distinction between public and private schooling in these terms, emphasizing accessibility rather than control, you are likely to conclude that a voucher system, far from destroying the public sector, would greatly expand it, since it would force large numbers of schools, public and private, to open their doors to outsiders.

A third objection to vouchers is that they would be available to children attending Catholic schools. This is not, of course, a necessary feature of a voucher system. The courts, a state legislature, or a local EVA could easily restrict participation to nonsectarian schools. Indeed, some state constitutions clearly require that this be done. The federal Constitution may also require such a restriction, but neither the language of the First Amendment nor the legal precedent is clear on this issue. The First Amendment's prohibition against an "establishment of religion" can be construed as barring payments to church schools, but the "free exercise of religion" clause can also be construed as requiring the state to treat church schools in precisely the same way as other private schools. The Supreme Court has never ruled on a case of this type (e.g., GI Bill payments to Catholic colleges or Medicare payments to Catholic hospitals). Until it does, the issue ought to be resolved on policy grounds. And since the available evidence indicates that Catholic schools have served their children no worse than public schools,[5] and perhaps slightly better, there seems no compelling reason to deny them the same financial support given other schools.

The most worrisome objection to a voucher system is that its success would depend on the EVA's willingness to regulate the marketplace vigorously. If vouchers were used on a large scale, state and local regulatory efforts might be uneven or even nonexistent. The regulations designed to prevent racial and economic discrimination seem especially likely to get watered down at the state and local level, or else to remain unenforced. This argument applies, however, to *any* educational reform, and it also applies to the existing system. If you assume any given EVA will be controlled by overt or covert segregationists, you must also assume that this will be true of the local board of education. A board of education that wants to keep racist parents happy hardly needs vouchers to do so. It only needs to maintain the neighborhood school system. White parents who want their children to attend white schools will then find it quite simple to move to a white neighborhood where their children will be suitably segregated. Except perhaps in the South, neither the federal government, the state government, nor the judiciary is likely to prevent this traditional practice.

If, on the other hand, you assume a board which is anxious to eliminate segregation, either for legal, financial or political reasons, you must also assume that the EVA would be subject to the same pressures. And if an EVA is anxious to eliminate segregation, it will have no difficulty devising regulations to achieve this end. Furthermore, the legal precedents to date suggest that the federal courts will be more stringent in applying the Fourteenth Amendment to voucher systems than to neighborhood school systems. The courts have repeatedly thrown out voucher systems designed to maintain segregation, whereas they have shown no such general willingness to ban the neighborhood school. Outside the South, then, those who believe in integration may actually have an easier time achieving this goal with voucher systems than they will with the existing public school system. Certainly, the average black parent's access to integrated schools would be increased under a voucher system of the kind proposed by the Center. Black parents could apply to any school in the system, and the proportion of blacks admitted would have to be at least equal to the proportion who applied. This gives the average black parents a far better chance of having their children attend an integrated school than at present. There is, of course, no way to compel black parents to take advantage of this opportunity by actually applying to schools that enroll whites. But the opportunity would be there for all.

THE PROPOSED DEMONSTRATION

The voucher plan described above could in theory be adopted by any local or state jurisdiction interested in increasing diversity in schools and parental choice in selection of schools. In the long run it is not much more expensive than the present system. But the Center has recommended to OEO that a demonstration project be financed first, carefully regulated to ensure that the proposed rules are followed, and carefully monitored to test the effects of dispensing public education funds in the form of vouchers. The Center has recommended that at least 10,000 elementary school students be included in the demonstration site, and that the demonstration city (or part of a city) should contain a population which is racially and economically heterogeneous. Ideally some alternative schools should already exist in the selected area, and the prospects for beginning other new schools should be reasonable.

In March 1970, staff and consultants of the Center embarked on an extensive investigation of the feasibility of conducting a demonstration project. Superintendents of schools in all cities with a population in excess of 150,000 in the 1960 census, which were not under court or administrative order to desegregate their school systems, were contacted by mail. Expressions of interest were followed up. Meetings were held in interested cities around the country. Local and state school administrators were contacted, as were interested school officials, teachers' groups, parents' organizations and nonpublic schools.

As of November 1, 1970, five communities had decided to apply for preliminary planning funds. If one or more of these cities decides to conduct a demonstration of the voucher program, we may have a chance at last to test what contributions a voucher program could make to improving the quality of education available to children in this country. If, on the other hand, the National Education Association and the American Federation of Teachers have their way, we shall have no test at all.

NOTES

1. Fuchs, E., "The Free Schools of Denmark" in *Saturday Review*, (August 16, 1969).

2. For a complete description of the Center proposal, see *Education Vouchers: A Report on Financing Education by Payments to Parents* prepared by the Center for the Study of Public Policy (Cambridge, Massachusetts: December 1970).

3. For other discussions of the need to encourage alternatives to the present public schools, see Clark, K., "Alternative Public School Systems" in *Equal Educational Opportunity* (Cambridge: Harvard University Press, 1969); Coleman, J. S. "Toward Open Schools" in *The Public Interest*, (Fall, 1967); Downs, A. "Competition and Community Schools" written for a Brookings Institution Conference on the Community School held in Washington, D.C., December 12-13, 1968 (Chicago, Illinois, revised version, January 1969); Friedman, M., "The Role of Government in Education," in *Capitalism and Freedom,* (Chicago: University of Chicago Press, 1962); Jencks, C., "Is the Public School Obsolete?" in *The Public Interest,* (Winter, 1966); Krughoff, R. "Private Schools for the Public" in *Education and Urban Society* Vol. II (November 1969); Levin, H.M., "The Failure of the Public Schools and the Free Market" in *The Urban Review* (June 6, 1968); Sizer, T., and Whitten, P., "A Proposal for a Poor Children's Bill of Rights" in *Psychology Today* (August 1968); West, E. G., *Education and the State* (London: Institute of Economic Affairs, 1965).

4. School management has been increasingly concentrated in the hands of fewer educators and school boards. The number of school districts, for example, declined from 127,531 in 1930 to less

than 20,440 in 1968. The number of public elementary schools dropped from 238,000 to less than 73,000 in the same period. The concentration is particularly striking in urban areas. The New York City School Board alone is responsible for the education of more students than are found in the majority of individual states. Los Angeles has as many students as the state of South Carolina; Chicago as many as Kansas; Detroit as many as Maine. Nearly half of all the students in public schools are under the control of less than 4 percent of the school boards. See U.S. Department of Health, Education, and Welfare, Digest of Educational Statistics (1969).

5. Greeley, A., and Rossi, P., *The Education of Catholic Americans* (Chicago: Aldine, 1966).

Black English for
Black Schools:
A Call for
Educational Congruity

Consider the following situation: A number of black
children are at home with one or more of their parents and
a number of other adults who may or may not be
relatives.[1] The adults, conversing in Black American
English, discuss a variety of topics of interest to them.[2]
The children also communicate among themselves in Black
American English as they sit on the periphery of the adult
group. Although they appear readily to understand what is
being discussed by the adults, the children do not
participate in the adult communication system. The adults'
communications are open to the children only so long as
they do not disrupt them. If a child, or group of children
does interrupt, the adult responds either with a frown
carrying negative overtones or else a short and curt reply
indicating a negative evaluation of the interruption. In
short, adults in the home consider children to be unacceptable participants in the adult communication system; they
are only to be seen, and not heard. The adults appear to

believe that by the age of puberty the children will be viable members of the communication system and will have learned the language and its uses within the low-income black community.[3]

Consider also this situation: A classroom in an urban school is comprised of 33 students and one female teacher, all of whom are black. Within the classroom, the teacher, using Standard American English, speaks directly to the students both individually and in groups with extended series of connected sentences. The children are expected to respond to the teacher with complete sentences and are to use Standard American English in speaking with her and with other students while they are in the classroom. There appear to be two linguistic groups of children within the class. One group appears to be bidialectal: its members speak Standard American English as well as Black American English; they are also quite facile in "code switching" between the two dialects. These children are primarily from middle-class families. The second group is comprised of children (described in the previous home situation) who are monodialectal: they speak only Black American English. The teacher refuses to allow any child in the classroom to speak unless he speaks in Standard American English ("I don't want to hear your mouth again unless you talk right"). By the end of the school year, there is very little communication between the teacher and those children who speak only in Black American English, so little as to prompt the teacher to suggest several children should be "tested" to learn "why they will not talk in class."

By the teacher's failure to recognize and allow variations in linguistic communication among the various groups of children within her classroom, she significantly contributes to insuring lack of academic success and advancement for the monodialectal low-income, black child.[4] The only legitimate linguistic pattern in the classroom was significantly different from that used by the low-income black children in their homes. Children who came to school speaking only Black American English were forced to compete with other black children who were able to speak Standard American English—the language of the teacher and the textbooks. Given the number of other difficulties that low-income black children have in the public schools, being forced to speak in what is essentially a "foreign language" within that school is no small thing.

THE STRUCTURE OF LANGUAGE IN THE PUBLIC SCHOOL

In the public school where this study was conducted, the curriculum was clearly defined and established for each grade level. The books, workbooks and teacher handbooks that were used also happened to be used in every other school within the city. All of these books, printed material on the walls, notes to be taken home—in short, all written communication between teacher and pupils or teacher and parents—employed Standard American English. No aspect of the public school allowed for use of Black American English.

Marshall Durbin has summarized a number of the basic assumptions concerning the transmission of information within the school. He notes:

1. Usually one female teacher presents the material to be learned.
2. The teacher's main technique for presentation is through verbal reward. If a child is verbally active as regards the lesson, he is rewarded verbally and highly praised to other students, other teachers and to his parents. He goes on to become a good student since his "level of motivation is high."
3. The content of the lesson is explained through language to children in great detail. The children are expected to disgorge the material in equally great detail. The greater the detail, the higher the verbal rewards.

4. Patience, good manners and always keeping the children first in mind are the keynotes to successfully teaching children because children can only learn by careful, patient and detailed communication directed at them. In short, the public school teaching techniques in America are directly analogous to the Middle Class American socialization process. The teacher acts and behaves as regards verbal behavior and learning exactly as a parent acts. [5]

Each of these points bears some discussion as it relates to the experience of the low-income, monodialectal, black child in the public school. The first and most obvious fact is that the learning situation for the monodialectal black child within the public school is, in nearly every respect, quite different from that within his home.

In school the material is usually presented by a single female teacher (in this particular school 24 of the 26 teachers were female), but in the low-income child's home, information is presented by a number of adults, only some of whom are female. While in the home communication is received *indirectly* from a number of sources, each reinforcing and strengthening the other, in the school the child must interpret communication *directed* toward him from a single source. Not only information is communicated, but various inflections, intonations, forms of syntax and morphological differentiations crucial to linguistic sophistication. In the school, the low-income child is presented only one dialect of English from only one adult who at no point attempts to interpret or note similarities between her English and that used by the majority of students in her class.

The teacher in the class observed continually encouraged verbal participation within the classroom between herself and the students albeit on her own terms. Those students who communicated in a manner acceptable to her received praise and often were held as models the remainder of the class would do well to emulate. Meanwhile, in the home of the low-income, monodialectal child, no rewards are given for interaction between adult and child; in fact, it is quite likely to be punished. Questions are often answered with one-syllable responses, negative in character and occasionally personally derogatory. If he comments to adults, as opposed to questioning them, the child is usually ignored. What rewards are given to him are often indirect, through comment to other adults present in the room about "how quiet" the child is and thus, "how good" he is. Even this reward, then, is rarely spoken directly to the child but most often to another adult.

In the classroom, the teacher's instructions to students were extensive and quite detailed. They were always given in series of complete sentences. Likewise, the students' answers or responses were accepted only when given in complete sentences. The teacher was intolerant of answers given either in phrases or in Black American English. (Note the insistence by the teacher, "I don't want to hear your mouth again unless you talk right.")

Early in the school year in which observations were made, the class was divided into two groups. The division was in part based upon whether or not the child could respond in a manner linguistically acceptable to the teacher. Teacher-pupil interaction over time narrowed to only that group of children who were able to conform to the desires of the teacher. This group of children happened to be the middle-class students in the classroom. Little interaction occurred between the children who did not use Standard American English and the teacher. These children, however, continued to communicate frequently with one another. The teacher repeatedly asked the monodialectal students to "quit whispering" among themselves. But when the teacher called on one of the monodialectal students, the student usually gave no response.

Lilly stands up out of her seat. Mrs. Caplow asks Lilly,

for example, what she wants. Lilly makes no verbal
response to the question. Mrs. Caplow then says
rather firmly to Lilly, "Sit down." Lilly does. However, Lilly sits sideways in the chair (so she is facing
the teacher). Mrs. Caplow instructs Lilly to put her
feet under the table. This Lilly does. Now she is
facing directly away from the teacher and tbe black-
board where the teacher is demonstrating to the
students how to print the letter "O". (the names of
teacher and student are pseudonyms.)

Those children within the classroom who were monodialectal were recorded as not responding to questions and
inquiries from the teacher at a rate nearly five times that
of the bidialectal students.

The teachers within the school said that they perceived
it was their "duty" to teach the children how to speak. In
fact, the teachers felt that they were not only required to
teach the children how to speak, but to teach them how to
speak "correctly." Within the classrooms teachers paid
special attention to the verbalization of the bidialectal
students to insure that they learned correct pronunciation.
The same attention was not given to the monodialectal
students. When questions were asked by the bidialectal
students, lengthy explanations were given, especially to the
"why" questions. When it was necessary to give negative
responses to the bidialectal students, lengthy explanations
were included. Basically, the teacher was performing the
same type of tasks reported by Durbin in the homes of
bidialectal students. With the middle-class students, the
linguistic patterns in the school and the home were
congruent. The teacher did not perform similarly with the
monodialectal students in her class. Her communication
with the bidialectal students followed the pattern established in their home, but there was strong dissonance
between the teacher's communication patterns and those
of the parents of the monodialectal children.

If one accepts John Dewey's dictum that the learning experience in the school should be highly congruent with the experiences and conditions of learning in the home, then one can agree that there is a basis for change in the present system of communication in the public schools. So long as a significant group of black students use Black American English as their system of communication, then the schools' refusal to employ such a system in teaching these children presents a discontinuity between the child's two significant learning centers—the home and the school.

A PROPOSAL FOR REFORM—LEGITIMATIZATION OF BIDIALECTALISM

One major change in the use of language as a communication system within the black school might be the use of Black American English as the major system during the first years of schooling. As the children who come to school speaking Black American English progress through the grades of elementary school, Standard American English should be taught as a "second language." Perhaps by the fifth grade the originally monodialectal children would become bidialectal, speaking both Black and Standard American English as their middle-class roommates do. From the time that the children can adequately deal with Standard American English, it should be adopted as the primary linguistic system in the classroom. This would probably be necessary to prepare the children to deal with the economic, cybernetic and technological structures of American society. Black American English appears to have developed as a "restricted code" which has not incorporated conceptualizations from industrialized American society.[6] Durbin notes that Black American English has developed within a segregated and isolated community that has been denied entrance to many institutions of the larger society.[7] If low-income black children who speak only Black American English are to have the opportunity to "navigate" the larger society, they must be taught Standard American English, as one would teach a foreign language. This is particularly important given the high degree of linguistic conformity and uniformity demanded of blacks who participate in the larger white society.

I do not mean to imply that the linguistic code of the child who speaks Black American English is responsible for the overwhelming presence of poverty among his family and peers. The plight of the poor black cannot be attributed to the fact that he possesses a linguistic code different from that of white society. The opposite appears to be more nearly the case: the restricted code arose from the realities of segregation and discrimination of blacks by whites. But the question is not really the role of linguistic codes in poverty. The fact is that the thrust of the American occupational structure is towards increased professionalization and skilled technological expertise. This, in turn, necessitates the use of Standard American English. If the monodialectal black child is to have access to the larger structures of American society, his ability to deal with the language appears to be a distinct advantage. Language is not a vehicle to change the stratified (and racist) occupational schema in this society, nor will merely knowing Standard American English ensure adequate employment for the black child in his adult years. It will, however, remove one roadblock to such employment.

FURTHER POLICY CONSIDERATIONS

If one were to use Black American English to teach children in black urban schools from the first day of kindergarten, the argument might be raised that middle-income black children who are proficient in Standard American English would be penalized. I do not believe that this would be the case, however, for the middle-class black children I studied also knew and could communicate in

Black American English. What would happen is that one criterion for the differentiation of children within the classrooms could be removed, because both middle-income and low-income black children would be using the same linguistic code. There would no longer be stratification of children according to this variable. With the introduction of Standard American English, over time the low-income children would gain bidialectalism and in the higher grades would no longer be at a linguistic handicap.

A second objection to this proposal may be raised if low-income black children will be in schools with white children who do not know Black American English. But Engelmann has noted:

> The child who originally speaks a non-standard dialect must be taught the standard one, but the child who originally speaks the standard dialect also must be taught at least one nonstandard one. If we do not follow this course of action, we do not get rid of the utterly unwarranted implication that the standard dialect is, after all, the superior one. The problem we are facing in this respect is similar to the one we are struggling with in the teaching of Negro history. If we teach it only to black rather than to all American students, we shall, in fact, continue the obnoxious tradition of cultural discrimination.[8]

If, indeed, two groups of children within one classroom do not possess a commonly understood linguistic system, it may be necessary to separate the children into different groups for at least part of the substantive lessons in the classroom. Though, at first, the time spent in separate groups might be significant, the need for separate groups would continually decrease as each group became proficient in the linguistic code of the other.

When one group of students speaks Standard American English and another speaks Black American English, the divisions within the classrooms appear to follow those of the larger social class system of the society. The data suggest that only by first recognizing that children within the same classroom do possess significantly different linguistic patterns can the various groups of children be effectively taught. The myth of the "melting pot" has led the public schools to apparent fear of admitting linguistic differences lest they prevent everyone from "melting" appropriately.

Low-income black children will continue to be taught ineffectively as long as they are forced to participate in classes where the teaching patterns are geared for children who speak Standard American English. Recognizing differences in linguistic patterns is not to be taken as a basis for establishing schools based solely on social class criteria. Rather, the use of Black American English in the curriculum during the early grades with Standard American English taught as a second language, is viewed as a means to aid in equipping low-income students to participate in the larger structures of American society. Such a proposal is offered as an alternative model to present classroom conditions, which clearly hinder social and economic mobility.

Recognizing that a number of value assumptions are implicit in this proposal, it is only fair to mention a criticism of the fundamental premises. Sledd notes:

> The basic assumption of bi-dialectalism is that the prejudices of middle-class whites cannot be changed but must be accepted and indeed enforced on lesser breeds. Upward mobility, it is assumed, is the end of education, but white power will deny upward mobility to speakers of black English, who must therefore be made to talk white English in their contacts with the white world. . . . The fact is, of course, that Northern employers and labor leaders dislike black faces but use black English as an excuse.
> Because approval goes to upward mobility, every-

body should be upwardly mobile; and because upward mobility is impossible for underdogs who have
not learned middle-dog barking, we must teach it to
them for use in their excursions into the middle-dog
world. There is no possibility either that the present
middle class can be brought to tolerate lower-class
English or that upward mobility as a national
aspiration will be questioned. Those are the pillars on
which the state is built, and the compassionate
teacher, knowing the ways of his society, will change
the color of his students' vowels although he cannot
change the color of their skins.[9]

Several comments should be made in response to Sledd,
though this is not the place to detail them extensively.
First, he does not dispute the assumption that in fact there
are two viable and quite different English dialects present
in a large number of elementary school classrooms.
Second, he does not suggest how low-income black
children are to be taught in the classroom if only Standard
American English is used. Nor does he discuss how
children are to be introduced to conceptualizations, for
example, in "new" math, if they are taught only in Black
American English, for this code does not presently permit
such mathematical formulations. Third, is not bidialectalism desirable, even as attacks are made to break down the
racist structure of American society, so that the child can
grasp more fully the nature of his world—for example, in
the daily newspaper—rather than view it through a dark
glass of "foreign languageness"? Finally, given the present
international trend towards the use of Standard English as
the primary mode of communication, whether it be in
banking, physics or sociology, may not the rejection of
bidialectalism for the low-income black child effectively
isolate him from the seemingly dominant current of the
last part of the twentieth century?

At least two other possible reservations about the

approach outlined in this essay must be commented upon. The first concerns the effects upon low-income mono-dialectal black children of television and other media that communicate Standard English, which are present in nearly every black home. The argument could be made that children in these homes are in fact learning Standard English and that this learning from the home only needs to be transferred to the classroom. Frederick Williams, in a paper prepared for the Institute for Research on Poverty at the University of Wisconsin, presented data which appear applicable to this issue and noted:

> If the distinctive language habits of the lower socioeconomic classes serve in the socialization of children in those classes, then what is the potential for the language of the mass media to counter this effect? Based upon what sketchy data now exist, television seems to have no significant effect upon the lower class child's learning of varying styles of language and, in particular, his learning of the more-or-less standardized English which is heard in television programs.[10]

Williams' subjects were picked on the basis of class characteristics, however, with half of the sample comprised of black children and half comprised of white children. His emphasis upon the class basis of linguistic characteristics downplays the importance of race and suggests (as does Engelmann) that a strong similarity exists between the linguistic patterns of low-income whites and blacks. (If such is the case, my contentions may be broadened to include any schooling situation where there are children of different social-class backgrounds. Since my research took place in a black school, I am not unequivocally prepared to make the extension in the framework of analysis.)

A second reservation revolves around the possible detrimental effects of using Black American English in the schools with regard to the assimilation of blacks into the social and economic mainstream of American society. I contend that using Black American English in the early grades with low-income monodialectal black children will not retard their assimilation but distinctly enhance it if they do choose to opt for assimilation. With Black American English, the child will begin schooling with a communication system that is accepted and used in the classroom. He will be able to participate and engage in learning within the classroom that would not be possible were he forced to use an unknown dialect. Second, with the introduction of Standard American English, over time the child is introduced to the communication system of the larger society in such a manner that he will be able to gain proficiency in that system. Third, the use of Black American English would diminish in direct proportion to the increase in the use of Standard English within the classroom.

Finally, and in a somewhat different vein, I have never been convinced that schools have served effectively as agents of socialization to enhance upward mobility for immigrants coming to the United States with different linguistic systems. What socialization schools did accomplish was merely enough to enable the new arrivals to "get by." The dominant power configuration at the time of the immigrant arrivals was surely not going to provide sufficient tools for assimilation for the immigrants to be in a position to threaten their own privileged positions! One must look to the arenas of political and economic activity, in my estimation, to account for the mobility that immigrants have achieved. Given the tenacity with which ethnicity maintains itself in the United States, one could conclude that the schools' attempt to homogenize immigrants has failed and that a large crack remains in the melting pot. Likewise, Black American English cannot be held responsible for the plight of the low-income black person in America. On the other hand, the ability to use

Standard American English may serve as an asset for the low-income black in the attempt to achieve mobility.

A PEDAGOGICAL NOTE: CLASSROOM INSTRUCTION

Concurrent with any suggestion of change in the pattern of linguistic communication now used in the urban black school is the need for change in the pattern of classroom instruction, particularly for the low-income black child. Classroom observations indicate that teachers within the urban black schools employ direct interaction between themselves and the students when teaching substantive material. The teachers speak to the children, ask them a specific and direct question, and indicate that they expect a direct response by a single child, all in the mode of one-to-one interaction. This pattern of teaching appears to fit very well with the experiences of the middle-class children who came from homes where there is a great deal of direct parent-child verbal interaction, where parents are accustomed to speaking to the children directly and receiving direct responses from them.

This pattern was not observed within the homes of children from low-income families (note the situation described at the beginning of this chapter). Though there appears to be little or no direct interaction between low-income adults and children, the children seemed to listen and also grasp the information shared among the adults. I have termed this mechanism of learning through indirect interaction as "secondary learning."[1 1]

Just as exclusive reliance on Standard American English within the classroom appears to be detrimental to the learning of low-income children, so also does the manner in which the material is taught. The low-income black student does not come to the classroom having experienced learning in direct one-to-one interaction with adults. Rather, information has been grasped by employing secondary techniques whereby the child merely listens and does not actively participate in the adult discussion. The low-income black child would have Dewey's optimal congruence between his home and his school when the teachers spoke in Black American English and did not speak directly to him, but rather spoke to another adult and allowed the child simply to sit and listen. Such is the pattern by which the low-income black child appears to learn in the home and such could be the pattern within the school if attempts were made to establish congruity between home and school experiences.

The above techniques could be employed in the school as the sole manner of instruction if all pupils are low-income black children. When there are also middle-class children present, as was the case in my study, modifications in the teaching techniques would have to be introduced. The children could be taught on the basis of whether their previous learning experience had been in the mode of personalized adult-child interaction or whether it had been primarily through mechanisms of secondary learning where there is little adult-child interaction. Such a situation of differential patterns of learning was observed in the study, especially when the high reading group (comprised of the middle-class students) was being taught and those at the remaining two tables (low-income children) listened to the teacher as she taught the others. This may be an important technique that could be expanded in use within the classroom. The teacher could conduct personalized interaction learning with the one group of children while at the same time fostering secondary learning with another group. But those children who do not presently employ direct interaction in their learning must be aided and taught to do so to achieve options in a society and school system that places high value on direct and immediate responses to questions and comments in one-to-one interaction.

Ironically, as the teachers observed in this study ignored the low-income children (because, in the words of one teacher, "they have no idea of what's going on . . .") and spent their time teaching the middle-class children, they were, almost in spite of themselves, teaching the low-income children. The process of secondary learning was allowed to exist in the class, not through a direct and rational decision of the teachers, but as a consequence of their decision to concentrate their teaching time with the middle-class students.

In fact, had the teachers decided to spend more time with the low-income children in one-to-one personalized interaction, the learning situation might not have been so conducive. In a sense, the low-income children experienced a partially optimal learning situation. Had the teachers also spoken in Black American English as they taught the middle-class students, the low-income children would have had a learning situation they were familiar with.

Significant changes are needed in both the linguistic and pedagogical aspects of the current school situation for the low-income black child who comes to school speaking Black American English and who understands his environment and the world around him through secondary learning. Failure to recognize that the low-income black child comes to school with a number of unique linguistic and pedagogical attributes may only exacerbate the current conditions in urban black schools. For so long as the school continues to accept only one manner of speaking and learning, the low-income black child will be at a significant handicap. The public schools are in the paradoxical position of espousing egalitarian ideals and ideological commitment to an equal opportunity for all children, but in fact sustaining class barriers among different groups of children. This can only contribute to inequality in the social and economic conditions of American society.

NOTES

1. This essay is based upon research aided by a grant from the United States Office of Education, Grant No. 6-2771. Original Principal Investigator, Jules Henry (deceased), Professor of Anthropology, Washington University. Current Principal Investigators, Helen P. Gouldner, Professor of Sociology, Washington University, and John W. Bennett, Professor of Anthropology, Washington University. The author wishes to acknowledge the many substantive discussions related to questions of the importance and impact of Black American English in urban schools with John Bennett, Marshall Durbin, Helen Gouldner and Carol Talbert. It is difficult to indicate the points at which at least one of the above mentioned persons has not contributed to the clarification of the position presented within this paper.

2. Though the term "Black American English" is used throughout this essay, Engelmann employs the term, "Rural Southern English," which appears to be nearly synonymous. Engelmann writes, "Rural Southern English . . . spoken largely by rural black southerners, in the South and also in the northern ghettos, is also used by some whites. . . . It is an English dialect, as valid, viable, and necessary in its own social context as Standard American English. In fact, rural southern is not a spoilage of Standard American any more than the latter is a disfigurement of British English." H. Engelmann, "The Problem of Dialect in the American School" in *Journal of Human Relations* 16 (Winter 1968).

3. Durbin, M., "The Linguistic Socialization of a Black Child" Unpublished (Social Science Institute, Washington University, St. Louis, Missouri: 1970).

4. Rist, R., "Student Social Class and Teacher Expectations: The Self-Fulfilling Prophecy in Ghetto Education" in *Harvard Educational Review* (August 1970) pp. 411-51.

5. Durbin, *op. cit.*

6. Bernstein, B., "Social Class, Linguistic Codes and Grammatical Elements" in *Language and Speech* Vol. 5 No. 4 (Oct.-Dec. 1962) pp. 221-33; and Lawton, D., *Social Class, Language and Education,* (New York: Schocken, 1968).

7. Durbin, *op. cit.*

8. Engelmann, H., *op. cit.*

9. Sledd, J., "Bi-Dialectalism: The Linguistics of White Supremacy" in *English Journal* (December 1969) pp. 1307-15.

10. Williams, F., "Social Class Differences in How Children Talk About Television" Unpublished (Institute for Research on Poverty, University of Wisconsin, Madison, Wisconsin: 1968).

11. Rist, R., *op. cit.*

The Right to Learn
vs.
The Right to Read

NORMAN E. SILBERBERG
and MARGARET C. SILBERBERG

Back in 1969, when he was United States Commissioner of Education, James E. Allen, Jr., declared that for the quarter of our population who do not do well in reading, "education, in a very important way, has been a failure, and they [the failures] stand as a reproach to all of us who hold in our hands the shaping of the opportunity for education." In the same speech, Allen further pointed out that "one of every four students nationwide has significant reading deficiencies," and "in large city school systems, up to half of the students read below expectation." He went on about the "knowledge and inspiration available through the printed word" despite the fact, or because of it, that a Gallup poll showed that 58 percent of the American people admit that they have *never* read a book. Allen then

Reprinted with the permission of **Society** magazine (formerly *trans*action) Vol. 8 No. 9-10, July/August 1971. Copyright © Transaction, Inc.

demanded the public and political recognition of "The Right to Read."

With all the studies done on reading, we still don't know why some children do not read efficiently. It is difficult, when a parent asks why a child can't read well, to suggest (in professional language, of course) that "That's not his bag." Yet, that is what most such appraisals often come down to. There are thousands of diagnoses of what is "wrong" with a child who does not read efficiently, and nearly as many supposed "cures" for these problems, but no one seems to have considered the possibility that we may be barking up the wrong tree in *expecting* all children to read well. These studies have identified many correlates of inefficient reading, but in none has a causal relationship been satisfactorily demonstrated. For example, although there is high correlation between socioeconomic class and reading skills, closer inspection of the terms reveals that the same thing may be lurking under the middle classes' "learning disabilities" and the poor's "cultural deprivation." For the poor, home environment is blamed for inefficiency in reading. For the rich, it is brain damage, which is presumably less reversible. In neither case do we really know why children in all socioeconomic classes read inefficiently—only that they do.

More important is the fact that, by definition, 50 percent of children must read at grade level or below, since grade level only means the median level achieved in a particular grade. Thus, it is not too surprising that Commissioner Allen finds as many as 50 percent of children who are encountering difficulties in reading. As long as grade equivalent is used as a criterion of reading skill, there has to be 50 percent who are below the median in this skill area. One could question the statistical appropriateness of labeling 50 percent of the population as "abnormal," but the real point is that we as a society are attempting to narrow the range of acceptable learning behavior to a specific point, which we have predetermined as appropriate conformity. This seems, at least, a self-defeating task.

We have found seven longitudinal studies of remedial reading. Not one shows any long-term beneficial effect. The current administration is also rather skeptical of these efforts. In a speech given early in 1970, President Richard Nixon described the results after almost $1 billion had been spent yearly on reading programs under Title I of the Elementary and Secondary Education Act of 1965: "Before-and-after tests suggest that only 19 percent of the children in such programs improve their reading significantly; 15 percent appear to fall behind more than expected, and more than two-thirds of the children remain unaffected—that is, they continue to fall behind." There is currently no evidence that one can "remediate" reading as long as reading is measured in relative rather than absolute terms. We can strive to move the whole reading curve up, but we cannot possibly eliminate its bottom half. Research on the cost effectiveness of such efforts, however, indicates, as they would say at the Pentagon, there is not much bang obtained for the remedial buck.

The better we get at measuring school learning skills, the better able we are to describe them. As the social sciences amass more and better measurements of behavior, we can define with good accuracy what percent of children will have difficulty in reading, what percent of children will have behavior problems and so forth. The only thing that we cannot do is to predict into which family such a child will fall. When parents come to us and ask why their child does not achieve or adjust properly in school, we are often tempted to tell the parents it's just their tough luck. What else can we tell them?

The only other response, it seems to us, is the reminder that bearing or adopting children guarantees parents nothing. We—as a society—have not communicated to parents the probabilities of their having children who do not conform to our predetermined narrow range of achievement. Someone should tell parents that they stand at least a 50 percent chance of having a child who will not be successful in school. This is not as difficult for most people to take as one might expect. Parents, for example, are not particularly shocked if it is suggested to them that their children are likely to resemble them in school learning abilities. (In speeches to upwardly mobile suburban parent groups, our suggestion that the parents pull their old report cards out of the attic to hang on the refrigerator as an inspiration to their children is always met with embarrassed laughter.) Unfortunately, however, parents and teachers take personal responsibility for altering a child's behavior so that he conforms to the standards set forth by the media, industry, the whole striving ethos of our culture. We have had parents of children accept the diagnosis of poor school achievement but fall to pieces when told the child should *not* attend college.

American society is moving more and more toward establishment of academic skill as the *sine qua non* of acceptance within that society. Even though we are, for all intents and purposes, attempting to provide some form of academic education to the total society, our demands become less and less realistic. In 1941, the median educational level in this country was ninth grade. Now we keep almost all of our children through tenth grade. Thus, those children who, in our parents' days, were not learning in school and left in sixth grade to work in mines or on farms are now forced *by law* to sit in school for three or four years longer. While they sit in school, they are usually offered either watered-down versions of the same reading-based curriculum the more talented children receive, or woodworking and shop courses which, it is realized by both teachers and students, provide no entry to a meaningful occupation. Even much of the curriculum research for educable retarded children is aimed not at the experience unit, but rather at ways of improving literacy in this group of persons whose tested language skills are in the bottom 5 percent of the population.

Despite the fact that academic potential (IQ) and intelligence (ability to survive in the environment) are very poorly related in many individuals, more and more sectors of the society are being forced into the high school graduate and college craze. We hear reports that companies will not even interview high school dropouts, even though there is no demonstrated relationship between the job task and academic achievement. A local chain of stores insists that their carry-out boys take a *written* test to get this job, even though the only reading required is occasionally setting a price on a stamp which is then used to stamp hundreds of cans. Carole Williams found that

> only 5 percent of the graduates of inner-city high schools are placed in colleges, jobs, or job-training programs by fall, while 50 percent of the dropouts scheduled to be graduated with the same class have found employment. . . . Inner-city schools don't teach these youngsters job skills, so they seek jobs as unskilled workers—jobs that have already been grabbed by the dropouts. In effect, they have been betrayed by the myth that they should stay in school.

Do these young people need an academic education, or do the personnel managers need an education into the types of skills needed for these jobs?

One example of the frustration encountered because of this thinking is a ninth-grade, 15-year-old boy recently evaluated at the Kenny Institute. He had academic potential within the average range, but, despite years of remedial help, he was still reading at about beginning fourth-grade level and was, of course, flunking most of his courses. He did not make friends easily, so it was not too surprising that when his family moved he refused to attend the new school. He could not bear to demonstrate his "dumbness" to the other students who, not atypically for their age, teased him. He was artistically gifted and good at working with things. What could we do for him? There were no vocational schools where he lived, and even if there had been, most such schools insist on passing grades in academic courses before admission. He was too young for the Department of Vocational Rehabilitation, which also usually encourages high school graduation or else sends the client back for additional course work in books. We could not locate a place where he might study art below a college level. Apprenticeship programs were not available for a high school dropout, as this boy was soon to become. Thus, we had a child who logically could contribute to society, but, because of his reading, was barred from education for an occupation—or rather was barred because the agencies that could help him would not because of their insistence on academic competence.

No one is attempting realistically to assess the wide variations in abilities and talents that exist among young children. Elitists claim that IQ differences among children are not only quantitative, they also represent qualitative differences: a child with a higher IQ is "smarter" than a child with a lower IQ. The trouble with this view is that it expects too much of IQ tests, which do only what they are supposed to do: predict success within an academic curriculum. In addition, it does not recognize the fact that academic curricula were developed for a small portion of the society and cannot be expected to be appropriate for everyone. Elitists regard children with low IQs as dead-wood; one influential government official was recently quoted as saying, "Let's teach them to turn a lathe and leave it at that."

On the other side, we find equalitarians whose philosophy is diametrically opposed to that of the elitists. They seem to view people as having equal potential. Thus, we can teach anyone anything, if our teaching techniques are appropriate and if the reward system is appropriate.

We feel the truth lies somewhere between these two points of view. Unquestionably, there are innate differences between individuals. It is also true that most people learn to survive quite well in this society, independent of their success in school. The problems come, however, because society places hierarchical values upon these differences. Higher IQ does not mean "better," it only means "different." Children with lower IQs can learn to do many things that are possibly more important and appropriate to a modern society than the tasks performed by college professors.

Most agencies and professionals exist to satisfy the parents or the school. Most also accept the narrow limits of behavior considered appropriate for children, and then try to fit the individual child into these narrow limits. But who is to speak for the child? What is needed is an advocate for the child.

The function of the advocate is not to attempt to satisfy unrealistic demands by parent or school or government. Rather, the advocate should interpret the child realistically to all concerned and attempt to help the child make it through childhood with the least possible stress. He should focus on the strengths of the child, rather than attempting to remake his weaknesses. Children are not clay; they have their own personalities, traits and talents, as do adults. Parents and the school must begin to recognize these individual differences, and appreciate them, rather than attempt to change them. Options must be made available for those children who are unable to conform, whatever the reason. To view those children who read poorly as defective and requiring a "cure" only increases the frustrations and unhappiness of these children, many of whom are already suffering from the pressure of overzealous parents and educators. A child's advocate would try to relieve this pressure and bring reality into planning for the individual.

If one is willing to accept this point of view, one can then reassess the child. Does the child truly have a learning disability, or, alternatively, do we as a society have a teaching disability? Most of the children we see in clinics or private practice are not incapable of learning. Many of them are incapable of reading comfortably, and many of them, often because of this inefficiency in reading, are unable to behave in a conforming manner. The relationship of poor school achievement to antisocial behavior is well documented. The question is, should we be devoting so much effort to changing the children, or should we be channeling some of our efforts into changing how and what we teach them? Does a child have a right to read, or does he have a right to learn?

As we have pointed out earlier, many children can be taught by other means. One can easily imagine a bookless curriculum which teaches through media other than the printed word, while the teaching of reading takes place much as other skills, such as lathe work, are taught. Art is taught as a skill, but nobody thinks of a child's proficiency in this medium as important to his education. Nevertheless, one should keep in mind that reading is only one skill in a vast repertoire of skills possessed by most children. If we could find ways to teach children by presenting them with more curricular options, we might reduce the stress on them and possibly reduce their rejection of the learning situation as well.

John Dewey, decrying the fetish of reading, recommended that books be thrown out of the elementary grades while we get on with the business of educating children. We are not advocating the burning of books or the elimination of reading instruction. Rather, reading should be taught as is any other specific skill, while other available resources are used to ensure that children are not excluded from education. The use of experience units, films, field trips, records, tapes, observation, readers (good readers can put books on tape), verbal interaction between children, and verbal interaction with teachers can be learning experiences.

Education need not be an either-or situation, where a child either learns by the narrow methods traditionally used in schools (book learning) or is shunted off to something called "job training." In a democracy, it is exceedingly important that each citizen be afforded the opportunity to be educated in the fullest sense of the word. Different responses to one skill such as reading should not bar children from a serious education in the name of training. The assumption that the inefficient reader and/or verbally less proficient child is unable to learn or cannot be educated is specious and cruel.

To rid ourselves of this assumption requires not only the restructuring of education but the restructuring of society with its artificial literary requirements. Let us look at some examples of how this could be done. The United States Department of Health, Education, and Welfare, in its request for research proposals relating to "The Right to Read" Program (RFP 70-6), describes a "reading task" in the following way:

Reading task: A real-life incident which creates an internally or externally imposed requirement for an individual to perform a discrete, observable operation which is highly dependent upon his having satisfactorily read a specific passage of written material. Examples of reading tasks are: (a) looking up a telephone number; (b) following written directions which tell how to assemble a toy or appliance; (c) responding to a written social invitation; and (d) completing a written job application.

Now, seldom, if ever, does one encounter a truly word-blind person. Even inefficient readers can look up telephone numbers, and for those who cannot, there is always "Information" (if you can get it) through the telephone itself. Following written instructions is a stickier matter. Many of us who read well are totally unable to comprehend the written instructions that come with appliances. And there are many other people, good at working with things, though not talented in the use of language, who can assemble appliances with minimal instruction in language. If records can be produced cheaply enough to put them on the backs of breakfast cereal boxes, it would seem logical that recorded instructions could be included *with* the written directions as an option. As for written social invitations, we will let Tiffany's worry about that.

The problem of the written job application is most critical. Current practice screens out people who want to work on assembly or other non-language-based tasks—tasks that can be and usually are demonstrated by the foreman without benefit of text, without determining if there is a relationship between filling out an application blank and the skill required for that job. Application blanks could be mailed out on telephone request so that the inefficient reader can get help from friends or family in filling it out, with options provided on the job (records, demonstrations and the like) to eliminate the need to read print. The current unemployment or underemployment of many Ph.D.'s raises the question of whether higher education guarantees financial security. Despite the fact that close to 50 percent of high school graduates attend college, less than 20 percent graduate. Vocational school is now becoming more and more a college level program, which means that persons who want to work in nonacademic vocations must first achieve academically for 12 years before they are even permitted access to training. For the first time, society is demanding that schools instruct today's total population of children as successfully as when less than ten out of 100 children entered high school. Unfortunately, "The Right to Read" suggests that we educate our masses *in the same way* as we used to educate a small number of children who were talented in reading.

We therefore propose that people who are concerned about the academically underachieving child switch their focus. Rather than functioning as agents of changing the child, we need more people to stand up for these children. We must advocate change so that these children can be included in society as they are, so that they can be valued for persons as they are and so that they can be proud of what they are. If parent groups and professionals become advocates for the child, demanding that schools and industry focus on ways of including these children rather than developing more requirements to exclude them, some change might be achieved.

The "that's not his bag" approach is not a pessimistic one. The focus switches to defining the limits in expected variations of specific behaviors within the population. It then becomes the responsibility of the schools to alter their curricula to fit the characteristics of the entire population, rather than attempt to restructure the population to fit society's descriptions of how children *should* perform. In this technological age, it is difficult to understand why literacy has maintained such importance. With education focusing almost solely on a curriculum based on literacy, we are excluding a sizable number of potentially capable citizens from an opportunity to be educated, informed and employed in meaningful jobs.

Educators must decide what it is they want to teach children. Must education continue to emphasize the value of traditional academic education to the exclusion of all else? Couldn't we reorder our priorities so that the teaching of reading requires less of the educator's time and energies? Can't we teach children about the world around them, their own and other cultures, the similarities and differences of other peoples, the social and ecological needs of people, past, present and future? The child's right to learn these things should outweigh his right to read.

The Search
for an
Educational Revolution

S.M. MILLER and FRANK RIESSMAN

BREAKTHROUGHS AND BREAKDOWNS

A revolutionary vision has emerged in American education. This vision is to educate the "disadvantaged," for education today is central to security and status. The issue today is how to promote this vision into deep-seated change and effective practice. We need to move from an image of what we wish to its realization in practice.

Each year a new major educational breakthrough is heralded. One year it is programmed instruction. Another year it is team teaching. Later, prekindergartens for the "culturally deprived" became the answer. Educators and citizens hunger for a one-shot, magic potion.

We vacillate between two reactions to these claims and efforts. On one hand, we feel that little is known about

Reprinted from "The Search for an Educational Revolution," F. Riessman and S. M. Miller, in *Urban Education and Cultural Deprivation* by C. W. Hunnicutt. Copyright A-795823 (October 15, 1965).

how to do an effective job of educating the new working-class youth. On the other hand, we feel that if what we know were implemented we would be much further along the line. In either case, we really cannot talk about programs unless we have assurance that we have an educational structure and citizen and professional pressure to implement them. We are not utilizing what we know, as Alvin Eurich has contended about the neglect of educational television. Demonstration and pilot projects often do not grow into national practice, even when they prove out.

Despite the "breakthroughs," the vaunted "educational revolutions," we are disturbed about what is going on. We feel that we are not advancing very rapidly toward the goal of effective education for low-income groups in the United States.

Despite all the hoopla about higher horizons, educational saturations, change agents, we are not really achieving much. The breakthroughs rapidly break down. True, there has been considerable change in some schools and some low-income youth have benefited, but the change is not very great nor does it tend to be continuing.

SOME DANGERS IN THE NEW EDUCATION TREND

It would be surprising indeed, if, in the context of past discrimination, patronization and ignoring of the poor, the new positive shift toward interest in the education of the new working class were to appear uncontaminated by the negative history of the issue. Hence, there are a great variety of potential regressions as well as new dangers to be guarded against:

1. The danger of overemphasizing vocational, non-academic education for children of low-income background, because of their physical style. The intellectually relevant aspects of the physical style are ignored and

misunderstood in this approach, and the physical style is seen simply as preparatory for physical occupations.

2. The danger of aiming for no more than bringing disadvantaged youngsters up to grade level, as though this were some lofty aim. Overlooked here is the positive style and creative potential of the low-income child.

3. The danger, currently quite prevalent, of stressing the deficits, the weaknesses in the background of the low-income child. If the deficits are seen in the context of the strengths of low-income culture and style, then a full-scale attack on the weaknesses (lack of school know-how, test-taking ability, anti-intellectualism) will be beneficial; but divorced from this framework there is strong likelihood that the low-income youngster may develop a negative self-image because of the constant accent on his deficiencies.

4. The danger involved in proposals for new separate tracks for the previously segregated and deprived Negro children, who, it is argued, will be damaged by the demands of the integrated classroom and pace of the white middle-class pupils. Unspoken, or less frequently mentioned, is the fear that the disadvantaged child will retard the middle-class child. Again, this view is rooted in the one-sided stress on the deficiences of the low-income child and the unwillingness of the school to adapt to the styles and needs of non-middle-class children.

5. The danger involved in stressing one-way communication from the school to the parents of the disadvantaged, in order to stimulate the parents to encourage their children to have a more interested, less estranged orientation toward the school. Actually, it is through two-way communication, in which the parents can genuinely influence the school (actually participating in vital policy decisions), that the alienation and estrangement will be broken down.

6. The danger involved in searching for gimmicks,

cure-all techniques for teaching low-income youngsters, rather than focusing on teacher abilities and the imparting of knowledge regarding the cultures and style of low-income groups. In the context of teaching know-how and changed attitudes, new techniques can be very useful, especially in aiming toward far-reaching intellectual growth of low-income pupils; however, by themselves, techniques and gimmicks will probably have limited effectiveness and can easily serve to obscure serious issues. For example, role playing degenerated into just another gimmick where it was applied without awareness of why and how it can be the basis for a completely new approach to teaching the low-income child.

7. The danger of relying upon team-teaching devices and teaching machines to solve teaching problems in connection with low-income children. Many applications of team teaching with "slow" children actually watered down the subject matter, lowered standards, and made negative assumptions about the slow child to the effect that he is less capable of understanding intellectual material, and therefore requires more "practical" subject matter. In one high school where Russian history is taught on a team-teacher basis, the "slow" group spent more time on Russian cooking and the like, while the other students did much more intellectually relevant research.

Teaching machines also are no panacea. While the low-income child likes the game dimensions and the physical dimensions of the teaching machine, he is quickly disillusioned as he comes to realize that this is "just another reader," and reading is not the best medium through which to appeal to the low-income person's style.

8. The danger arising from oversimplified, mechanical efforts at correcting traditional errors, such as the early efforts at revising the white middle-class oriented Dick-and-Jane readers. Initially, the old readers with Dick and Jane in a lovely suburban home were modified by simply

blackening the faces of some of the families. The old themes, setting and language remained, but the faces were now black. (Bank Street College has now developed urban readers with new and broader themes.)

9. The danger of assuming that in order to educate a low-income youngster it is going to be necessary to middle-classize him—to give him middle-class values. Part of this error lies in failing to understand that low-income groups, and Negroes in particular, have very positive attitudes toward education (although they may have highly critical attitudes toward the school), and they do not have to be middle-classized in order to appreciate and desire education. An important deterrent to this trend would be the recognition of the positive elements in the mental styles of low-income people, and the inclusion of these styles in a modified school culture—rather than one-sidedly attempting to change the children to fit the traditional middle-class school culture.

10. A most crucial danger that must be guarded against is the possibility that the current wave of interest in the poor may simply become a fad without impact. Many people who never evidenced much serious interest in the problems of poverty have suddenly jumped on the bandwagon; what will happen when some other issue becomes au courant? It should be noted that programs such as Higher Horizons and Headstart, despite all their excellent intentions, contain the risk that they are rooted too much in short-run zeal and special extra effort that cannot easily be maintained for long periods of time.

Unfortunately, the failure to achieve great educational advance in the face of the new vision of the mssion of the schools is leading to scapegoating of low-income children. Frequently, the struggle to aid children who do not easily fit into the school situation is given up. For example, we do not find the concept of "cultural deprivation" a useful one. It leads people into confusing ways of beginning to analyze the problem. People are different—but the obligation of the school system is to learn how to deal with people who are quite different in terms of their ways of dealing with the learning situation.

The emphasis should not be upon people measuring up to a standard before we deal effectively with them, but rather upon professionals' learning to deal effectively with people who are quite different in outlooks, experiences and capacities. The obligation is not in the people who are different. Rather it is in the professional to learn to deal with a wide variety of students. If a physician's patient is not successfully treated with penicillin, he moves to sulpha or to another form of treatment. The medical model is that the obligation is the physician's to do something about the problem. We submit that this obligation attaches to all professionals. Professionals have to avoid the stance that problems rest fundamentally with clientele. Patients or clientele do not fail; only practitioners do. The use of a term such as "cultural deprivation" leads us away from looking at ourselves as practitioners. We begin to scapegoat those with whom we are having difficulty.

We fear that we are beginning to move toward the possibility of a do-nothing policy in regard to making sweeping changes in the school. For example, the present emphasis upon prekindergarten education as basically necessary for the advance of low-income children is terribly exaggerated. Obviously, there is an important role for it, but we should not act as though it is a panacea that obviates other changes.[1]

We do not think that this view is valid. This ideology bars schools from moving in more flexible, adaptive directions. The escape from failure, the fear of defeat, is leading to a search for gimmicks, for movement without change. We are trying to avoid upsetting the old ways as we paste on some new ways. At its worst, we are subjected to a series of public-relations maneuvers masquerading as educational programs. We need fewer public-relations announcements and more internal reorganization of the schools.

We are basically looking for a technology to solve our problems with the disadvantaged. Technological changes such as prekindergarten programs, team teaching, or reading machines and the like will be an important part of any educational revolution. But we doubt very much that they will be the most important part of the revolution today. And we emphasize today. Different times, different problems, different procedures. Today, something else is needed in addition to new technologies. Just as we may have false gods, so may we have false revolutions.

Although many issues spur an educational revolution, this chapter emphasizes the currently neglected role of administration: the need for adaptability and flexibility and for an effective school climate.

THE NATURE OF THE EDUCATIONAL REVOLUTION

Everybody knows why Rome fell—the Goths came down from the north and took over the city. Many explanations stress the external forces that subjugated the mighty Roman Empire. However, Vladimir Simkhovitch, economic historian and author of *The Fall of Rome*, had another approach: Rome fell because of the declining marginal productivity of the land. Rome was no longer able to support itself agriculturally; this weakened the population. The tensions which existed within Rome emerged out of its economic plight. The important element in the demise of Rome's imperial grandeur was not the coming of the Goths, but its internal stresses. The questions were: What was happening within Rome to weaken it? What were the kinds of tensions, the schisms, that were taking place, making it possible for an outside group to be victorious?

We think this mode of analysis is appropriate to education. What are the problems within educational institutions today? We have to look increasingly toward the internal structure and operation of education. This is particularly important now, for many of the new technologies and new programs require a new kind of administrative structure which permits and facilitates these programs.

The administration of a school impregnates every nook and cranny of the school. Frequently, after a half-hour stay in school, one can describe what the chief administrator is like without ever meeting him. Walk along the halls, look into classrooms, and the style of the institution is clear. It has an atmosphere and climate, a way of operating, which affects everything that takes place. The superintendent or principal sets this style.

Many programs of innovation succeed because they really are changes in school administration, and sometimes school administrators, rather than because of the specific content of the program changes. For example, we suspect that a core element of the positive phase of progressive education was that its supporters devotedly provided an effective climate for the teachers and found school administrators who made it possible for teachers to be flexible and imaginative. To some extent, at its beginning, progressive education was a revolution in educational administration, permitting teachers to be experimental and adaptive.

In the absence of an appropriate organizational base, innovational programs fail. For example, in the summer of 1963, President Kennedy provided funds for the U.S. Office of Education to encourage school dropouts to return to school. In the month of August, counselors went out into some communities to talk to dropouts; and a sizable number of youth did return to school. From what one can learn, many, if not most, of those who returned to school dropped out shortly afterward. This gung-ho campaign did not accompany any change in schools. Dropouts went back to the same kind of situation they were in before. They were returning exiles. Shortly, they again became expellees and refugees from the school—the displaced persons of the affluent society.

Many innovations require an atmosphere, an organization, a structure, which permits them to take root. For example, many schools in low-income areas are now emphasizing school-community relations, getting parents more involved in the educational outlook of their children and closer to their schools. In one school, this increased contact backfired. The low-income parents grew more alienated from the school than ever before. Through greater intimacy with the school, they learned how the school operated and how their children were treated by teachers and administrators. And they did not like what they regarded as the punitive behavior of school personnel. Increased parent contact with the schools, if it is to be effective, may be more important in changing the attitude and behavior of school personnel than those of parents!

New technology and procedures are needed, but they will tend to have limited effects without organizational change. New technologies will rapidly become calcified without such changes. Fortunately, the new technology can be a leverage for organizational change.

ADMINISTRATIVE IMPERATIVES

What are the ingredients of the needed changes in educational administration?

Today we need administrators and teachers who have an authentic commitment to low-income youth. The commitment has to be clear, honest, dedicated and implemented. It has to include sizable amounts of new money for schools, especially those in low-income areas. Parents and the community have to share in policy decisions. Against these fundamentals, we should examine school outlook, organization and climate.

First, the schools have to adapt to the variations in students. No one method works with everybody. Variability and flexibility of programs and approaches are central if we are right in our theme about the variety of perspectives and needs among the "new" working class.

Second, schools have to provide satisfactions to students. If schools operate as or are perceived as prisoner-of-war camps, then we think Edgar Z. Friedenberg and Paul Goodman are correct in their defense of the dropout. The honorable course for a prisoner of war is to break out of camp. School climate and effective school programs are obviously crucial here in building satisfactions in the school.

Third, more effective teachers are needed. We have routinized and overorganzied schools, making it very difficult for teachers to be effective. Sometimes the basic perspective in administering schools appears to be that the task is to make it possible for morons to teach idiots. This view can be a self-fulfilling prophecy. The teacher's role has been overly circumscribed and tightly determined from on top. Standardization, routinization and accountability have been positive steps in the development of schools, as they have been in industrial practice. But the present situation calls increasingly for flexibility and individualization within the school. This is a general problem of large-scale organization.

FLEXIBILITY AND ADAPTABILITY

What is involved in moving toward more organizational flexibility and adaptability?

Assumption A: Education Today Is Not a Continuous Process But a Discontinuous One. Increasingly, the educational process is going to be discontinuous. People will be dropping out of public schools and returning; college students will drop out and return—this is already exceedingly common. With changing occupational demands, people are going to have to be retrained—"redeveloped," in a sense—at different points of their lives. Education and training are not one-time, one-shot activities. Leaving and returning to education and training at different points of one's life will be the typical practice. We need many entry and re-entry points to the school system and training. This is especially true of those who have difficulty in making the educational grade. We need programs which fit the unique development and experience of individuals at the time they re-enter school. The tenth grader who has dropped out and worked for a couple of years and returned to school differs from the tenth grader who never did. We need new bridges and linkages between school and the outside. It is not enough to open a few re-entry doors; the returning student has to be provided an experience which is individually useful.

Assumption B: People Vary. There is tremendous difference among youth today, whatever the social-class level. In any given socioeconomic level there are many different kinds of youths. Upper middle-class progeny are both hippies and Reaganites. Some school dropouts are able to get decent jobs, while others are candidates for permanent economic dependence. Variations in experience and outlook mean that different people need different things at various points in their lives. No one method works equally effectively with everybody. This is our experience with teaching reading. Adherents of some educational practices are members of religious cults, vying in protestations about which cult has the revealed truth. The unfortunate truth is that everyone has the revealed truth, but only a small part of it. Certain methods work very well with certain groups, but they do not work very effectively with others.

We cannot be bound to method. To some extent,

arguments about methods are controversies about different ends. Obviously, different ends may require different means. The more frequent situation is that we do not recognize that there may be many different routes to the same end. We have become bound up in the means. The teaching of reading, for example, should be based on a set of empirically based generalizations. What procedures work with whom? If a procedure does not work with some, then we have to learn ways that are more effective with them. The teaching of reading today is ideologically rather than scientifically based.

One of the central issues in achieving effective differentiation is how to avoid stigma. The less "normal," less "typical" tracks tend to become stigmatized. In turn, stigma leads to degradation and low-quality education. Those recruited to do the low-prestige teaching jobs tend to be of lower quality; they frequently do not have much pride in what they are doing. Many youth who are receiving special attention in school or out are stigmatized because of this attention. Consequently, the help they receive from the new programs is very slight indeed.

The need in our society is for differentiation without stigma. Historically, though, perceived differences are attached to a scale of values, and honor and stigma are parceled out accordingly. We need differentiation in society—we certainly would not want everyone to be like us—but the criteria of the present distribution of honor and stigma are certainly questionable. Perhaps, too, the intensity of feeling about honor or stigma might well be reduced.

These are large issues. For the school administrator, their immediate mandate is to treat as a major task the achievement of individualization and differentiation without producing stigma.

Assumption C: Good Teachers Emerge When They Have Enough Independence and Scope to Permit Personal Style to Flourish. There is no one best type of teacher, or one all-purpose teaching approach. Teachers have to be permitted more independence, more scope and more initiative. A perplexing difficulty here is how to build teachers' accountability for performance at the same time that individual teacher variations are encouraged. In order to attain teacher accountability, school systems have determined what the teacher puts into the system: the boundaries of the syllabus, the class plan and so on. When, for example, class plans are stressed, then inputs are central and individual initiative curbed. The end product, the output in terms of students' achievements, is often given less attention than the input. This occurs because of disagreements about goals and the means of measuring movement toward them, and the fears of a clear-cut evaluation. If outputs are emphasized as the mark of success, then teachers can have wider latitude and still be held accountable for their behavior. New administrative outlooks are necessary.

Assumption D: No Permanent Solutions Exist. Too much of the feeling persists that following a particular policy or procedure would solve our problems for all time. Different times, different places, different issues require different policies. Change and adaptability, assessment and appropriateness are the continuing imperatives. No one-time change will safeguard us forevermore. We constantly have to adapt to new circumstances. As our political climate changes, as our economy moves in new directions, as education becomes the prime route to social mobility in America, as we develop a new poor, we have new demands upon education. Educational systems have to move. All organizations, including educational systems, have to adapt or become anachronistic. There is no necessarily enduring value in any particular strategy or procedure.

The orientation to change runs the danger of falling into novelty and faddism for change's sake. The question is can

we become adaptive and flexible without becoming fad-
dists and novelty hunters, thrill seekers of the new?

ORGANIZATIONAL CLIMATE

What ingredients are required for innovational programs to
succeed? The climate of the school is of great importance.
It affects—as well as is a product of—the behavior of
students and teachers. In consequence, it is paramountly
the administrators' responsibility to improve it.

In analyzing the important ingredients of a "positive"
school climate, personal biases are inevitable, since values
determine to a large extent the definition of what is
positive. We need a pluralism in our quest for desirable
ends. What is the best way depends upon particular
circumstances. What is positive in some group or situation
may not be positive for others. Nor do we know enough to
be definitive about what builds the different types of
effective climates. It is important to recognize many
different kinds of positive school climates and the diverse
roads to each.

One of the basic ingredients in a positive school climate
is *respect*. Students have to be respected. Teachers have to
be respected, particularly by school administrators who
frequently implicitly denigrate their staff by such devices
as time clocks.

Our impression of many programs aimed at low-income
youth is that school personnel not only have meager
understanding of these youth, but that they really do not
like them. We doubt that you can go very far with a youth
whom you do not like. Thus, the attitude of the school
toward disadvantaged youth—who are disturbing to the
more affluent in part because they are disadvantaged—is
essential to effective programs.

Learning and knowledge have to be respected, which is
not always true in our schools. We are sometimes more

respectful of particular teaching methods than we are of knowledge itself. There are many different kinds of positive school climates, many different ways of achieving this condition. Respect has many different doors.

A second important theme of a positive school climate is *authenticity*. The faculty and administration have to stand on what they say. Edgar Z. Friedenberg in his *The Vanishing Adolescent* and elsewhere has been trying to show us the inauthenticity in the relationship between schools, school personnel and students. Frequently, school administrators are phonies. Youth recognize that they do not say what they mean. Little is going to work as long as inauthentic relationships prevail. If a school changes, its people have to believe in what they are doing. The changes cannot be for public-relations effectiveness alone. There has to be a real commitment to the changes.

The third theme of a positive school climate is the fostering of *competence*. The school has to be able to do the job it sets out to do. Youth generally, and low-income youth particularly, do not respect authority figures who are incompetent, who make promises which they cannot achieve, who have goals which have little relationship to the outside world. The school situation has to be built on competence.

The fourth need is for *consistency* and *predictability* in a school. Many schools do not have predictability. The prison experience is interesting. Prison riots usually occur when the practiced, predictable rules, the formal and informal procedures, are broken by the warden. In most prisons the inmates have taken over a good deal of the functioning of the prison. This is known by the warden and it is permitted. It is an easier way to run a prison. In fact, it is difficult to run it any other way. When the warden is forced to change procedures because of a break or the insistence of the board of overseers, he begins to get tough, to put the screws on, to break up the informal groups; the informal loci of power are prevented from operating as they did before. Then a food riot or strike may occur. The predictable modes of behavior have been supplanted and prevented from operating in their usual way. We do not want to liken schools to prisons, although highly controlled institutions have many similar characteristics.[2]

Predictability and consistency are essential to any positive school climate. Consistency is perhaps the most important element in the personality or outlook of those who are effective with low-income youth. A wide diversity of personality types, not just the hearty athlete or the "one of the boys" types, can do well. We think of a dandified, pedantic little Frenchman whom few would predict could be effective with tough New York City boys. Yet—he showed respect for them even when he forced them to take off their hats; his behavior was always predictable and consistent. And he was effective.

Fifth, the school has to have purpose and direction. It has to believe in something. It has to have a *mission*. A school is unlikely to have a positive climate without a mission. If the theme is just that everyone love everyone else and there is no tie beyond that, the love won't last very long. A good deal of the positive impact of programs aimed at low-income youth depends on the Hawthorne effect on school personnel. They believe in what they are doing; they are consulted and involved in the new programs. Morale is high in the pursuit of a common goal.

Finally, school programs have to be *relevant* to low-income youth. They have to see that what the school is doing has come relationship to their own lives.

Important developments are occurring in the United States. We are learning important things. But we are not sufficiently implanting them. We are moving toward a more positive school situation for center-city youth, despite hesitations and obstacles. The greatest lag is in the area of internal school organization.

New technology may produce revolutionary changes in the schools, introducing new dynamics. This result is more likely when the technology forces changes in the relationships among administrators, teachers, and students who are involved through the technology. We think this is the crucial point to understand. New technology is necessary to work more adequately with low-income youth, but this technology will be inadequate unless facilitating administrative change occurs.

IMPLEMENTATION

How is the kind of educational revolution that we need going to be produced? Pressure from within the educational establishment and from without are both necessary. The needed external pressure for change is more apparent than the internal drive for transforming schools. The Negro revolution and the war on poverty have focused attention on schools, asking how well they are doing the job of educating low-income students. Many changes have resulted from these pressures. We expect them to continue and to be sharpened in their specificity and sophistication. But are we doing enough?

The recent availability of funds for education of the "culturally deprived" is leading many who have had no interest in disadvantaged youth to begin to manifest a concern so that they can drink at the new financial trough. With the smell of poverty money, many are running to the youth they have long neglected. Our initial response to this phenomenon, we must confess, had been a moralistic one: Repugnance at the new-found "mission" that money can now buy but social responsibility did not. But more reflective friends have convinced us that the achievement of change requires giving people a reward, a material interest, in moving in new directions; altruism cannot be depended on. Poverty money is providing school systems, schools of education, and affluent professors, with a stake in doing new things about the poor. Sometimes the interest in low-income youth comes out of unloving things such as developing good public relations, or obtaining money to do other things under the guise of helping the poor, or striving to reduce politically important pressures. But the most important result is that more attention is being given to low-income youth. Nevertheless, these activities have to be policed—held accountable—to see that they actually benefit those to whom we dedicate ourselves in the preambles to our projects.

External pressure is thus leading to increased attention to low-income youth, although not without difficulties. But have teachers done all they could to bring about change? Teachers' organizations—both the unions and the professional organizations—have paid inadequate attention to the reorganization and rededication of schools so that they can deal more effectively with low-income pupils. It is important that teachers and their organizations take the responsibility of initiating and demanding action for the improvement of schools, especially those in low-income areas. Teachers' initiatives in securing modifications in the schools are of grave importance.

One of the frequent complaints of fledgling teachers is that they cannot implement their good ideas because the school authorities resist them. Schools of education are caught in the bind of preparing students for what is desirable practice, which may lead to strain in the actual teaching situation, or to reduce their goals to what is acceptable practice to many school officials. This is a widespread problem in American life, having many different faces.

The encrustations of professionalization and the rigidities of bureaucratic organizations force dedicated professionals to be in tension with the organizations in which they work. *They have to subvert as well as live with their bureaucracies.* Every large organization has a bureaucratic underground, a group resistant to the existing practices of the organization. Much of what we learn about American foreign policy is leaked out by dissident groups within the State Department. Some of us will have to be provocative, raising questions and following policies which are not fully acceptable to the organizations in which we work, if we are to fulfill our responsibilities to our students and to our society. We need courageous, creative discontent.

Increasingly, as we live in bureaucracies, we shall have to face the Eichmann question: What is our individual responsibility for what our organization does? To what extent does organizational loyalty supersede personal morality and require us to ignore or protect incompetence and irresponsibility? Should not teachers, singly and in association, publicly and privately, criticize what their schools are doing when youth are victimized?

Obviously, such pressure is insufficient to swing the battle to the rapid improvement of conditions for low-income youth. But it is one of the the things that can be done.

We have stressed that respect for students and competence are important elements in successful teaching of low-income youth. Does this imply that teachers have to have "mature" personalities or exceptional intellect; that we can succeed only if we have more restricted criteria of admission to teaching, thereby aggravating the teacher shortage? No one, of course, can argue against the desirability of getting more feeling teachers into the system; this may happen as salaries and the status of the profession increase. But this is unlikely in the short run. Nor will we be getting the intellectual giants who made lycées and gymnasiums the superior schools they have been; the special factors leading learned persons into lower levels of education do not exist in our society. What are our possibilities of getting better teachers in the immediate situation?

Few of us can consistently rise above our surroundings.

In a fascinating study of physicians, it has been shown that those with the high-level training do not do well in poor medical settings. More important than the training of a physician is whether or not he is in a hospital situation which permits and pushes him into quality medical practice. Similarly, for teachers, the community and organizational setting of a school affect whether or not teachers can have authentic relationships with their students. If a community does not have commitment to low-income youth, few authentic responses can occur. Authenticity occurs not only because of personality and value characteristics of the teachers, but from the situation as well. Some people can triumph over adverse conditions and demonstrate devotion and respect. But for most of us, if the situation indicts authenticity or does not encourage it, then authenticity will be a rarity.

TEACHER TRAINING

Nonetheless, much more can be done to promote teachers' positive feelings about low-income youth. The emphasis, we have asserted, is that teacher training should lead to the development of each individual's style rather than to the emulation of one grand style of teaching. People have different ways of developing and of expressing their style. Many teachers have to become more aware of how they can more effectively use themselves in the teaching situation. We do not mean that they need psychotherapy, but that they lack adequate mirrors in their training so that they can learn their strengths and weaknesses. They are not aided in discovering useful leads to develop teaching approaches with which they are creative. Much of this can be learned. And we think that teachers and prospective teachers can be provided experiences and knowledge about low-income youth that will build positive feelings and respect.

We have to shed the straitjacket of thought about the process of teaching teaching and the overemphasis on formal credentials, a mark of our uncertainty about what is effective performance. Research has to be conducted in a serious way. Studies of school dropouts fill us with oceanic despair; many are almost criminally incompetent.

The cookbook approach to pedagogy, research and administration prevents teachers and administrators from learning how to think imaginatively about their problems. Underlying much of the teaching in schools of education is an absence of respect for the students and their potential. Lacking, frequently, is a sense of vitality and enthusiasm about teaching itself.

Schools of education—like medical schools—have a tremendous impact on practice. A mission to work with the disadvantaged is needed—and a willingness to forego comforting clichés, to face the anxiety and adventure of discovering how to deal effectively with low-income youth and to build school institutions which attract rather than repel.

CONCLUSION

If we agree "that loyalty to petrified opinions never yet broke a chain nor freed a human soul," then we must beware of the persistent danger of traveling on old roads and triumphing on old fields, lacking the courage to take off from where we are. We hope for great breakthroughs in pedagogy. Perhaps they will soon come; probably not. In either case, the educational revolution largely depends on the outlook and behavior of the educational establishment.

NOTES

1. We are not discussing Martin Deutsch's useful programs, but the way in which an ideology is being built around a useful idea. See Alvin W. Gouldner's discussion of this process in "The Metaphysical

Pathos of Bureaucracy," *American Political Science Review* (1953).

2. This is reflected in René Clair's great movie, *A Nous la Liberté*, the predecessor of Charlie Chaplin's *Modern Times* which has a fascinating sequence where the camera moves between a factory's mass-production line and a prison, showing the similarity between the pace and control of the prison and the production line.

PART II

ALTERNATIVES
TO
THE PRESENT
EDUCATIONAL SYSTEM

Freedom and Learning:
The Need for Choice

PAUL GOODMAN

The belief that a highly industrialized society requires 12 to 20 years of prior processing of the young is an illusion or a hoax. The evidence is strong that there is no correlation between school performance and life achievement in any of the professions, whether medicine, law, engineering, journalism or business. Moreover, recent research shows that for more modest clerical, technological or semiskilled factory jobs there is no advantage in years of schooling or the possession of diplomas. We were not exactly savages in 1900 when only 6 percent of adolescents graduated from high school.

Whatever the deliberate intention, schooling today serves mainly for policing and for taking up the slack in youth unemployment. It is not surprising that the young are finally rebelling against it, especially since they cannot

Reprinted from "Freedom and Learning: The Need for Choice" by Paul Goodman in *Saturday Review*, May 18, 1968. Copyright © 1968 Saturday Review, Inc.

identify with the goals of so much social engineering—for instance, that 86 percent of the federal budget for research and development is for military purposes.

We can, I believe, educate the young entirely in terms of their free choice, with no processing whatever. Nothing can be efficiently learned or indeed learned at all—other than through parroting or brute training, when acquired knowledge is promptly forgotten after the examination— unless it meets need, desire, curiosity or fantasy. Unless there is a reaching from within, the learning cannot become "second nature," as Aristotle called true learning. It seems stupid to decide a priori what the young ought to know and then to try to motivate them instead of letting the initiative come from them and putting information and relevant equipment at their service. It is false to assert that this kind of freedom will not serve society's needs—at least those needs that should humanly be served; freedom is the only way toward authentic citizenship and real, rather than verbal, philosophy. Free choice is not random but responsive to real situations; both youth and adults live in a nature of things, a polity, an ongoing society, and it is these, in fact, that attract interest and channel need. If the young, as they mature, can follow their bent and choose their topics, times and teachers, and if teachers teach what they themselves consider important—which is all they can skillfully teach anyway—the needs of society will be adequately met; there will be more lively, independent and inventive people; and in the fairly short run there will be a more sensible and efficient society.

It is not necessary to argue for free choice as a metaphysical proposition; it is what is indicated by present conditions. Increasingly, the best young people resolutely resist authority, and we will let them have a say or lose them. And more important, since the conditions of modern social and technological organization are so pervasively and rigidly conforming, it is necessary, in order to maintain human initiative, to put our emphasis on protecting the young from top-down direction. The monkish and academic methods which were civilizing for wild shepherds create robots in a period of high technology. The public schools which did a good job of socializing immigrants in an open society now regiment individuals and rigidify class stratification.

Up to age 12, there is no point to formal subjects or a prearranged curriculum. With guidance, whatever a child experiences is educational. Dewey's idea is a good one: It makes no difference *what* is learned at this age, so long as the child goes on wanting to learn something further. Teachers for this age are those who like children, pay attention to them, answer their questions, enjoy taking them around the city and helping them explore, imitate, try out, and who sing songs with them and teach them games. Any benevolent grownup—literate or illiterate—has plenty to teach an eight-year-old; the only profitable training for teachers is a group therapy and, perhaps, a course in child development.

We see that infants learn to speak in their own way in an environment where there is speaking and where they are addressed and take part. If we tried to teach children to speak according to our own theories and methods and schedules, as we try to teach reading, there would be as many stammerers as there are bad readers. Besides, it has been shown that whatever is useful in the present eight-year elementary curriculum can be learned in four months by a normal child of 12. If let alone, in fact, he will have learned most of it by himself.

Since we have communities where people do not attend to the children as a matter of course, and since children must be rescued from their homes, for most of these children there should be some kind of school. In a proposal for mini-schools in New York City, I suggested an elementary group of 28 children with four grownups: a licensed teacher, a housewife who can cook, a college senior and a teenage school dropout. Such a group can meet in any storefront, church basement, settlement house or housing project; more important, it can often go about the city, as is possible when the student-teacher ratio is seven to one. Experience at the First Street School in New York has shown that the cost for such a little school is less than for the public school with a student-teacher ratio of 30 to 1. (In the public system, most of the money goes for administration and for specialists to remedy the lack of contact in the classroom.) As A.S. Neill has shown, attendance need not be compulsory. The school should be located near home so the children can escape from it to home and from home to it. The school should be supported by public money but administered entirely by its own children, teachers and parents.

In the adolescent and college years, the present mania is to keep students at their lessons for another four to ten years as the only way of their growing up in the world. The correct policy would be to open as many diverse paths as possible, with plenty of opportunity to backtrack and change. It is said by James Conant that about 15 percent learn well by books and study in an academic setting, and these can opt for high school. Most, including most of the bright students, do better either on their own or as apprentices in activities that are for keeps rather than through lessons. If their previous eight years had been spent in exploring their own bents and interests rather than being continually interrupted to do others' assignments on others' schedules, most adolescents would have a clearer notion of what they are after, and many would have found their vocations.

For the 15 percent of adolescents who learn well in schools and are interested in subjects that are essentially academic, the present catchall high schools are wasteful. We would do better to return to the small preparatory academy, with perhaps 60 students and three teachers—one in physical sciences, one in social sciences, one in humanities—to prepare for college board examinations. An academy could be located in and administered by a university and staffed by graduate students who like to teach and in this way might earn stipends while they write their theses. In such a setting, without dilution by nonacademic subjects and a mass of uninterested fellow students, an academic adolescent can, by spending three hours a day in the classroom, easily be prepared in three or four years for college.

Forcing the nonacademic to attend school breaks the spirit of most and foments alienation in the best. Kept in tutelage, young people, who are necessarily economically dependent, cannot pursue the sexual, adventurous and political activities congenial to them. Since lively youngsters insist on these anyway, the effect of what we do is to create a gap between them and the oppressive adult world, with a youth subculture and an arrested development.

School methods are simply not competent to teach all the arts, sciences, professions and skills the school establishment pretends to teach. For some professions—social work, architecture, pedagogy—trying to earn academic credits is probably harmful because it is an irrelevant and discouraging obstacle course. Most technological know-how has to be learned in actual practice in offices and factories, and this often involves unlearning what has been laboriously crammed for exams. The technical competence required by skilled and semiskilled workmen and average technicians can be acquired in three weeks to a year on the job, with no previous schooling. The importance of even "functional literacy" is much exaggerated; it is the attitude and not the reading ability that counts. Those who are creative in the arts and sciences almost invariably go their own course and are usually hampered by schools. Modern languages are best learned by travel. It is pointless to teach social sciences, literary criticism and philosophy to young-sters who have had no responsible experience in life and society.

Most of the money now spent for high schools and colleges should be devoted to the support of apprentice-ships; travel; subsidized browsing in libraries and self-directed study and research; programs such as VISTA, the Peace Corps, Students for a Democratic Society, or the Student Nonviolent Coordinating Committee; rural recon-struction; and work camps for projects in conservation and urban renewal. It is a vast sum of money—but it costs almost $1,500 a year to keep a youth in a blackboard jungle in New York; the schools have become one of our major industries. Consider one kind of opportunity. Since it is important for the very existence of the republic to countervail the now overwhelming national corporate style of information, entertainment and research, we need scores of thousands of small independent television sta-tions, community radio stations, local newspapers that are more than gossip notes and ads, community theaters, highbrow or dissenting magazines, small design offices for neighborhood renewal that is not bureaucratized, small laboratories for science and invention that are not central-ly directed. Such enterprises could present admirable opportunities for bright but unacademic young people to serve as apprentices.

Ideally, the polis itself is the educational environment; a good community consists of worthwhile, attractive and fulfilling callings and things to do, to grow up into. The policy I am proposing tends in this direction rather than away from it. By multiplying options, it should be possible to find an interesting course for each individual youth, as we now do for only some of the emotionally disturbed and the troublemakers. Voluntary adolescent choices are often random and foolish and usually transitory; but they are the likeliest ways of growing up reasonably. What is most essential is for the youth to see that he is taken seriously as a person rather than fitted into an institutional system. I don't know if this tailor-made approach would be harder or easier to administer than standardization that in fact fits nobody and results in an increasing number of recalcitrants. On the other hand, as the Civilian Conservation Corps showed in the thirties, the products of willing youth labor can be valuable even economically, whereas accumulating Regents blue books is worth nothing except to the school itself.

(By and large, it is not in the adolescent years but in later years that, in all walks of life, there is need for academic withdrawal, periods of study and reflection, synoptic review of the texts. The Greeks understood this and regarded most of our present college curricula as appropriate for only those over the age of 30 or 35. To some extent, the churches used to provide a studious environment. We do these things miserably in hurried conferences.)

We have similar problems in the universities. We cram the young with what they do not want at the time and what most of them will never use; but by requiring graded diplomas we make it hard for older people to get what they want and can use. Now, paradoxically, when so many are going to school, the training of authentic learned professionals is proving to be a failure, with dire effects on our ecology, urbanism, polity, communications and even the direction of science. Doing others' lessons under compulsion for 20 years does not tend to produce professionals who are autonomous, principled and ethically responsible to client and community. Broken by processing, professionals degenerate to mere professional personnel. Professional peer groups have become economic lobbies. The licensing and maintenance of standards have been increasingly relinquished to the state, which has no competence.

In licensing professionals, we have to look more realistically at functions, drop mandarin requirements of academic diplomas that are irrelevant, and rid ourselves of the ridiculous fad of awarding diplomas for every skill and trade whatever. In most professions and arts there are important abstract parts that can best be learned academically. The natural procedure is for those actually engaged in a professional activity to go to school to learn what they now know they need; re-entry into the academic track, therefore, should be made easy for those with a strong motive.

Universities are primarily schools of learned professions, and the faculty should be composed primarily not of academics but of working professionals who feel duty-bound and attracted to pass on their tradition to apprentices of a new generation. Being combined in a community of scholars, such professionals teach a noble apprenticeship, humane and with vision toward a more ideal future. It is humane because the disciplines communicate with one another; it is ideal because the young are free and questioning. A good professional school can be tiny. In *The Community of Scholars* I suggest that 150 students and ten professionals—the size of the usual medieval university—are enough. At current faculty salaries, the cost per student would be one-fourth of that of our huge administrative machines. And, of course, on such a small scale contact between faculty and students is sought for and easy.

Today, because of the proved incompetence of our adult institutions and the hypocrisy of most professionals, university students have a right to a large say in what goes on. (But this, too, is medieval.) Professors will, of course, teach what they please. My advice to students is that given by Prince Kropotkin, in "A Letter to the Young": "Ask what kind of world do you want to live in? What are you good at and want to work at to build that world? What do you need to know? Demand that your teachers teach you that." Serious teachers would be delighted by this approach.

The idea of the liberal arts college is a beautiful one: to teach the common culture and refine character and citizenship. But it does not happen; the evidence is that the college curriculum has little effect on underlying attitudes, and most cultivated folk do not become so by this route. School friendships and the community of youth do have lasting effects, but these do not require ivied clubhouses. Young men learn more about the theory and practice of government by resisting the draft than they ever learned in Political Science 412.

Much of the present university expansion, needless to say, consists in federal- and corporation-contracted research and other research and has nothing to do with teaching. Surely such expansion can be better carried on in the Government's and corporations' own institutes, which would then be unencumbered by the young, except those who are hired or attach themselves as apprentices.

Every part of education can be open to need, desire, choice and trying out. Nothing needs to be compelled or extrinsically motivated by prizes and threats. I do not know if the procedure here outlined would cost more than our present system—though it is hard to conceive of a need for more money than the school establishment now spends. What would be saved is the pitiful waste of youthful years—caged, daydreaming, sabotaging and cheating—and the degrading and insulting misuse of teachers.

It has been estimated by James Coleman that the average youth in high school is really "there" about ten minutes a day. Since the growing-up of the young into society to be useful to themselves and others, and to do God's work, is one of the three or four most important functions of any society, no doubt we ought to spend even more on the education of the young than we do; but I would not give a penny to the present administrators, and I would largely dismantle the present school machinery.

Race and Education:
A Search for Legitimacy

CHARLES V. HAMILTON

An essay on public policy, race and education in the
United States cannot overlook the clear existence of
tremendous ferment taking place in the various black
communities in this country. The nature of that ferment
is such that, if we would devise relevant policy for
educating vast numbers of black people today, we cannot focus merely, or even primarily, on achievement
in verbal and mathematical skills as criteria for educational
improvement. At one time, possibly to the mid-1960s, it
was possible to talk about educational policy largely in
terms of "integration" (or at least, desegregation) and
assume that plans to implement integration would be
dealing with the core of the problem of educational
deficiency. This is no longer the case.

Reprinted from "Race and Education: A Search for Legitimacy" by
Charles Hamilton, *Harvard Educational Review*, Vol. 38, No. 4, Fall
1968. Copyright © 1968 by the President and Fellows of Harvard
College.

Today, one hears wholly different demands being raised in the black community. These demands are better represented by the kinds of resolutions coming out of the workshops of the newly formed (June 1968) National Association of Afro-American Educators than by the conclusions reached by the report on *Equality of Educational Opportunity* (Coleman Report). These demands are reflected more clearly in the demonstrations of black high school students in many cities for more emphasis on Afro-American history and culture and for better science lab facilities than by the findings of the United States Commission on Civil Rights (*Racial Isolation in the Public Schools*). These demands are more clearly illustrated in the positions taken by the Harlem chapter of the Congress of Racial Equality (CORE), calling for an independent school system for Harlem, and by many of the Concerned Black Parents groups than in policy recommendations found in the statement issued by the Board of Education of Chicago, Illinois in August 1967 (Redmond Report).

First, I would like to indicate why it is more important at this time, from a sociopolitical point of view, to put more credence in the wishes of the black community than in the statements and findings of the experts. Second, I would like to give examples of the kinds of things on the minds of some of those black people taking an active interest in new directions for education in the black community. Third, I want to present a sketch of a proposal for dealing with some of the problems in some of the large urban areas. I am not sanguine that the proposal will be applicable in all places (I assume it will not be), but neither do I believe it possible or necessary to develop one model to fit all occasions. My proposal attempts to combine some of the fervent wishes of a growing number of black people with the clear need to think in wholly new institutional terms. I am fully aware that public policy in this area has been influenced by such dichotomies as "integration vs. segregation" (*de jure* and *de facto*) and "integrated education vs. quality (compensatory) education." My presentation will not use these terms as primary focal points, but it is clear that the main thrust of my proposal will support the involvement of more parents in the school system and the improvement of educational opportunities within the black community. Some critics will view this as an "enrichment" proposal, or as an effort at "compensatory" education, or even as a black power move to maintain and further divisiveness in the society. I simply acknowledge these criticisms at the outset and intend to let my proposal stand on its own merits.

A CRISIS OF EDUCATIONAL LEGITIMACY

It is absolutely crucial to understand that the society cannot continue to write reports accurately describing the failure of the educational instutions vis-à-vis black people without ultimately taking into account the impact those truths will have on black Americans. There comes a point when it is no longer possible to recognize institutional failure and then merely propose more stepped-up measures to overcome those failures—especially when the proposals come from the same kinds of people who administered for so long the present unacceptable and dysfunctional policies and systems. Seymour Martin Lipset once wrote:

> Legitimacy involves the capacity of the system to engender and maintain the belief that the existing political institutions are the most appropriate ones for the society. The extent to which contemporary democratic political systems are legitimate depends in large measure upon the ways in which the key issues which have historically divided the society have been resolved.

> While effectiveness is primarily instrumental, legitimacy is evaluative. Groups regard a political system as

legitimate or illegitimate according to the way in which its values fit with theirs.[1]

And in another place, he has written:

All claims to a legitimate title to rule in new states must ultimately win acceptance through demonstrating effectiveness. The loyalty of the different groups to the system must be won through developing *in them* the conviction that this system is the best—or at least an excellent—way to accomplish their objectives. And even claims to legitimacy of a supernatural sort, such as "the gift of grace," are subjected on the part of the populace to a highly pragmatic test—that is, what is the payoff?[2]

The United States gradually acquired legitimacy as a result of being *effective*.[3]

The important point here is that loyalty, allegiance, is predicated on performance. What decision-makers *say* is not of primary importance, but it is important what black people *believe*. Do they believe that the school systems are operating in their behalf? Do they believe that the schools are *legitimate* in terms of educating their children and inculcating in them a proper sense of values? With the end product (i.e., their children graduating from high school as functional illiterates) clearly before their eyes at home and with volumes of reports documenting lack of payoff, it is not difficult to conclude that black people have good reason to question the legitimacy of the educational systems.

They begin to question the entire process, because they are aware that the schools, while not educating their children, are at the same time supporting a particularly unacceptable situation. They know that the schools are one of the major institutions for socializing their children into the dominant value structure of the society. V. O. Key, Jr. concluded in his book, *Politics, Parties and Pressure Groups:*

In modern societies the school system, in particular, functions as a formidable instrument of political power in its role as a transmitter of the goals, values and attitudes of the polity. In the selection of values and attitudes to be inculcated, it chooses those cherished by the dominant elements in the political order. By and large the impact of widely accepted goals, mores, and social values fixes the programs of American schools. When schools diverge from this vaguely defined directive and collide with potent groups in the political system, they feel a pressure to conform.[4]

The relevance of all this is that makers of policy and their advisers must recognize that there is a point beyond which vast numbers of black people *will* become alienated and will no longer view efforts on their behalf, however well-intentioned, as legitimate. When this happens, it behooves decision-makers, if they would search for ways of restoring faith, trust and confidence, to listen to the demands of the alienated. The "experts" might see integration as socially and educationally sound and desirable, but *their* vision and empirical data might well be, at this juncture, irrelevant. Unless this is understood, I am suggesting that public policy might well find itself in the position of attempting to force its programs on a reluctant black community. And this is hardly a formula for the development of a viable body politic.

A clear example of a paternalistic, objectionable policy is contained in the report of the Chicago Board of Education, *Increasing Desegregation of Faculties, Students, and Vocational Education Programs,* issued August 23, 1967. The Report called for busing black children into all or predominantly white schools. It contains the very revealing paragraph:

> The assignment of students outside their neighborhood may be objected to by Negro parents who prefer that their children attend the segregated

neighborhood school. This viewpoint cannot be ignored. Prior to implementation of such a transfer
policy the administration must take steps to reassure
apprehensive sending area parents that transfer will be
beneficial not only in terms of integration but of
improved education for their children. The generation
of a favorable consensus in the designated sending
area is important. *If such a consensus is unobtainable,
the transfer program would have to proceed without
a popular base.* In the light of the dismal alternatives
such a program perhaps should proceed even without
consensus, but every effort should be made to attain
it.[5]

This is a perpetuation of the pattern of telling the black
community what is best for it. My point is that this
position will only increase alienation, not alleviate it. At
the present time, when the educational systems are
perceived as illegitimate, it is highly unlikely that such a
policy could lead to success. In order for the program to
work, support *must* be obtained from the black community. This means that educational achievement must be
conceived more broadly than as the mere acquisition of
verbal and mathematical skills. Very many black parents
are (for good reason) quite concerned about what happens
to the self-image of their black children in predominantly
white schools—schools which reflect dominant white
values and mores. Are these schools prepared to deal with
their own white racism? Probably not, and a few summer
institutes for white, middle-class teachers cannot prepare
them. Are these schools prepared to come to terms with a
young black child's search for identity? Will the black
child indeed acquire certain skills which show up favorably
on standardized tests, but at the same time avoid coming
to grips with the fact that he or she should not attempt to
be a carbon copy of the culture and ethos of another racial
and ethnic group? Virtually all the social scientists,

education experts and public policy-makers who emphasize integration overlook this crucial, intangible, psychological factor. Many concerned black parents and teachers do not overlook it, however. And their viewpoint has nothing to do with black people wanting to perpetuate "separate but unequal" facilities, or with attitudes of "hate whitey." This concern is simply a necessary reaction to the fact that many white (and black) liberal, integration-oriented spokesmen are tuned in to a particular result and overlook other phenomena. They fail to understand that their criteria for "educational achievement" simply might not be relevant anymore.

What I am stating (in as kind a way as possible) is that setting criteria for measuring equal educational opportunity can no longer be the province of the established "experts." The policy-makers must now listen to those for whom they say they are operating; which means of course that they must be willing to share the powers of policy-making. The experts must understand that what is high on the liberal social scientist's agenda does not coincide with the agenda of many black people. The experts are still focusing on the effectiveness of existing educational institutions. Many black people have moved to the evaluation of the legitimacy of these institutions.

American social scientists generally are unable to grasp the meaning of alienation when applied to certain groups in this country. (Most of the recent perceptive literature on alienation and modernization deals with new nations of Africa and Asia.)[6]

Consequently, Grant McConnell, in an important book, *Private Power and American Democracy,* could write:

> In general the use of government has depended on a particular group's capacity to isolate the relevant governmental agency from influences other than its own and to establish itself as the agency's constituency—at once giving an air of validity to its own

ends and endowing it with the added disciplinary power of public authority over its own members.[7]

And later:

... farm migrant workers, Negroes, and the urban poor have not been included in the system of "pluralist" representation so celebrated in recent years.[8]

Then finally:

It can be readily agreed that if explosive mass movements are a genuine threat to America, a politics of narrow constituencies might be desirable to counter the danger. Small associations probably do provide order and stability for any society. In the United States some associations may serve in this manner to a greater degree than others. The American Civil Liberties Union and the League of Woman Voters have given notable service to American democracy. Trade unions and farm organizations have undoubtedly also been similarly useful at various times. Nevertheless, it should be clear that a substantial price is paid for any guarantee against mass movements provided by a pattern of small constituencies. That price is paid in freedom and equality. Although the price would be worth paying if the danger were grave, it can hardly be argued that such an extremity is present.[9]

There are voices in the black community (accompanied, as we well know, by acts of expressive violence) saying precisely that the danger *is* grave and that the extremity *is* present. The educational systems are particularly vulnerable, because of their very conspicuous inability to "pay off."

AN ALTERNATIVE AGENDA

It is instructive, then, to examine some of the major items presented by certain voices in the black community.

Clearly, one source of constructive ideas would be black teachers, those persons who not only teach in ghetto schools, but whose children attend those schools (in most instances), who, themselves, grew up in the black community, and who, for the most part, still live in black communities.[10] Approximately 800 such teachers met in Chicago, June 6-9, 1968, in a national conference and formed the National Association of Afro-American Educators. They did not spend the four days discussing the Coleman Report or the report of the U.S. Civil Rights Commission. One could identify four particular areas of concern at that conference, and these areas coincide to a great extent with the issues raised by associations of Concerned Black Parents as well as various Afro-American History clubs in the high schools around the country.

Control. It was generally concluded that the existing educational systems were not responsive to the wishes of the black community. Therefore, those structural arrangements now operating should be changed substantially. The decision-making process in most ghetto school systems was challenged. The workshop on the black school and the black community issued the following statement:

—Whereas, the educational systems of this nation have criminally failed the Black youth of this country,

—Whereas, Black parents have not had a voice in determining the educational destiny of their youth,

—Whereas, the Black youth and Black parents are demanding relevant education to meet their needs,

—Therefore, be it resolved that we encourage, support and work to organize local communities to control their own schools through local or neighborhood school boards and further that this organization go on record to immediately implement such plans.

—The goal of the National Association of Afro-American Educators should be Black control of the Black Community schools.[11]

One hears these kinds of statements increasingly among

newly politicized people in the black communities. The focus has shifted; emphasis is now on viable ways to gain enough leverage to drastically revise a system. Black people, having moved to the stage of questioning the system's very legitimacy, are seeking ways to create a new system. This is difficult for most Americans to understand precisely because they have assumed the continuing legitimacy of the present educational system.

Parent Involvement and Alliance with Black Teachers. It is becoming clearer and clearer that the major agents of control should be black parents in the community working closely with the teachers in the school. For this reason, if no other, many black spokesmen do not favor various compulsory plans for busing black children out of their communities into white schools, in some instances miles away from home. Are we to assume that black parents, likewise, will travel miles across town in the evenings to attend PTA meetings—frequently to be surrounded by a sea of white faces, more articulate and with more organized voting strength? The principle of busing over-looks the very important factor of facilitating black parent participation in the child's schooling. If in fact the home has a critical role to play in the educational process, then we would be well advised not to pursue policies which would make that role more difficult.

The participation of black parents in the child's schooling is one of the points high on the agenda of some black people. And it is clearly at odds with one of the stated objectives of the Redmond Report: to bus black children into white schools, but to maintain a quota (no white elementary school would be over 15 percent black; no high school over 25 percent black), in order to guard against the possibility of a white exodus. James Redmond, Superintendent of Schools in Chicago, said: "Chicago will become a predominantly Negro city unless dramatic action is taken soon. . . . School authorities (must) quickly achieve and maintain stable racial proportions in changing fringe areas."[1] [2] Trying to placate whites simply is not a matter of top (or high) priority to many black people, especially if it must be done by manipulating black children.

Discussion of parental involvement and control has serious implications for the standards of professionalism we adopt. Black parents might well have different notions about what is methodologically sound, what is substantively valuable. They might well be impatient with some of the theories about teaching reading and writing. And at this stage who is to say that their doubts are not valid? The present approaches have hardly proved efficacious. Therefore, when we get sizeable black parental participation, we are opening up the profession to question and challenge about what constitutes educational legitimacy. No profession welcomes such intrusion from laymen. This is quite understandable; professionals have a vested self-interest. All those years of college courses and practice teaching and certifying exams, all those credentials of legitimacy may be going by the board. But that is precisely what happens in societies which are modernizing, in societies where new groupings—alienated from traditional norms—rise to make new normative demands. It is disturbing, disruptive, painful. It is change. And this is the phenomenon American social science has been unable to come to terms with in the latter half of the twentieth century—especially with reference to the issue of race relations.

Psychological Impact. A third matter of concern to these new black voices is the psychological impact of educational institutions on the black children. Many black people are demanding more black principals in predominantly black schools, if only because they serve as positive role models for the children. Children should be able to see black people in positions of day-to-day power and authority. There is a demand to have the schools recognize *black* heroes with national holidays. There is concern for emphasizing group solidarity and pride, which is crucial for the development of black Americans. And there is very serious question whether a predominantly white, middle-class ethos can perform this function. Again, the Coleman data measure verbal skills and mathematical abilities, but there are other areas of equal importance. One should not assume that symbols of cultural pride are unimportant. Lipset was correct when he described the impact of these symbols, but he was incomplete when he applied them to the United States—when the growing awareness of black Americans is taken into account. He wrote:

> A major test of legitimacy is the extent to which given nations have developed a common "secular political culture," mainly national rituals and holidays. The United States has developed a common homogeneous culture in the veneration accorded the Founding Fathers, Abraham Lincoln, Theodore Roosevelt, and their principles.[13]

The schools serve as a major instrument to transmit such a common homogeneous culture. And yet, we are beginning to see black Americans call for the recognition of other heroes: Frederick Douglass, Martin Luther King, Jr., Malcolm X and so forth. Students are demanding that the traditional Awards Day programs at their schools include such awards as a Malcolm X Manliness Award, a Marcus Garvey Citizenship Award, and Frederick Douglass and Martin Luther King, Jr. Human Rights Awards. We see black writers challenging the idea of a common secular political culture. John Oliver Killens and Lerone Bennett, Jr. are two prominent examples. Killens captured the mood when he wrote:

> We (black Americans) even have a different historical perspective. Most white Americans, even today, look upon the Reconstruction period as a horrible time of "carpet-bagging," and "black politicians," and "black corruption," the absolutely lowest ebb in the Great American Story. . . .

We black folk, however, look upon Reconstruction as the most democratic period in the history of the nation; a time when the dream the founders dreamed was almost within reach and right there for the taking; a time of democratic fervor the like of which was never seen before and never since. . . .

For us, Reconstruction was the time when two black men were Senators in the Congress of the United States from the State of Mississippi; when black men served in the legislatures of all the states in Dixie; and when those "corrupt" legislatures gave to the South its first public-school education. . . .[14]

Even our white hero symbols are different from yours. You give us moody Abe Lincoln, but many of us prefer John Brown, whom most of you hold in contempt as a fanatic; meaning, of course, that the firm dedication of any white man to the freedom of the black man is *prima-facie* evidence of perversion or insanity.[15]

And Lerone Bennett, Jr. challenged much of American historical scholarship when he challenged the role and image of Abraham Lincoln:

Abraham Lincoln was *not* the Great Emancipator. As we shall see, there is abundant evidence to indicate that the Emancipation Proclamation was not what people think it is and that Lincoln issued it with extreme misgivings and reservations.[16]

A growing number of black Americans are insisting that the schools begin to reflect this new concern, this new tension. We simply cannot assume a common secular political culture. If we continue to operate on such false assumptions, we will continue to misunderstand the very deep feeling of alienation in the black community. And misunderstanding cannot be a viable basis for enlightened public policy. Likewise, it is not only important that Afro-American history be taught in the black schools, but that it also be incorporated into the curriculum of white schools throughout this country. It is not sufficient that only black children be given an accurate historical picture of the race; all Americans must have this exposure—in the inner city, the suburbs, the rural schools.

Who can predict what the "tests" will show when we begin to expose black children to these kinds of innovations? What sort of impact will this have on the motivation of those "slow learners," those "high risks," those (and here is the misnomer of them all) "culturally deprived?" The legitimacy of the "standardized tests" must be questioned as long as they overlook these very essential components.

Curricula and Instructional Materials. Closely related to the third point is a concern with the kinds and content of materials used, especially in black schools. How are black people portrayed? Do the textbooks reflect the real experience of black Americans in history and in contemporary society? The workshop on instructional materials at the Afro-American Educators Conference concluded:

> In each local community black educators must develop a criteria for selection of materials which will be presented to the Board of Education, to local textbook committees, and to the major publishing houses which provide text and supplemental materials to that community. It is incumbent upon us, if we are to serve this society, that instructional material which we select be both educationally sound and incorporate a strong black orientation.
>
> Black classroom teachers must help black students to speak the language of the marketplace and assist them as they move back and forth between "their own thing and a white American thing." Since all groups usually speak two languages, one at home and within their group and another in the economic world; by nurturing and respecting our own language and effectively manipulating the other we will become a

truly bilingual people. This is necessary to achieve a
viable economic base. . . .

Black teachers must become connected with major
textbook publishing firms as authors, editors and
consultants to create the materials available on the
market. We must pressure major publishers to reflect
the needs of black children in schools. We will work
for a factual inclusion of the scientific contribution
of black scientists to medical and scientific advancement. For example, Dr. Daniel Hale Williams (open
heart surgery) and Dr. Charles Drew (developer of
blood plasma) must receive their rightful place in
elementary and secondary science texts.[17]

These are some of the things on the agenda of many black
people as they consider possible solutions of our vast
educational problems. It is far too soon to evaluate the
results of most of these proposals—in some instances they
have not even been implemented. And in most cases they
are in the embryonic stage. We are without precedent in
these matters, and it would be presumptuous of American
social scientists to attempt to prejudge results, or even to
suppose that they could. Black people are searching for
new forms of educational legitimacy, and in that kind of
modernizing atmosphere the traditional criteria for measuring effectiveness might well be irrelevant and anachronistic.

AN ALTERNATIVE MODEL

The rhetoric of race and education, as stated earlier, is
prolific with dichotomies of segregation vs. integration,
quality education vs. integrated education, compensatory
programs vs. busing, and so forth. Too much is assumed by
these simplistic terms, and a superficial use of these labels
frequently restricts and predetermines discussion at the
outset. While this is unfortunate, it is probably unavoid-

able, given the historical context and the highly emotional atmosphere. Those persons favoring "neighborhood" schools and opposing busing have traditionally been, in the North, white parents and taxpayer groups, usually identified as anti-Negro in their basic racial views. These groups would normally be found opposing open housing laws as well. Therefore their motivations are questioned when they argue that they are essentially concerned about "educational standards" and property values. When it is pointed out to them that white students do not suffer academically and (if panic selling is avoided) property values do not go down, they do not listen. And their intransigence leads their opponents to label them as racial bigots and segregationists.

Proponents of busing and integration see a positive academic and social value in racially heterogeneous classrooms. Integration to these people is virtually synonymous with quality. And black people who once worked for desegregated schools but who no longer do so are viewed as having given up the fight, as having joined the white racists and, indeed, as having become black racists and advocates of "Black Power separatism."[18]

I state this simply to acknowledge an awareness of some of the positions taken before I proceed to suggest an alternative educational plan. The fact that my ideas would appear more closely akin to the views of some white segregationists whose ultimate goal is to deny educational opportunity to black people is an *appearance* I cannot avoid. It is important however to point out that a close examination of the ultimate goals of my suggestions will indicate a clear divergence from views held by the segregationists. In other words I am motivated by an attempt to find an educational approach which is relevant to black people, not one that perpetuates racism. The plan I am suggesting is not a universal panacea; it is not applicable in all black ghettos. Where it is feasible—particularly in the large urban communities—I strongly propose it for consideration.

This is a model which views the ghetto school as the focal point of community life. The educational system should be concerned with the entire family, not simply with the children. We should think in terms of a Comprehensive Family-Community-School Plan with black parents attending classes, taking an active, day-to-day part in the operation of the school. Parents could be students, teachers and legitimate members of the local school governing board. A similar plan is already in operation in Chicago: the Family Education Center. There are two centers, the Westinghouse and Doolittle Centers, which provide basic adult education, prevocational and vocational training, and work experience programs.

Mr. William H. Robinson, Director of the Cook County Department of Public Aid, has stated:

> The Center's most unique feature is the Child Development Program for the students' (parents') pre-school children, who come to school with their mothers and spend the day in a well-equipped, professionally staffed nursery school. Mothers can attend classes with the assurance that their children are receiving proper care and mental stimulation. Thus, the program makes participation in an educational program possible for many recipients who were prevented previously because they could not obtain adequate child care services.[19]

Since the inception of the program two years ago, 1,300 adults and 500 children have been involved in the centers.

This concept should be expanded to include fathers as well, those unemployed and willing to obtain skills. Many of these parents could serve as teachers, along with a professional staff. They could teach courses in a number of areas (child care, auto mechanics, art, music, home economics, sewing, etc.) for which they are obviously now trained. The Comprehensive Plan would extend the school program to grades through high school—for adults and children—and it would eliminate the traditional calendar year of September to June. (There is no reason why the educational system could not be revised to take vacations for one month, say in December of post-Christmas, and another month in August. The community educational program would be a year-round function, day and evening.)

The school would belong to the community. It would be a union of children, parents, teachers (specially trained to teach in such communities), social workers, psychologists, doctors, lawyers and community planners. Parent and community participation and control would be crucial in the hiring and firing of personnel, the selection of instructional materials, and the determination of curriculum content. Absolutely everything must be done to make the system a functioning, relevant part of the lives of the local people. Given the present situation of existing and growing alienation, such involvement is essential.

If it can be demonstrated that such a comprehensive educational institution can gain the basic trust and participation of the black community, it should become the center of additional vital community functions. Welfare, credit unions, health services, law enforcement and recreational programs—all working under the control of the community—could be built around it. Enlightened private industry would find it a place from which to recruit trained, qualified people, and could donate equipment and technical assistance. The several advantages of such a plan are obvious. It deals with the important agencies which are in daily, intimate contact with black people; it reduces a vast, fragmented service bureaucracy which now descends on the black community from many different directions, with cumbersome rules and regulations, uncontrolled by and unaccountable to the community. It provides the black people with a meaningful chance for participation in the very important day-to-day processes affecting their lives; it gives them educational and vocational tools for the future. All these things reflect the yearnings and aspirations of masses of black people today.

The Comprehensive Plan envisions the local school as a central meeting place to discuss and organize around community issues, political and economic. All of the establishments functioning under the plan would provide relevant intermediary groups to which people could relate. The size of the community involved would vary, with several factors to be considered: geography, number of participating agencies, available funds (from federal, state and local governmental sources) and manageability. At all times, the primary concern would be about the active involvement of people and about their possession of real power to make decisions affecting the Comprehensive Plan. They would hire consultants and experts whose legitimacy would be determined by their relevance to the community, not by a predetermined set of criteria superimposed from outside.

The proposed Comprehensive Plan attempts to come to grips with the understandable alienation discussed in the first section and with the appropriateness of the agenda items described in the second section of the paper. This plan is better understood when one keeps in mind the premise presented earlier: black people are questioning, evaluating the *legitimacy* of existing educational institutions, not simply searching for ways to make those institutions more effective. I am suggesting that we are at a point in the process of modernization and social transformation when we must begin to think and act in wholly new normative and structural terms.

NOTES

1. Lipset, S. M., *Political Man: The Social Bases of Politics* (New York: Doubleday, 1963) p. 64.

2. Lipset, S. M., *The First New Nation: The United States in Historical and Comparative Perspective* (New York: Basic Books, 1963) pp. 45-6. (Emphasis added).

3. *Ibid.,* p. 59. (Emphasis in original.)

4. Key, V. O., Jr., *Politics, Parties and Pressure Groups* (New York: Thomas Y. Crowell, 1964) pp. 12-3.

5. Board of Education, City of Chicago, *Increasing Desegregation of Faculties, Students, and Vocational Education Programs* (August 23, 1967) p. B-20. (Emphasis added.)

6. See: Weiner, M., ed., *Modernization, The Dynamics of Growth* (New York: Basic Books, 1966); Apter, D., *The Politics of Modernization* (Chicago: University of Chicago Press, 1965); Eisenstadt, S. N., *Modernization: Protest and Change* (Englewood Cliffs, N. J.: Prentice-Hall, 1966); Shils, E., *Political Development in the New States* (New York: Humanities Press, 1964); Hodgkin, T., *Nationalism in Colonial Africa* (New York: New York University Press, 1957); Silvert, K. H., *Expectant Peoples: Nationalism and Development* (New York: Random House, 1964); Pye, L. W., *Politics, Personality and Nation Building: Burma's Search for Identity* (New Haven: Yale University Press, 1962).

7. McConnell, G., *Private Power and American Democracy* (New York: Random House, 1965) pp. 346-7.

8. *Ibid.,* p. 349.

9. *Ibid.,* pp. 355-6.

10. In a column entitled "Quality Teaching in Decentralized Slum Schools," Fred M. Hechinger, education editor of the *New York Times,* wrote: "It seems more realistic and, for the long pull, more constructive to face the fact that part of the answer to the crisis must come through the efforts of Negro teachers. If young Negro college graduates can be channeled into these schools and if their greater identification with the children's and the parents' own background can more easily gain the pupils' confidence and attention, then to sacrifice some of the present licensing requirements may be a small price to pay." (the *New York Times,* April 29, 1968).

11. Excerpt from mimeographed notes of discussion and reports of workshops of National Association of Afro-American Educators (Chicago: 1968).

12. Quoted in an editorial in *Chicago Sun-Times*, January 12, 1968, p. 27. The editorial, which favored the Redmond Plan, further stated: "That part of the Redmond Plan that has excited opposition calls for fixing immediately a balanced racial enrollment in those all-white schools that are in the way of the Negro expansion. It would be roughly 90 per cent white, 10 per cent Negro. The Negro pupils (who are from middle-class families) would be acceptable to white families and keep them anchored in the neighborhood, whereas they would flee to the suburbs if the Negro proportion became greater than 25 per cent. The plan may not work. If it does it is at best only a holding action until the entire metropolitan area faces up to the demographic realities of our time. But it should be tried."

13. Lipset, S. M., *Political Man*, p. 68.

14. Killens, J. O., *Black Man's Burden* (New York: Trident Press, 1965) pp. 14-5.

15. *Ibid.*, p. 17.

16. Bennett, L., Jr., "Was Abe Lincoln a White Supremacist?" *Ebony*, 23, No. 4 (February, 1968) p. 35.

17. Excerpt from mimeographed notes and discussion and reports of workshops of National Association of Afro-American Educators (Chicago: 1968).

18. An example of this attitude was contained in the report of the President's civil disorders commission (Kerner Commission). "The Black Power advocates of today consciously feel that they are the most militant group in the Negro protest movement. Yet they have retreated from a direct confrontation with American society on the issue of integration and, by preaching separatism, unconsciously function as an accommodation to white racism."—*Report of the National Advisory Commission on Civil Disorders* (New York: E. P. Dutton, 1968) p. 235.

19. Cook County Department of Public Aid, *The Challenge of Change* (Annual report, Chicago: 1967) p. 11.

Private Schools
for Black Children

CHRISTOPHER JENCKS

The public school system of New York City is on the brink of collapse. No compromise between the teachers' union and the school board is likely to resolve the fundamental conflicts between the school staff and the advocates of black community control. Until the basic political framework of public education in New York City is altered, strikes and boycotts—or both—are likely to recur on an annual basis.

Nor is New York unique. It is simply first. All the forces which have brought New York City to its present condition are at work elsewhere, and the New York story will certainly be repeated in dozens of other major cities around the country during the next decade.

The origin of the crisis is simple. The public schools

have not been able to teach most black children to read and write or to add and subtract competently. This is not the children's fault. They are the victims of social pathology far beyond their control. Nor is it the schools' fault, for schools as now organized cannot possibly offset the malignant effects of growing up in the ghetto. Nonetheless, the fact that the schools cannot teach black children basic skills has made the rest of the curriculum unworkable and it has left the children with nothing useful and creative to do for six hours a day. Ghetto schools have therefore become little more than custodial institutions for keeping the children off the street. Nobody, black or white, really knows what to do about the situation.

The traditional argument of both black and white liberals was that the problem could be solved by integrating black children into predominantly white schools, but experience has shown than many whites are reluctant to allow this, and that many blacks are not willing to move into white neighborhoods or bus their children across town even if the opportunity is available. Furthermore, studies such as the one done in New York City by David Fox have shown that most black children's academic performance improves only a little or not at all in integrated schools. Most people have therefore abandoned integration as a solution, at least in big cities.

Most educators are now concentrating on "compensatory" and "remedial" programs to bring academic competence in all black schools up to the level of all white schools. Unfortunately, none of these programs have proved consistently successful over any significant period. A few gifted principals seem to have created an atmosphere which enables black children to learn as much as whites in other schools, but they have done this by force of personality rather than by devising formulas which others could follow. Programs like More Effective Schools in New York City may eventually prove moderately effective, but evaluations to date have not provided grounds for great optimism.

The widespread failure of both integration and compensation has convinced some black nationalists that the answer is to replace white principals and teachers with black ones. But experience with this remedy is also discouraging. The schools in Washington, D. C., for example, have predominantly black staffs, and yet their black pupils learn no more than in other cities. So, many black militants are now arguing that the essential step is not to hire black staffs but to establish black control over the schools. There is little evidence one way or the other on this score, but the schools in America's few predominantly black towns are not especially distinguished.

The available evidence suggests that only a really extraordinary school can have much influence on a child's academic competence, be he black or white. Within the range of variation found in American public schools—and by traditional criteria this range is quite broad—the difference between a "good" school and "bad" school does not seem to matter very much. James S. Coleman's massive *Equality of Educational Opportunity* survey, conducted for the U. S. Office of Education, demonstrated this point in 1965. Coleman's work was much criticized on methodological grounds, but most subsequent analyses have confirmed his conclusions. Indeed, recent work at Harvard suggests that Coleman probably overstated the effect of school quality on student achievement. This means that the gap between black and white children's academic achievement is largely if not entirely attributable to factors over which school boards have no control.

There are, of course, both educators and scholars who disagree with this conclusion and who argue that the schools play a substantial role in perpetuating inequality between the races. Such skeptics must, however, explain two facts documented by the Coleman survey and never seriously disputed since.

First, Coleman's work confirmed previous studies showing that even before they enter school black children perform far less well on standard tests than white children. The typical black 6-year-old in the urban North, for example, scores below five-sixths of all white 6-year-olds on tests of both verbal and nonverbal ability. These tests obviously measure performance on tasks which seem important to educators and psychologists, not tasks which seem important to the children being tested or most of their parents. But for precisely this reason they provide a fairly accurate indication of how well any particular cultural group is likely to do at such "white-middle-class" games as reading and long division. In the case of poor black children, the tests predict disaster.

The prediction, moreover, is all too accurate. Twelve years later, after the schools have done their best and their worst, the typical black 18-year-old in the urban North is still scoring at about the fifteenth percentile on most standard tests. The schools, in short, have not changed his position one way or the other. This obviously means that his absolute handicap has grown, for he is 12 years older and both he and his classmates know far more than before, so there is more room for differentiation. Thus a first-grader who scores at the fifteenth percentile on a verbal test is less than a year behind his classmates; a twelfth grader who scores at the fifteenth percentile is more than three years behind.

The second fact which must be reckoned with is that while black children go to many different sorts of schools, good and bad, integrated and segregated, rigidly authoritarian and relatively permissive, their mean achievement level is remarkably similar from school to school. By the sixth grade, for example, the typical lower-class northern black child is achieving a little above the fourth-grade level. There is a great deal of individual variation around this average, both because black lower-class families vary considerably in the amount of support they give a school child and because individual children differ in native ability. But there is very little variation from one school to another in such children's average level of achievement. The black lower-class average is within one grade level of the overall black lower-class average in nine schools out of ten. This uniformly depressing picture cannot be attributed to uniformly depressing conditions in the schools Coleman surveyed. Many of these schools were predominantly white, and some had excellent facilities, highly trained and experienced teachers, relatively small classes and high overall levels of expenditure. These differences show no consistent relationship to the mean achievement of black elementary school pupils.

The last word has certainly not been written on this subject. Indeed, a group at Harvard is planning another whole book on it. But at the moment I think the evidence strongly indicates that differences in school achievement are largely caused by differences between cultures, between communities, between socioeconomic circumstances and between families—not by differences between schools.

None of this provides any adequate excuse for the outrageous and appalling things which are often done in ghetto schools. But it does suggest that even if black schools had the same resources and the same degree of responsibility to parents that the better suburban schools now have, ghetto children would still end up much less academically competent than suburban children.

It follows that the pedagogic failure of the ghetto schools must not be blamed primarily on the stupidity or malice of school boards or school administrators. It must be blamed on the whole complex of social arrangements whose cumulative viciousness creates a Harlem or a Watts. This means that, barring a general improvement in the social and economic positions of black America, black children's school achievement is unlikely to improve much in the foreseeable future, no matter who runs the schools or how they are run.

Some will challenge this depressing conclusion on the ground that black children's achievement scores could be substantially improved if really radical changes were made in the character and organization of black schools. This may well be true, but such changes are unlikely. Nor is it clear that they would be worth the cost. Despite a great deal of popular mythology, there is little real evidence that improving black children's academic skills would help any appreciable number of them to escape poverty and powerlessness.

On the contrary, studies by Otis Dudley Duncan at the University of Michigan suggest that academic competence probably explains only 10 percent or 15 percent of the variations in men's earnings. Research by Stephan Michelson at the Brookings Institution likewise indicates that staying in school is not likely to be much help to a Negro who wants to break out of poverty unless he stays through college.

In these circumstances, it seems to me that we should view the present urban school crisis primarily as a political problem, and only secondarily as a pedagogic one. So long as militant blacks believe they are the victims of a conspiracy to keep their children stupid—and therefore subservient—the political problem will remain insoluble. But if we encourage and assist black parents with such suspicions to set up their own schools, we may be able to avert disaster.

These schools would not, I predict, be either more or less successful than existing public schools in teaching the three Rs. But that is not the point. The point is to find a political *modus vivendi* which is tolerable to all sides. (After that, the struggle to eliminate the ghetto should probably concentrate on other institutions, especially corporate employers.) How, then, might independent, black-controlled schools help create such a *modus vivendi?*

The essential issue in the politics of American education has always been whether laymen or professionals would control the schools. Conflict between these two groups has taken a hundred forms. Professionals always want more money for the schools, while laymen almost always want to trim the budget. Professionals almost always want personnel hired and promoted on the basis of "fair" and "objective" criteria like degrees, examination results and seniority. Laymen are inclined to favor less impersonal criteria, such as whether the individual has roots, whether they personally know and trust him, whether he gets on well with his colleagues, and so forth. Professionals almost never want anyone fired for any reason whatever, while laymen are inclined to fire all sorts of people, for both good and bad reasons. Professionals want a curriculum which reflects their own ideas about the world, and this often means a curriculum that embodies "liberal" ideas and values they picked up at some big university. Laymen frequently oppose this demand, insisting that the curriculum should reflect conservative local mores.

The development of big-city public schools over the past century has been marked by a steady decline of lay control and an increase in the power of the professional staff. Until relatively recently, this has meant that control was exercised by administrators. Now the teaching staff, represented by increasingly militant unions and professional associations, has begun to insist on its rights. This is, however, an intraprofessional dispute. It has done nothing to arrest the staff's continuing and largely successful resistance to nonprofessional "intervention" by parents, school-board members and other laymen. About the only thing such laymen can still decide in most big cities is the overall level of expenditures.

The extent to which the professional staff gets its way seems to be related to the size of the administrative unit in which it works. Laymen usually have more power in small school districts, while the staff usually has more power in big districts. Until relatively recently, most liberals saw this as an argument for bigger districts, since they thought that the trouble with American education was its excessive deference to local interests and its lack of professionalism. In the past few years, however, liberals and radicals have suddenly joined conservatives in attacking bigness, bureaucracy and the claims of enterprise. Most people on the Left are now calling for more participation, more responsiveness, more decentralization and less "alienization."

Liberal thinking on this question is in large part a response to black nationalism. More and more Negroes believe there is a cause-effect relationship between the hegemony of what they call "white middle-class" (read professional-bureaucratic) values in their schools and the fact their children learn so little in those schools. So they think the best way to improve their children's performance would be to break the power of the professional staff. This, they rightly infer, requires Balkanizing big-city systems into much smaller units, which will be more responsive to parental and neighborhood pressure. (There are, of course, also strictly administrative arguments for breaking up systems as large as New York City's into units the size of, say, Rochester. But that would not do much for parental control.) So black militants want to strip the central board of education and central administrative staff of authority, elect local boards, have these boards appoint local officials, and then let these locally appointed officials operate local schools in precisely the same way that any small-town or suburban school system does.

This scheme has been attacked on two grounds. First, given racial and economic segregation in housing, localism in education means *de facto* segregation in schooling. In New York City, for example, almost everyone agrees the so-called "Bundy Plan" would foreclose any serious effort to reduce racial and economic segregation in the schools. Furthermore, if big-city school systems are broken up, the more affluent neighborhoods will presumably pursue the logic of Balkanization a step further by asking for fiscal as well as administrative autonomy. This demand would be politically difficult to resist. Yet if it were met, the expenditure gap between Harlem and Queens would almost certainly become wider than it now is.

The second common objection to the Balkanization of big-city school systems is that it would produce more parental "interference." (The distinction between "participation" and "interference" is largely a matter of where you think parents' rights end and staff prerogatives begin.) Parental interference would, it is plausibly argued, make it even harder to recruit staff members whose values are significantly at odds with the community's. This would make schools even more homogenized and parochial than they now are. Indeed, a local district which does not give its staff substantial autonomy is likely to have some difficulty recruiting even teachers who have grown up in the neighborhood and share the parents' values, simply because most teachers do not want parents constantly second-guessing them. Once the first flush of idealistic enthusiasm had passed, locally controlled schools in poor areas would probably have a harder time getting staffs than they do now. Like small rural districts confronted with the same problem, small impoverished urban districts would probably have to depend mainly on local people who could not get better jobs elsewhere.

These two arguments against local control of big-city schools naturally carry little weight with black militants. They have little patience with the liberal claim that the way to make black children learn more is to give them more white classmates and more middle-class teachers from Ivy League colleges. When liberals oppose decentralization on the grounds that it would legitimize segregation, the black militants answer: "So what? Integration is a myth. Who needs it?" When professional educators add that decentralization would create working conditions unacceptable to highly trained (and therefore potentially mobile) teachers, the black militants again answer: "So what? Teachers like that don't understand black children.

Who wants them?"

Differences of opinion like this probably cannot be resolved by "experimentation"—though more reliable information about the consequences of various school policies would certainly help. For reasons already indicated, the solution must be political.

In seeking such a solution, however, we should bear in mind that a similar crisis arose a century ago when Catholic immigrants confronted a public school system run by and for Protestants. This crisis was successfully resolved by creating two school systems, one public and one private.

It seems to me that the same approach might be equally appropriate again today. Since such an idea is likely to shock most liberals, it may be useful to recall certain neglected features of the parochial school experiment.

The motives of the Catholic immigrants who created the parochial school system were different in many important respects from the motives of the black nationalists who now want their own schools. Nonetheless, there were also important similarities. Just as today's black nationalist does not want his children infected by alien, white "middle-class" values, so many devout Catholic immigrants did not want their children to imbibe the alien values of white Protestant "first families." Just as today's black nationalist deplores the public schools' failure to develop pride and self-respect in black children, so, too, many Irish immigrants felt they needed their own schools to make their children feel that Catholicism and Irishness were respectable rather then shameful. And just as many black parents now want to get their children out of public schools because they feel these schools do not maintain proper discipline, so, too, many Catholics still say that their prime reason for sending their children to parochial schools is that the nuns maintain order and teach children "to behave."

Why, then, did not devout Catholics press for Balkanization of big-city school systems? Why did they not turn their neighborhood schools into bastions of the faith rather than creating their own separate system?

The answer is that there were very few neighborhoods in which literally all the residents were Catholic. Even where everyone was Catholic, not all Catholics wanted their children educated in self-consciously Catholic schools. Some Catholics, especially those of Irish ancestry, were extremely suspicious of the Anglo-Protestant majority, were strongly attached to the church, and eager to enroll their children in church schools. But others, of whom Italian immigrants were fairly typical, felt as suspicious of the Irish who dominated the church here as of the Anglo-Saxons who dominated the rest of America. Such Catholics were often anticlerical, and they wanted to send their children to schools which would stick to the three Rs and skip ideology.

Thus, even in the most Catholic neighborhoods, there was a large minority which thought priests, nuns and theology had no place in the local schools. This minority allied itself with the Protestant majority in other parts of the same state. These state-wide majorities then kept strict limits on local control so as to prevent devout Catholics from imposing their view of education on local Protestant (or lax Catholic) minorities. In particular, most state constitutions contain some kind of prohibition against the introduction of church personnel and teaching into the local public schools. When they do not, it is only because the federal First Amendment was thought sufficient to prevent the possibility.

This points to a difficulty with neighborhood control which black militants have yet to face. Blacks are not a majority in many of the areas where they live, at least if these areas are defined as large enough to support a full school system. Nor are black Americans of one mind about Balkanization and its likely consequences. Some black parents still believe in integration. They think the only way to get the social and material advantages they want is to stop being what they have always been, however difficult and painful that may be, and become culturally indistinguishable from the white majority. They therefore want their children to attend integrated schools, to study the same curriculum as white children, and to have teachers from good colleges (most of whom will be white for the foreseeable future). What these families want is thus very similar to what the present professional staffs of big-city school systems want.

Other black parents feel that they can never become indistinguishable from whites, that attempts to acquire white culture only make black children feel miserable and incompetent, and that if such children are to succeed they will have to develop their own style. Such parents want their children to attend schools which try to develop distinctive black virtues and black pride and which maintain the discipline which is so sorely lacking in the public schools. This cannot, I fear, be reconciled with what the present professional staff wants (or knows how to do).

For convenience, I will label these two sorts of black parents "integrationists" and "nationalists"—though the flavor of the distinction is perhaps better captured in the militants' rhetorical distinction between "Negroes" and "blacks."

Balkanizing big-city school systems would clearly be a victory for the nationalists at the expense of the integrationists. Schools in predominantly black neighborhoods would almost certainly end up with fewer white students and teachers. Local control would also make it easier for white neighborhoods to resist open enrollment, busing and other devices for helping black integrationists send their children to predominantly white schools. The curriculum might or might not be substantially revised once black neighborhood boards held power, but whatever revisions were made would certainly please the nationalists more than the integrationists.

Yet for this very reason state legislatures are unlikely to let black separatists exercise complete control over "their" schools. Just as legislatures earlier protected the rights of Protestant and anticlerical Catholic minorities in devout Catholic communities, so they will almost certainly protect the rights of white and black-integrationist minorities in predominantly black neighborhoods.

If, for example, the local Ocean Hill-Brownsville board wins control over the schools in that part of New York City, the New York State Legislature will almost surely go along with union demands for tight limits on the local board's right to discriminate against whites in hiring teachers and principals. (No such discrimination appears to have taken place in Ocean Hill-Brownsville's hiring of teachers, but the local board does seem to have had a strong and entirely understandable prejudice in favor of black principals.) State certification requirements are also likely to be strictly enforced, so as to restrict black local boards to hiring teachers who have enough respect for white culture and white standards of competence to have got through four or five years of college. New restrictions are also likely to be put on the curriculum, perhaps in the form of a law against teaching "racial hatred," so as to keep LeRoi Jones, etc., out of black schools. Such action would be defended on the same grounds as the rules barring religious teaching in public schools.

Restrictions of this kind are both reasonable and necessary in public institutions which must serve every child in a community, regardless of his race or his parents' outlook on life. They are, however, likely to mean that black nationalists end up feeling that, even though they have a majority on the local board, they do not really control their schools. Once again. Whitey will have cheated them of their rightful pride. Local control is, therefore, likely to enrage the professional educators, work against the hopes and ambitions of the integration-minded black and white parents, and yet end up leaving black nationalists as angry as ever. An alternative strategy is badly needed.

The best alternative I can see is to follow the Catholic precedent and allow nationalists to create their own private schools, outside the regular public system, and to encourage this by making such schools eligible for substantial tax support.

The big-city school systems could then remain largely in the hands of their professional staffs. (A major change in the distribution of power between teachers and administrators would still be required and some decentralization of big cities would also be advisable on bureaucratic grounds, but these are negotiable issues.) The public system would continue to serve white and black integrationists. Separatists who found this system unacceptable would have the option of sending their children to other schools at relatively low cost.

The beginnings of such a parallel system can already be seen in some big cities. Black middle-class parents are already far more likely than their white counterparts to enroll their children in private schools. A number of private "community schools" have also sprung up in the ghettos during the past few years. The Muslims run several schools. These schools have found many black parents are willing to make considerable financial sacrifices in order to send their children to a school they think superior to the public one. What these ventures lack, however, is substantial political and financial support. Without this they are likely to remain isolated and relatively unusual.

Some will ask why an independent black school system should need or deserve white support when the parochial schools get no such support. The most relevant answer is that, without the unity and legitimacy conferred by religion, the black community cannot go it alone. It is, perhaps, an unfortunate historical accident that black America lacks its own church, but it does—and even the Muslims have not been able to remedy the situation. Yet black America still needs its own schools, free to serve exigencies of black nationalism. Given the inevitable hostility of both professional educators and laymen who believe in integration, black nationalists are unlikely to be able to create such schools within the public sector.

Is there any justification for funding black private schools without funding other private schools on the same basis? My answer is no!

Indeed, it seems to me that the only way a black private-school system could hope to get tax subsidies would be to ally itself with a parochial school system in demanding federal and state support for all private schools. Many traditional liberals feel this would violate the constitutional separation of church and state. The Supreme Court has never ruled on this question, however; until it does, it seems reasonable to assume that there is no constitutional objection to federal or state subsidies for private schools—so long as these subsidies are earmarked to achieve specific public purposes, and so long as the schools are accountable for achieving these purposes.

An analogy may clarify this point. Back in the nineteenth century, the Supreme Court ruled that the government could legally contract with Catholic hospitals to care for public charity patients, and today only the most strict separatist would argue that the federal government cannot contract with a Catholic university or a Catholic hospital to carry out scientific research. Why, then, should it not contract with a Catholic school to teach physics to 16-year-olds or reading to impoverished six-year-olds?

Private schools should, of course, be required to show that they had actually done what they promised to do, rather than devoting public funds to the construction of chapels or the production of antiwhite propaganda. But accountability of this kind is essential with all tax subsidies, whether to private schools, private corporations or local government.

Even if a coalition between the church and the black

community were put together, is it realistic to suppose that white Protestant America would actually support black schools? My guess is that it would, so long as the financial burden remains within reason. Remember, I am not proposing that white legislators should help create a private system for blacks which would be more expensive than the one now attended by whites. I am only proposing that black children who attend private schools should be eligible for at least part of the tax subsidy which is now available if they choose to seek an education in the public system. Far from increasing the overall tax bill, then, a scheme of this kind would actually lower it. In particular, it would help slow the rise in local property taxes by providing black parents with state and federal incentives to withdraw their children from locally supported schools, thus cutting local costs. Many local white taxpayers would probably greet such a development with considerable enthusiasm. It would also reduce some white parents' anxiety about the public system's being "overrun" by black children. (It would not actually diminish integration-minded blacks' interest in desegregation, but if it reduced overall black enrollment, it might make desegregation seem a little less threatening and more practical.) In addition, the creation of an independent black school system might strike many whites as a relatively easy and painless way to buy political peace and sweep the whole racial problem under the rug. I doubt if it would succeed in doing this, but it might at least help shift the focus of racial conflict away from the schools and into other more critical arenas.

At this point, somebody always says, "Well, what about private schools established by white supremacists to escape integration?" The answer to that question is already clear. The Supreme Court has held subsidies for such schools unconstitutional, and neither legislatures nor Congress should provide them.

Indeed, I would go further and argue that the state should not subsidize any school which is not open to every child who wants to enroll—regardless of race, religion or ability. Not many non-Catholics want to attend parochial schools, but some already do and others will. Their admission should certainly be a precondition for public subsidies. Similarly, black schools should be required to admit white applicants in order to get tax support. No rush of applicants need be anticipated.

One final objection to the establishment of independent black schools should be mentioned. Many whites fear that such a system would preach black nationalism and racial hatred, and that this would make racial reconciliation even more difficult than it now seems.

This is a reasonable fear. The same objections were raised against the Catholic schools for more than a hundred years. Yet despite all sorts of horror stories about anti-Semitism and other forms of prejudice in Catholic schools, a 1964 survey by Andrew Greeley and Peter Rossi of the University of Chicago demonstrated fairly conclusively that Catholics who attended parochial schools were no more intolerant, narrow-minded or socially irresponsible than Catholics who attended public schools. Indeed, the survey suggested that, all other things being equal, parochial schools had a more liberalizing effect on Catholics than did public schools.

And similarly, the Greeley-Rossi survey suggests that the black schools would not have to be especially affluent to do an acceptable job. While the parochial schools spent far less per pupil than the public schools, used less extensively trained teachers, had much larger classes, were housed in older buildings, had smaller libraries and relied on a curriculum even more medieval than did the public schools, their alumni did at least as well in worldly terms as public-school Catholics.

All other things being equal, parochial-school Catholics ended up with slightly more education and slightly better jobs than public-school Catholics. The only really significant difference Greeley and Rossi found between the two groups was that parochial-school products were more meticulous and better informed about their religious obligations. This suggests that fears for the future of black children in black-controlled schools may also be somewhat exaggerated.

The development of an independent black school system would not solve the problems of black children. I doubt, for example, that many black private schools could teach their children to read appreciably better than white-controlled public schools now do. But such schools would be an important instrument in the hands of black leaders who want to develop a sense of community solidarity and pride in the ghetto, just as the parochial schools have worked for similarly placed Catholics.

Equally important, perhaps, the existence of independent black schools would diffuse the present attack on professional control over the public system. This seems the only politically realistic course in a society where professional control, employee rights and bureaucratic procedures are as entrenched as they are in America. The black community is not strong enough to destroy the public-school bureaucracy and staff. Even if it did, it now has nothing to put in its place. What the black community could do, however, would be to develop an alternative— and demand tax support for it.

Some radicals who expect black insurgency to destroy the whole professional hierarchy in America and create a new style of participatory democracy will regard this kind of solution as a cop-out. Some conservatives whose primary concern is that the lower orders not get out of hand will regard it as an undesirable concession to anarchy. But for those who value a pluralistic society, the fact that such a solution would, for the first time, give large numbers of non-Catholics a choice about where they send their children to school, ought, I think, to outweigh all other objections.

Another Look
at Student Rights
and
the Function of Schooling

PARENTS and STUDENTS of the
ELIZABETH CLEANERS STREET SCHOOL

Within a system of legal precedent and reasoned interpretation, the courts consider issues of student rights as raised in formal lawsuits and appeals. What is the correspondence of this very special judicial world to the everyday world in which students and their parents are searching for definitions of their rights, responsibilities and relationships within the schools that exist in their own communities?

One aspect of correspondence lies in the influence of the evolution of judicial decision as it has filtered through to the actual existence of students. How closely does practice follow the dicta of what should be? But there is another side to the correspondence. The day-to-day lives of students and their parents reveal sources of strain and emerging definitions of self and role that will eventually have to be translated into the terms of the judicial world. Are there indications of conceptions of student rights that outstrip what the courts have recognized thus far?

This second aspect of correspondence was our focus as we talked

Reprinted from "Another Look at Student Rights and the Function of Schooling," *Harvard Educational Review* Vol. 40 No 4, November 1970. Copyright ©1970 by the President and Fellows of Harvard College.

with students and parents of the Elizabeth Cleaners Street School. After years of participating in various public and private schools in New York City, they have come together and chosen a stance of truancy toward a system they judge to be inadequate in terms of both rights and learning. The students, who range in age from 12 to 17, are what used to be called "privileged kids" (though no current use of the term seems quite appropriate). With the active support of their parents, they have taken over a laundry storefront in a condemned section of buildings on Manhattan's West Side, joining there a number of impoverished Puerto Rican families who have become squatters in other condemned buildings. The Elizabeth Cleaners Street School began formally this fall, although parents and students must continue their search for funds and basic supplies.

As the opening of their school drew near, we asked them to share their concerns with us. Their analysis of the issues basic to the nature of learning suggests a concept of student rights extending beyond freedom of individual expression within an established structure. They raise the question of collective rights and responsibilities of students to control their own education within the context of a more direct relationship with the urban community of which they are a part.

Schools today consist of marks and tests. Teachers alienate children by acting authoritarian and superior to them. The dull rhetoric and inflexible dogma of schools not only alienate students, but also channel them into specific laid-out roles in society, both racist and sexist. Students have no say whatsoever in how the schools are governed, for example, in the hiring and firing of teachers. In short, control of schools has been placed in the hands of those whom school does not affect—bureaucratic administrators. All this makes us feel that change must come from outside the school system.

We are therefore creating an alternative high school that will be controlled, operated and governed by the students, which will include the responsibility of hiring and firing of teachers. Since it is our school we have made it available to ourselves at all times.

We feel that New York City is our most relevant classroom. The school will relate to the community that it is in. We are working for an ethnic balance of white, black and Latin students. We are creating a school that we believe will be very meaningful in today's society.

—from a statement written
by students of the Elizabeth Cleaners Street School

STUDENTS

The interview took place in July at a summer camp in western Connecticut. Present were Vashti Gittler, 13; Jeff Graham, 15; Jimmy Graham, 11; Lisa Mamis, 15; Betsy Reid, 15; Cathy Salit, 12; Peter Winston, 12. The interviewers were Ellen Solomon and Gregg Thomson of the Harvard Educational Review. *What has been your experience with student rights in the schools you're leaving?*

Betsy: I had no rights whatsoever in my school.

Was this a private school?

Betsy: Yes. And it was just like a Gestapo.

Lisa: I. S.———[1] also, where I used to go—they have a puppet student government. You know, people run for mayor, and secretary and treasurer. And they don't do anything—they don't do anything at all. It's just a total farce. I think it was last year, I heard that they decided just to hold off student elections. And then the students got upset. So the administration set up a supposedly real G. O. which supposedly has power. I really doubt how much it has. But there were never any student rights in the school.

Were there any confrontations about this lack of real rights?

Lisa: Not when I went to public school, although I hear they have them now. But when I went to Y———[2] last year in eighth grade, we all decided we were going to become very political and get a student government going, because there's never been a student government there. And so we set up this thing where each eighth-grade class would elect two officers to meet with the headmaster each week to

1. A public junior high school in New York City.

2. A private school in New York City.

discuss problems. And the kids in the class would tell their representative what the problems were.

The kids are too passive to recognize when they have any problems. If there's anything bothering them, they're too lazy to do anything. So that fell apart anyway. They don't want anything. All they want in Y—— is to smoke dope and get out at three o'clock.

Smoke dope in school?

Lisa: In school. Cause they have to. It's the only way they can live inside.

Well, should the right to smoke pot in school be a student's right?

Lisa: But nobody's asking for that. Sure, you can make up weird student rights. You can label anything a student right.

But that was what you said. They wanted to smoke dope—

Lisa: The majority of those students *are* interested in smoking dope and getting the fuck out because it's such a bad environment. That's what *they* want to do. But those aren't the kids that are actively working for students' rights.

Besides, that's the situation only in private schools. You can take a kid at Y—— , who has been there all his life and try to show him something. Because he's been isolated in the private school he can't see what's been happening in the public schools. The public high schools are, like, the most radicalizing places that exist. You become radical if you go to a public high school for a day. Private school kids are just beginning to get together over Kent. That got them upset because they could relate to white students getting killed.

Vashti: I don't think that's the way it is at my junior high. In my public school, the kids know how bad it is—they don't have any rights at all—but they just learn to live with it. And they don't even try to do anything. People try to arouse the kids' interest in—to get some things, but it doesn't seem to work. The kids are so used to it—they just try to forget about it by doing other things.

Wasn't there something about the flag?

Vashti: In another public school I went to, a lot of the kids didn't want to pledge to the flag. They didn't think that the pledge had any meaning. They just said, "We're not going to stand up." And they were suspended from school. So they got themselves a case in court and got the law changed. Now it's not illegal to sit down during the pledge. That was something. But when you're doing something like this, it takes so much work, especially when all the teachers are against you.

Are there other rights that are important to you?

Lisa: Well, decisions on curriculum and hiring teachers— the sort of things that are going on in the school. Like who gets expelled. For example, I remember an incident this year: we had a senior who was taking a test that he felt was a pretty uptight test and a lot of silly questions were being asked. So he put on the bottom "Why don't you fuck somebody—you'd feel a whole lot better." And the teacher took it to the school psychologist. And while she was in the office the headmaster said, "Hey, let me see that a minute." And it grew on from there that he was suspended. He met with the headmaster of the school to discuss what he had done and the headmaster said in the beginning, "I've already made the decision to suspend you. I'm just holding this meeting as a token." So everybody got very excited over this. And we met on a Saturday which is big for private schools. Like who sacrifices their Saturdays for school? So we all went to school on Saturday for a big meeting about strategy and how we were going to disrupt classes and not go to classes and have a student strike. We held up the lunchroom one day, and the teachers got very into it. And so we decided one day we were going to go to our classes and take a vote about discussing this kid. I went to my class and there were seven

in my class and we voted five to two for discussing him. So
the teacher comes in and he hadn't been at the meeting—
he didn't know what was going on so we explained it to
him. He said, "I don't give a shit what the fuck you're
talking about. This is *my* class and we're going to learn
grammar." So we were all pretty surprised at that, so we
ran up to the lunchroom and told everyone what had
happened. And the same thing happened in every other
class. Nobody was concerned. And parents got upset over
that, too. But it died down. And he was suspended . . . but
he came back.

Cathy: And then—then was when Lisa's brother Joshua
passed around petitions against the principal in I. S.——.
How did that work out?

Lisa: Well, there was a teacher strike that year, and people
that were against the strike broke into the building and
held the school. And they had a black teacher substitute as
the principal. And after the strike was over, they decided
that he was a much better principal. So Joshua circulated
petitions saying, "We, the students of I. S.—— , demand
that Mr. H—— has done a good job and should be our
permanent principal. Sign here if you agree." And some
kids came up to him in the lunchroom one day and asked
him if they could sign the petition and he said, "Sure."
And the acting principal or assistant principal saw this
happening and she took him to the principal's office where
he locked the door and interrogated my brother and
harassed him. So a teacher who heard about it called up
my mother and she called up the superintendent of schools
and there was a whole big thing about it. So he's suing.

Is the same principal still there?

Lisa: No, he got kicked up to a higher office.

*It seems like at least some teachers are helping you get
rights.*

Lisa: Some teachers, though not very many.

Cathy: Even some of the ones who do support them,

they're not really for them.

Why not? Why wouldn't a teacher be for student rights?

Lisa: Because most of the teachers employed in public schools are the kinds that have, like, that have been there for 30 years and have very old-fashioned ideas. And all the teachers that support students' rights are new and young and soon become disillusioned with the system and quit. So there aren't many of them.

How do the other teachers respond when you protest?

Vashti: They do things like give us bad marks and put us down on section cards; it's really disgusting.

Cathy: In private schools I think it's worse though, because like in my school, Y——, like they used to warn all the teachers about me, and I was marked in the school as a bad influence.

What sort of things had you done?

Cathy: I fought against the teachers because I didn't learn anything. I was being fed information, you know. And a whole lot of kids agreed with me, like Peter. We would try to do things to change it. Nothing would ever seem to work. My teacher taught like a computer. And of course, the whole administration stood up for *her*.

When you say you fought against the teacher and tried to do things, what did you try to do specifically?

Cathy: Well, we would constantly go to the principal and try to talk to him about doing something. And he would always tell us that everything would work out all right, because she was a *new* teacher. But after nine months, you know, she wasn't still a new teacher. And I remember one incident: one of the sixth-grade teachers—she never even had me in her class and didn't know me personally or anything—told the kids in her class that they could not have anything to do with me, because I had a negative attitude. I was a bad influence. And they did a whole lot of other things, you know. Like, it was very *obvious* that I was marked, though I had never even spoken to her. When my mother came to school, the first thing that teacher said to her was, "Do you know that Cathy hasn't said hello to me the *whole* time she's been in school?" You know, it's really crazy. The principal said the exact same thing—he said, "Cathy hasn't said hello to me."

Lisa: Yeah, that happened to me. I couldn't believe it. Mr. K—— complained to my parents that I never said hello to him in the hallway. Like, it's so incredible.

Your private and public schools seem to be similar in their attitude toward rights. Do private schools at least offer you better learning experiences?

Lisa: Well, Y—— is supposed to be a "progressive" school and you're taught the same thing you're taught in public school. I know from experience because I switched from public school to Y——. Their science courses are exactly the same. You don't learn anything in anything. You're just fed information, the same as you would be anyplace else.

What do you think should be happening instead?

Lisa: Well, they don't bother to sit down and ask you, "Well, what would you like to learn. Would you rather learn about India or would you like to learn about Red China?" See, Core class is a mixture of English and history. And they tell you at the beginning of the year that you're going to learn about India for a year. Like it's a whole year down the drain if you're not interested in India, or if you happen to be interested in Cuba or Red China or some other country.

Peter: You know, you take a negative attitude. You resent the fact that you had no choice in the matter at all.

Lisa: And any teacher that would do that in the first place is not going to teach that subject in such an exciting way that you would be turned on by it.

In other words, you say that you know better than the teachers what kind of things you should be learning?

Cathy: Of course!

Lisa: It's us that's doing the learning, and we know what we're interested in. And it's not true anymore that teachers know better. Nobody can know what's important to you.

Well, what are some of the things that you think are important to learn?

Lisa: Well, you know, *relevant* is a very overused word. But, you know, things that are relevant. Like everybody's very interested in Cuba, right? So instead of everybody learning about India for a year, you learn about Cuba. And you find out what's going on in terms of the Venceremos Brigade, things like that. It really relates to you.

Are science or math or things like that relevant?

Lisa: They could be. You know, you could *make* them relevant—if you're interested and have a good teacher.

Did you think about these things when you hired your new teachers?

Cathy: Definitely. Yes.

Lisa: We weren't looking for what they knew. We were looking more towards personality and overall rounded-out characters. We wanted people we could feel close to and talk to and relate to more, I guess.

Vashti: It always seems to me that if it's someone I'm close to or someone I like and respect, I learn much better. If my brother tries to teach me something that a teacher whom I dislike has already tried to teach me, my brother could always teach it to me much better. We picked them also because they knew so much more than we do, and I want them to kind of interest me in more things. Then I can decide what I want for myself.

Lisa: All the teachers we hired have the same kind of personality. They all like Chinese cooking, they all know urban problems, they're all into art and photography and pottery and things like that, and things like ecology and Cuba.

Cathy: If they don't know something, they'd say so. We'd learn together—it would be an exchange.

Lisa: Or we'd get a part-time teacher who could teach it.

Cathy: I have a question. There isn't any special time when you're supposed to go. It's open all the time, isn't it?

Lisa: It's open when you want it and when you arrange with the teacher.

Do the teachers know they've been hired for a 24-hour-a-day job?

Cathy: It's not a 24-hour-a-day job. I don't think you can say that at all.

Lisa: Well, it depends on the teacher's commitment. The full-time teachers wanted it to be a total commitment. Some of the part-time teachers also want it to be a total commitment. But they have less responsibility, I guess.

Around what age do you think students start thinking about wanting their rights?

Cathy: Twelve. Twelve is probably the best age that they should start. Once you get into junior high, that's when things really start happening. When you're in elementary it's kind of hard to understand all the shit that's being handed to you.

Lisa: And you still have to learn basics, things like reading and writing. It shouldn't necessarily be the way they're teaching it. But you do have to learn basics.

Why should a student have to learn how to read and write?

Lisa: Oh, if he doesn't want to? I don't know how to answer that. I guess that to function in an environment like the city, in order to be able to communicate, you've got to learn how to read and write.

Do you want to do more reading and writing?

Cathy: I'm interested—not the way it's being taught now.

Lisa: It depends on what's being written. You know, not the old-type books like *Silas Marner*. They're dead. But books like Jerry Rubin's are widely read.

Are you at all afraid that you're risking too much? That when you're about 35 and you find you didn't learn calculus because nobody made you, you're going to be lost?

Lisa: No. It's too important to be scared. You can't be scared.

Cathy: That's not true. That's not true at all—

Lisa: Yes, but you can't be a coward about it and say, "I'm dropping out and I don't want to drop out." If you really believe in it—you just try not to be scared.

Peter: I feel that I'm far beyond the time when someone has to expose me to different subjects. I think I'm capable of deciding what I want to learn.

Suppose you can't decide what you want to do—will you be able to ask for guidance?

Lisa: It's up to the student, the whole school is based on the student. I know when we first discussed setting up the school, a lot of us said that we didn't know what we wanted and could you help us? That would be the school—to expose us to things that we weren't getting exposed to in public school and Y——.

Do you think seriously about what kind of work you're going to do for your life?

Cathy: I'm not worrying about that yet.

Jeff: Sort of. Radio, photography, music.

Cathy: There was a guy I spoke to who has a theater. My mother talked to him also. He asked me how I felt about the school and everything. We asked him if we could work out kind of an apprenticeship and he said that would be a very good idea. Like being part of the theater—maybe doing scenery or whatever it is.

Would you see this as learning skills which later in your life you want to use in a job?

Cathy: Maybe.

Lisa: I see it as something I'm interested in now.

Betsy: But talking about films and photography is what I'd like to do. Possibly for a living. So I will be using it.

Vashti: Sometimes I don't think, like, I'm going to be doing work the way adults do it today. It doesn't seem like it's still going to be that way, that you'll have a job and

then go home to your family. Things will change and I will
be doing things differently. If I really need to earn money,
I'll do something I'm really interested in.

*Do you all have a vision of what the adult world will be
like? What would you like it to be?*

Vashti: People won't have a job and a certain role in life.
You do what you're interested in. I guess it's something
like the school. Everyone helps each other. And money
isn't the main thing in everyone's life. There will be other
things.

Jeff: I think our school is a preparation for better
education. I mean, learn what you're interested in.

But you think then you'll go to college?

Lisa: Well, it depends. I have three years left.

Jeff: Well, I don't want to go to college.

Why don't you want to go to college?

Cathy: Well, I'm only 12 now. By the time I'm of college
age I hope colleges will be more relevant to today's
society. Colleges now are so useless. The only way they're
useful as I see it to me is to get a job. And if I wanted to
get a job I guess I'd go to college. But why should colleges
only be for *that?*

Lisa: A lot could happen. The alternative school thing is
just starting and it's really growing, and it's a big booming
thing. Colleges could begin to accept the idea of alternate
schools and really begin to understand it. And colleges
have to be geared toward people coming from alternate
schools.

*Suppose you thought that starting this school meant that
you'd never be able to get into any good college? Any
college you really wanted to go to?*

Cathy: I know kids who've been in a school where there's
no science, and it's not accredited and they've gotten into
college. Like some of them got into Antioch and Goddard.

Lisa: You'd have to get into the progressive schools. You
can't get into the Ivy League schools.

*What about your parents? Do you feel that they really
have a good sense of what your rights should be? Do you
foresee any difficulties with them?*
Cathy: Difficulties? Not really. Not with my mother. I
think, maybe, with my father. I'm not sure he understands
everything that I want, but then I'm not sure I know
everything *he* wants either.
Vashti: At some of the first meetings some of the parents
get a little scared. Like the first time we started talking
about our rights, they kind of drew back.
Lisa: I don't think there were real difficulties. No, I think
the only thing—well, there was a big split over whether our
school should merge with another school, a community
school. That was a big split between students and parents.
Yeah, over accreditation. I think the majority of parents
wanted us to merge. Well, my parents did and Jeff's
parents did.
Jeff: Yeah, I think my father and mother did.
Then you have *made demands on your parents since this
all began? They weren't so willing in the beginning?*
Cathy: Not in the beginning.
Jeff: In the beginning my mother was more for the school
than I was. She just knew more about it, that's all.
Lisa: Yeah, a lot of parents dragged in kids.
Jeff: She didn't drag me.
Lisa: Yeah, but some did.
*Were there kids interested in coming to the school whose
parents wouldn't let them? Or did other kids not want to
come?*
Lisa: Well, some kids were scared. It's a scary thing to drop
out. We had trouble with a couple of parents whose kids
wanted to stay too.
And did those kids think of leaving home?
Lisa: Yes, one did. She left home. But things got cleared
up. There was a meeting held with the parents who were

having trouble and they got it cleared up. So the girl went home, and she's coming to the school.

Then most of the kids you know are working it out with their parents in some way? As far as you're concerned, then, is the whole "generation gap" just blown up?

Lisa: It was invented by the media. The generation gap was invented by an idiot. I'm sure it exists very little.

Cathy: I don't think it's a generation gap. It's an individual gap between parent and child, and parent and parent, or child and child. It's not a generation gap—that's such a *disgusting* way of putting it. I'm not sure, but I think the majority of kids in this school are a lot more radical than their parents are. I don't think the parents realize it either.

Vashti: One day my mother said to me, "Vashti, don't you want to go to a good private school?" I couldn't believe that! I was really angry. She wants me to go to a good college too. Sometimes she's kind of wistful. She's getting over it.

Lisa: It's like with Women's Liberation—my mother's into Women's Liberation—and she turned to me the other day and she said, "You know, there's one thing wrong with Women's Liberation—you don't have weddings." (laughter)

But you feel that your parents have supported the school, have allowed you to do this?

Lisa: Yes. But we would have done it anyway. Without their consent. Definitely. But it wouldn't have been as easy.

Cathy: But if our parents had felt much differently, we would have a different kind of environment around us. And maybe we wouldn't be so *into* this.

Lisa: Things might have worked out even better if we had to fund it. It could have made us stronger.

Did your parents always encourage you to think for yourselves, make your own decisions?

Lisa: Well, all my life this is the way it was. We used to live in Vermont, in the country, and even there we had a big stink. And my mother was always politically involved and we had friends from Africa and she ran for an office. And it was just always around me. So I never thought differently.

And were there conflicts as you grew up about things you wanted that your parents didn't want?

Vashti: Well, with me there was. I began to realize—it kind of started when I realized what was happening to me in the schools and how my mother kind of always decided how my life was going to be. I'd just say things like, "I'm my own self, and no one's going to run my life for me." And we still have fights—but I think I'm winning.

Cathy: I have conflicts sometimes with my mother. She's always saying, "Cathy, you're only 12 years old. And don't you forget it." As if I'm ever going to forget it if she keeps on reminding me! Politically, like with the school, we agree with each other almost completely. I don't know if there's anything political we disagree on.

Do you discuss everything with them?

Lisa: Yeah.

Jeff: No, not *everything* that goes on.

Lisa: It's a different thing—certain things that are private but that doesn't mean we don't discuss freely with them.

Vashti: I don't discuss freely with my mother things that I know she disagrees with me on. I don't want to get into hassles with her. But if it's something that affects me then I'll fight for it all the way. Like I do sometimes.

Can you envision any point at which your parents would tell you you had to do or be something?

Jeff: Well, I can't imagine my father coming to me and wanting me to be a lawyer. You know, I'll do what I want. And he's not going to tell me what my life's going to be.

Lisa: I don't think that any parents that would consent to letting their kid go to this school would actually make a demand on their kid, of what to do with his life. I mean, the whole thing with this school is that kids decide for themselves what they're going to learn and what they're going to do with their lives anyway.

Have you made any progress toward getting what you and your parents want—an ethnically balanced school?

Lisa: Yeah, we've tried, but we've been only partly successful. I mean, black and Puerto Rican kids have a different life to lead. For blacks and Puerto Ricans—they need a diploma.

Have you talked to blacks and Puerto Ricans who say that?

Lisa: Right. We have a white skin and that's a privilege, so we can use it the way we want. So it's scarier for them than for us to drop out and make it whatever way you make it.

Cathy: I mean society will at least accept us because we're white, you know.

Lisa: And middle-class.

Cathy: Well, naturally.

Lisa: Two poor whites called me up. It's almost as hard for them—I'd say it's as hard for them as it is for Puerto Ricans to drop out.

What about the parents of these kids you've talked to?

Lisa: Of the black and Puerto Ricans? We haven't talked to them. Except for one—I spoke to one Puerto Rican father. But his kid isn't coming into school because he's not interested. His father is.

Well, why should a black or Puerto Rican kid who needs a diploma so bad come to a risky school like this?

Lisa: Right. Well, that's where we're having problems. But the Puerto Rican or black kids that we get that *are* interested are into revolution and beating down the school system. And you know, you could devote your life in this school to what you want. You do in school what you want. If you want, what you do in the school is to work on school strikes, organize.

I was struck by someone's remark that being in public school is a radicalizing experience. Why do you want everyone into free schools then?

Lisa: You see, the schools destroy people. And like, you can take a prison up to a point. Like schools are prisons. When Huey Newton got out of prison, he was asked, "How does it feel to be free?" And he wasn't free. It was just another prison. That's the way it is in schools, too. You can take it up to a point. And you're radicalized the first day of school when the teacher tells you to take off that button you're wearing. Or to cut your hair or not show up again. You know, that's all you need.

Aren't there laws?

Lisa: There are laws, but the laws—you know. Who protects them? I mean, there are lawsuits, but it still happens.

Then you feel that by making your school and by developing yourselves as individuals, you're beating the system that way and you're saving your souls for the future.

Lisa: And encouraging other people to drop out too.

And the black revolutionary kids?

Lisa: Well, they have to get themselves together. And you know there're black schools and lower East Side schools that are for blacks and Puerto Ricans, and they get themselves together and we get ourselves together.

Cathy: One of our main ideas is that when we reach our limit of 30 kids and we can't accept any more kids, we'll be trying to work with other kids to start their own schools—as many as possible.

How did you decide that 30 kids would be the limit?

Betsy: That's all we could handle for space, and financially.

And how do you decide which 30 kids it will be?

Cathy: First come, first served.

There are no entrance qualifications?

Lisa: Uh-uh. But the ages are from 12 to 17.

How do you handle disputes among yourselves? Do you vote?

Lisa: No.

Cathy: Yes, we do. None of us really agrees about—

Lisa: We don't raise our hands and vote. We usually say, "Well, is that agreed?"

Cathy: And if somebody says, "No"—

Lisa: Well, when we were discussing whether Lin was going to be full-time, we discussed it with Peter and we said, "Well, is it agreed that since only one person wants Lin as full-time then he should be part-time?" and everyone said, "Yes."

Cathy: That's majority rule.

Do you foresee any areas in which you feel there might be serious splits? You can? What sort of things?

Lisa: We had one a while ago concerning ——'s[3] daughter. See, we had decided that we weren't going to take any more white kids into the school, and there was a question of whether or not to let her in. A lot of us felt so strongly about the moral courage her family had shown. But then she decided not to come. She's going to Y——.

Cathy: After we were arguing for three weeks—

Lisa: It was a heated, heated argument.

The vast majority of kids don't have parents with the values that your parents have. Do you think about those kids? Are they ever going to have a chance to get the kind of education that you're setting up for yourselves?

Lisa: It's got to be a personal decision on whether you're going to fight your parents. Last year my brother was involved in an alternate school. He and a girl were helping set it up. In mid-July they discovered that everybody was quitting the school except for the two of them. But come September when they advertised in the *Voice* and got a whole lot of students, this girl learned that her mother didn't want her to go to the school. Her mother had

---

3. A prominent pacifist and leader in the resistance to the war in Vietnam.

registered her in the U.N. school. And she fought her mother and just refused to go there. And so she went to *her* school. You have to fight.

Do you think other kids will be influenced by your idea of education?

Lisa: Yes, we can expose them to it. We can help them and tell them what we've done.

Vashti: It's sort of sad in my school. The kids realize what's happening, how they're being treated in the public schools. But they're so used to having it fed to them that they're just beyond doing anything about it. Instead of trying to make something new, they just kind of think about other things, like fights and little cliques and not going to classes. And those are the only things on their mind. But it wouldn't really occur to them to make some—

Lisa: But then you have to point it out to them.

Vashti: A lot of them are past hope.

Lisa: Nobody's past hope.

Perhaps the public schools themselves will begin to be influenced by the kind of education you're creating for yourselves.

Cathy: You'd never get it there. You could never do it. They wouldn't give it to you. And even if they said they would give it to you, they wouldn't go through with it. I mean they would just trick you. Anyway you wouldn't be able to function with 3,000 kids. . . .

Lisa: Look at the size of *this* school!

Cathy: . . . and overcrowding and conditions like prisons. And there, in the public schools, the whole idea is that it has to be *given* to you. No, you've got to *take* it. You've got to get it *yourself*.

Is that also a responsibility in terms of the whole society?

Vashti: You mean changing society? I don't think anyone *has* to do it. But as in setting up the school—if you care about where you live and everything, you probably want to change it and make it better.

Lisa: One of the responsibilities we're taking on is changing students' lives, you know, making lives liveable for students. By starting our own school, we destroy the system. So that's the responsibility we've taken.

PARENTS AND TEACHERS

The interview took place in July in a Manhattan apartment. Present were the full-time teachers of the school: Peter Leventhal, Elaine Louie and David Nassaw—and parents: Barbara Gittler, Jerry Graham, Jack Mamis, Peter Reid, Sema and Murray Salit and Florence Winston. The interviewers were Ellen Solomon and Gregg Thomson of the Review.

Let me ask you this: Why start the school in the first place? Weren't your children getting rather adequate education in their private schools or public schools?
Mr. Graham: No, no. Inadequate education. In *every* way. I personally don't believe—to use John Holt's term—in a "right answer" theory of education. Everything was wrong with their education. I wasn't motivated terribly by student rights so much as the whole concept of the educational system, the whole educational relationship between student and teacher and student and school administration.
Mr. Mamis: I think you can make a long case about how the administration and the teachers deprive students of their rights and use them, treating them as the enemy. We could go through that whole thing. But it goes after the fact that they are not being educated. The students don't feel like school is exciting, they don't feel that this is the place they want to go in the morning, and, as soon as that feeling arises, the conflict which creates the rights issues comes up. So we have all sorts of anecdotes about how their rights are infringed and the awful things the administrators did to assert their authority, but it still goes

back to the fact that they weren't getting anything out of school.

In other words, you're suggesting there wouldn't be any conflict of rights if the kids were really turned on by their education?

Mr. Mamis: Well, it's really a question of the chicken and the egg, but the teachers that turn the kids on don't have that kind of conflict, because they are understanding.

Mrs. Salit: I disagree with both of you and with the notion that you can separate kids' rights from inadequate education. I think what happened was that in all of their educational experience, someone was always trying to negotiate something that was not negotiable, which was their rights. And each time this came up there was a conflict. First it caused mild trouble—they would stand up and claim their rights. Then it got to be the whole action that was going on in school—they, defending their rights, and the administration, trying to negotiate with them.

What kind of rights are you referring to?

Mrs. Salit: Well, I think that, by and large, one of the ways kids learn is to ask questions, and this is their right. However, each time a provocative question was asked, it was suppressed one way or other. First they say things like "That's not in the curriculum; it's not going to be on the test so we can't deal with it." Then, as it got worse, their attitude would be, "You're being very disruptive," and then that led into all kinds of miserable—

Mr. Mamis: Still, I think of Josh going to public school where there are allegedly all sorts of problems with rights and where he has a very straight English teacher who teaches the subject, but makes it so exciting he wants to go to that class. There's no rights issue about whether he does his homework; he willingly follows many traditional aspects of what's going on in that class, because the class is very stimulating. He's treated much more like an adult than in the other classes.

Mrs. Salit: I think that if rights are respected, education takes place. I don't know what happened in this particular English class, but I would suspect that without it's ever being discussed, one person would have to be respecting the other person. They have to, in order to get anything out of it.

Your children have gone to both public and private schools. Is there a difference in terms of students rights?

Mr. Mamis: There's a distinct difference between the experience we had at the junior high school and the experience we had at the private school, where there seemed to be no rights whatsoever. No parental rights—it was conspicuous. You paid your money, you signed a contract with the school, and in effect, you had nothing more to say about it. The Board of Trustees and the people they designated to run the school had absolute control, whereas in the public school system you could scream and yell and say these people were responsible to you. You can't say that in the private schools, and I think that affected the kids that I know at the private school. The parents couldn't even help them, because the administration was so remote from them. And it created an entirely different attitude. I sense in my daughter who went to private school—"I've got to get out of here so I can have my own school with my own rights"; whereas I sense in my son, who's fighting for his rights in the junior high school, that it is compensatory. He can say, "Next year I'm going to try to do this and try to do that."

Can the struggle for rights be an educational experience?

Mrs. Salit: I don't think kids should have to spend all their time proving to teachers and administration that they know what their rights are and they're going to fight for them. It should just be an accepted thing. Otherwise the kids have to constantly prove their rights and there's no time for education to take place.

Mrs. Gittler: When Vashti and the children in her school

demanded their right not to stand for the Pledge of Allegiance, it was the first time she really ran into a bureaucracy. And it involved suspension and legal battles and the courts. And the children knew they were being put upon for something that was their right to start with and it colored their whole relationship with the teachers and with the school. They became "troublemakers." It affected their homework, their schoolwork, the interest the children had in their teachers. It just changed the whole atmosphere in the school.

Are you saying that before the eruption there were no problems?

Mrs. Gittler: Oh, there were many problems. But the kids were sort of battling it out, not knowing what the battle was all about, and suddenly they saw the whole problem: they had *no* rights at all according to the teachers and the system. They were battling for something they thought they had anyway, and they found that the system was really horrified that they thought they had these rights. So it became a really legal, heavy confrontation, apart from whether the teacher of the subject matter was really interesting or not. It certainly gave Vashti a whole other view of her school—in terms of herself and how much she could do herself, without the approval of the school, her teachers, grades and that sort of thing.

Mr. Mamis: But I think it takes a good many years of battling on Vashti's level before you have some self-confidence that you know what your rights are and that you know where the teacher is denying them to you. And that you're right. You don't run home to your parents and ask, "Did I do the right thing? I'm afraid."

Mrs. Gittler: But you still sound as if the more sophisticated you get, the better a demander you are, whereas I think what Vashti and our kids seem to be saying now is, "We don't want to have to demand any more. We don't have to make these explicit demands. We want to start from where we should be."

Mr. Mamis: Yes, but I think that's idealistic. Besides I think that there's a whole learning experience, that the struggle is educational, that there's something very exciting that these kids could develop for getting, as leaders of a school, more and more rights for the body of students. And I think really comes a point when the administration becomes so overbearing that these kids lose, they make no headway. Then you have dropouts; you have, perhaps, a new school like this. Or if you're lucky, you have some relationship, some breakthrough with the administration and you start getting some rights. As soon as you start getting some, then you really have something exciting in the school, even though it may be miserable and oppressive and all that. You start getting places.

Mrs. Salit: But I saw Cathy in a very ugly position in her school. I felt that the struggle had caused her to lose interest in anything educational. There were many things that ordinarily would not have bothered her. Somehow the struggle became the most important thing. I felt it was having a destructive effect.

Then do you think the Elizabeth Cleaners St. School will be a conflict-free experience for the kids? Or will the fights be different?

Mr. Reid: I think that they're only going to fight each other.

Mr. Graham: Right. The fights will be individual rights versus rights of the group—and which comes first.

Miss Louie: I can see your new school becoming very insular for the students, unless 99 percent of their activity occurs outside and they really become New Yorkers, so to speak. It's possible that students will have no conflict simply because there would be enough time, enough patience, enough reason, enough familiarity between enough people that they can just go right through it. A radical attitude that might have developed would be totally smothered because their rights will be taken for granted. "We got it, and we're only 13, 14 or 15, and we did it by ourselves." In a sense that's good, because they won't have personal struggles on a day-to-day level. On the other hand, the revolution isn't won, because it's only going to affect maybe 20 kids at this moment. So probably their emphasis on using the city as a school is one of their most important premises.

Your kids are undertaking a great deal. They're not starting just an individualistic Summerhill-type school— they're in the midst of an urban slum. Do you have fears for them?

Mrs. Salit: Yes, I have certain fears. At the moment I'm in a fortunate position, because my child still talks to me. I don't know how long this is going to last but, for example, the first weekend we were at school, there was an unfortunate incident. A young man had gone into one of the semi-abandoned buildings to get a refrigerator to bring to another apartment, and in the course of all of this, he was stabbed by the superintendent of the building. He came into our storefront and then was taken to a hospital. You know, everyone assured me that our kids were really all right. I wasn't there, but I had the suspicion that my own daughter must have been upset by it, because though she may have read about these things in the newspaper, she had never witnessed anything like this. I felt certain she was disturbed by it. When we spoke about it, she admitted that she had been frightened by it, and at that point I asked her if she felt that she really wanted to be a pioneer in this sort of thing. And she said that if she had a choice, she would rather go into a school like this that was already established; however, there was also something very exciting about starting it herself. And that, yes, if I would stick close by she would want to do it. And I assured her, too, that at any point she felt she wasn't capable of handling a situation like this, that we could change it. And I meant it. And that wouldn't mean that she would have to go back into any institution-type school. We would just find something else. But, yes, my kid was scared, and I think she's still apprehensive about what's going to take place there in September. And I think we are, too.

Mrs. Gittler: I found that a lot of the goals of starting a school like this—which were very much to do with education and learning—became very blurred when it came to community. Because really she felt, and I certainly did—because I'm a parent, and they're only 12 or 13—that the fear involved in choosing a place that's a very dangerous neighborhood to start with became part of what the school was about. And that worried me because I felt what the kids wanted in terms of education was being very mixed together with what the parents in the community wanted in terms of the community in which they had lived for a long time. And I felt that it went a long way toward diminishing the actual educational goal—"What are we going to learn and how are we going to learn it?" and "Who are our teachers going to be?" and "There's a whole world of things we want to learn about." It became very involved with—"What are we doing for the community?" and "Can we cope with this?" and "And are we going to be afraid or are we not?" and "What are we going to do when a junkie walks in the store?" Which I really felt was aside from the weight of starting a new school, and becoming truants, and bucking the whole system. And raising money was a great extra burden.

Mrs. Salit: I have those fears that you mentioned, but I don't have the fear that something was happening that took the place of what the kids had set out to do. Those kids had the best lesson in city government that they will ever have. Let's face it. Like, the guy who was stabbed brought charges against the superintendent. The superintendent was let off, the hospital wouldn't accept the wounded man, he was sent off to the Tombs with 45 stitches, and his bail was put at $2,500. How could the kids escape learning from that experience?

Mr. Salit: Barbara, you made it sound as if we guided the kids into this storefront. If you remember the several meetings before that when nothing was being accomplished, the kids unanimously agreed that what was the sense of talking about a white, middle-class school if we were to be a street school, and that we better find some way of doing something so that we had some balanced composition. The feeling then was that the best way to go out and get this was to literally go out and establish ourselves in the areas that we wanted to do the recruiting. So we didn't say, "Let's go to the most dangerous neighborhood in New York City." We said, "Let's go to a place that does represent the kind of ethnic balance that we're seeking, establish ourselves as part of this community." I think that that was the reason for doing it.

Mrs. Gittler: I just know that many times Vashti would come home and talk about the girls being worried about walking out in the street. Men would come by and, you know, they hadn't gone through this with men looking at them that way, or coming up close to them, or coming on to them and they didn't understand the language these men were speaking, which was a whole new thing. And I feel that to a child—12 or 13 years old—it becomes a thing wholly apart from their educational process.

I feel that the weight of learning and establishing a new kind of learning is very grave. It really is. I don't take that for granted for one second. They haven't been in a situation where they've chosen their own life styles or their own subject matter or their own course of learning before. And add to that a kind of fear of walking out of the school into the street.

Mr. Mamis: They've chosen their own life style for years, they've picked what they want to learn for years, they pick what kind of clothes they want to wear. Of course, they do—you just don't recognize it.

Mrs. Salit: I think what Barbara says is right. I think that if a kid is living in fear of something he really can't learn too much.

Mr. Mamis: You didn't hear what I said. What I said was that these kids have for many years picked their own life style. They pick the kinds of clothes they like, they pick the kind of hairdo they want, they choose the kind of books they want to read, they think what they like. You don't recognize it as picking their own life style because it remains under your wing.

Mrs. Gittler: I have yet to meet one child in this group whose life style doesn't reflect the views of the parent.

Mr. Mamis: In other words, they can't make choices if they relate to their parents' choices?

Mrs. Gittler: I'm not saying that at all. I'm saying they haven't really been on their own yet.

Mr. Mamis: I'm saying, quite clearly, they have made a number of choices as to what they like in life. And they have been doing that since they've been infants. I think that's what children do. They make those choices. And I think what frightens the parents now is that those choices now take on an aspect of being independent of their parents at an earlier age than we expected it would happen. And we're relatively unprepared for it.

Mrs. Gittler: What really frightens me is that something very important to my daughter, choosing her own kind of education, which I think she can handle, is extended to her choosing the kind of fear that she has to live with.

Miss Louie: On the one hand, to refer to your comment about the girls' not being able to understand men rapping with them on the streets, it probably was in Spanish. But on the other hand, the function of the school will literally be to explain the whole *Machismo* concept to them. Instinctually my feeling about the area was that it is not mini-skirt area, and the girls can make that decision in and of themselves.

Mr. Mamis: You make value judgments about the kinds of

fears these kids have. They also have fears if the college president walks in the door. Or if Governor Rockefeller walked in the door, they would have fears. They have fears when they have to call someone to help to raise money. They have to learn how to deal with these real things. And if they learn, if they can say with some confidence, "I'm no longer afraid to call some rich businessman on the phone and ask him for money," it's the same kind of solution that can say, "I'm no longer afraid to walk down that block. I know what these men are going to do."

Mr. *Graham*: I don't see how we can separate education in the classroom from life. To me that's what's been wrong with all of the schools. Kids have been told, "You must learn what's in these paragraphs. Don't worry about life. That's not your problem, you'll learn for life later." And now to me, this school offers a chance for a kid to be as dumb as he may have to be in order to learn something, make as many mistakes, be as open, go through whatever he has to go through. I believe that kids get scared in the hall of a private high school when a guy, suitably tough-looking, comes up and threatens a girl. One way or another, life is learning how to cope with that, with the guidance of teachers sensitive enough to see the problem and work with it.

Have you created procedures for dealing with disagreements among you? Are there certain guarantees you have formalized for the individual rights of the kids, parents and teachers?

Mr. *Leventhal*: You know this came up at—I can't remember what meeting—but this came up in general terms of conversation. In one meeting a boy was very insistent that these things get written down. But the general feeling in the group was that we don't really have to write them down because actually we're all working together. So you don't need to prescribe ways in which you can or cannot do certain things. And it occurs to me now that this is the only right that really exists—the right to have some sort of sympathetic correspondence. But at that time at that meeting—I may be wrong, maybe I picked this up wrong—but at that time the general feeling was that there was really no reason to describe exactly what the rights of individual persons were.

Mrs. Salit: But at every meeting somebody said we've got to identify our roles in this. This came up at every meeting.

Mr. Reid: You mean the students didn't want to write down a list. They wanted no part of laws, government structure, formality, even the vote.

Mr. Leventhal: Yes, and there's a very serious, classical, anarchic sort of feeling in terms of students getting together. I taught at a private school, and even there there's the feeling that if this state apparatus weren't there, then we wouldn't have to talk about this shit all the time.

It seems to me that the aspiration in this situation is to reach that point. The possibilities are such that you can reach that point, whereas in the other situation, no matter what you do, you can't. All the other schools tend to isolate them as units and not allow them to get together.

Mr. Mamis: I think that what creates whatever conflicts we've had so far is the desire of some students who feel very strongly that other students don't understand the community spirit and are being divisive and that they can't cope with it. "Why haven't they cooperated? Why aren't they coming into the thing instead of setting up a barrier?"

Have the students faced a situation that divided them?

Mr. Mamis: There was a meeting called to interview a teacher. Some students who didn't come to that interview insisted that, before any decision could be made, that they should also interview, and that it wasn't fair. Those who had attended felt the meeting had been openly announced, that they had met as a community group, and that their choices, feelings and opinions should be accepted as a community choice of opinion without the others feeling offended. But they scheduled another interview.

I have the feeling that they don't want something divisive to come up, and they're willing to go through that extra effort to keep it going as a community. They really want everybody to be feeling much the same about these things.

Mr. Graham: No, I don't think that at all. I think they're very shrewd and are really quite sensitive to that. The strong sense of who's uptight about learning specific things, uptight about the dangers, uptight about the money—they know that already.

Have there been any divisions between the parents and children? Have the kids wanted things you didn't?

Mr. Mamis: I felt considerable surprise when the students began to assert the demands for the rights that they wanted. "We want to pick our own teachers. We want to make that kind of decision." None of which I necessarily would have objected to. And I don't know if any other parent really would have objected, but it came very abruptly. It came all of a sudden.

Mr. Graham: Remember the tenor of us getting together at first—all of us getting together, and of the kids getting increasingly frustrated and increasingly losing their voice at these meetings and finally pulling themselves together and saying, "Well, finally, these are the rights we're going to have." And they really did that. All of a sudden, they made that shift, asserted the rights that they wanted, and they have not backed down in any sense.

Mrs. Gittler: I personally started feeling that it was important to identify goals in this vein, because we were headed for unnecessary trouble. If we were going to inflict what we thought was right for the school on the kids—

Mr. Mamis: Are you confusing what we think is right for the school with what our rights are as parents? In this school we have evolved a role because we were there at the

beginning. We existed as parents, we helped them. Whatever our role in the school really is, I think we're still going
to have enormous problems about our roles as parents. A
lot of these things about what we feel *should* be going on
at the school really are going to come up a lot of times.
But we really have a role as part of the school. We exist as
part of the school. We even want to be students in class.

Mrs. Gittler: That's up to the kids to decide. I don't think
they've—

Mr. Mamis: Whatever it is, I throw that out as my feeling. I
think that those things are going to come up, but we're
still part of the school. We are a part of the school in a lot
of ways.

Mrs. Salit: I think what's happening in our school is that
they have discovered that they can't do a lot of things by
themselves. But unlike a public school or a private school
where it would be pointed out to them, I think that we
took another posture in this case. I don't know how we
did it, but I don't find any animosity between the kids and
myself. But I also know that in order to get certain things
going, I have to set the date, I have to call them to remind
them—

Mr. Mamis: But they also plan meetings on their own and
tell *us* when they're scheduled. They're developing their
roles, and one of our roles is to help them. They're at ease
with the roles that we have so far as long as we have not
been domineering.

I feel considerably different about the situation than I
did when I started. I feel probably more extreme than
anybody else. I feel that Lisa right now in her own
head could very well operate without the school with my
consent. I think she'd do a lot of the things that the school
has in mind as an educational objective by herself if the
school didn't materialize. I think that at some point they
don't need academic learning, or they have to be made to
see the world as apprentices, and they have to start

functioning that way. And what I see her doing within this school is learning how to find out what she'd like to do, try out different things, mature. That's what I hope she'd develop in this school.

You say the kids are making all decisions themselves. How would you feel if they decided that they wanted to turn the school into a community center—a center for dropouts or an abortion advice center or something like that?

Mr. Graham: I do feel that 13, 14, even 15-year-olds, as most of these are, should have their rights to learn, should have much, much freedom. They also should have responsible, sympathetic adult direction that they can look to and respond to. I just am not prepared to turn a kid loose and say, "There's the world, go get it!" I think that the teachers will be all important in this school. And I think that kids want to learn. I think that people basically want to learn. The first thing you want to do is learn. I don't believe these kids are turned off from learning. They just want to learn in a reasonable way.

But I'm worried about knowledge. I'm worried about interest in education and learning and the learning process. Yes, I'm concerned about that. And I would not be terribly thrilled—though I don't believe that teachers would be in favor—if the kids decided, "Well, let's stop being a school and we will be an abortion center, or a dropout thing." Yet I think that almost any project can be so framed to encompass a lot of learning skills. I think that through, for instance, a dropout center my kid could learn a bit more about math, and, in order to do a dropout center correctly, do some research and study up on what is going on. And by its very nature he would have to read. All the learning potential is there.

Mr. Reid: Sometimes there's conflict between what they want to learn and what parents think they should learn.

Mr. Graham: Yes, I'm prepared for that. I don't have a set of preconceived things that I want Jeff or anybody to know on coming out of school. I don't believe many of us knew much when we came out of school. I think that those of us who were lucky only knew how to learn.

Then you don't feel you have a right to say to your child, "Look, I really think this *is more important than* that" *or "You need a sense of how the past relates to the present"?*

Mr. Mamis: I have a right to say, and have said, in loud tones, "God damn it, you never heard of Debs?" or "What the hell, they went through *that* in the thirties!" and all that. I expressed some shock that he didn't know the historical similarities between what had gone on and what he was trying to do. But in realistic terms he is, nevertheless, learning the same thing, developing how he feels about those problems, as if, or better than, had he read them in a book. It'll be a harder lesson and he'll make more mistakes, but he'll know much more strongly how he feels in practical situations about it than he would from having learned it from a book. That would be marvelous— if they could read the whole historical perspective and apply it to what is going on. But they can't—there's no time to do both things. You're given a choice. I feel much differently about the choice I've made now than I would have two years ago, and I really feel what they want to do is a more exciting thing. It makes them more exciting, makes them better people.

Do you feel that the age differences among the students should sometimes influence what happens to them individually?

Mr. Mamis: There are things I can see coming up which would give me great difficulty. I would feel differently with a 12-year-old than with a 15-year-old.

Mr. Salit: I guess that would depend upon what the parents' and child's previous experience was. Normally you would say, "Hey, we have a 12-year-old. What are we exposing her and ourselves to?" But based on our years of private school education, we are now willing to try this, to try it wholeheartedly. A year from now you might find me being more vocal about saying no to the things I didn't like that occurred. At this particular point, I can't honestly say I can anticipate any *no* because I'm committed to try anything. In our minds it can only be better. It can't be worse, and if we remain free and open about this—

Mr. Mamis: You were asking a specific question about age. If the teacher orients Lisa towards a dramatic group that's functioning, and the director says, "We're going out of town for a month, and we need our apprentices to come on up for the scenery," I would be apprehensive. I would say no to a 12-year-old—but not to a 15-year-old.

Mrs. Gittler: I would say no about going down to the Lower East Side by herself at midnight.

Mrs. Salit: The way I see the school there's no reason a child should be asked to do something that's not appropriate. In other words, Lisa, who's 15, will be doing things far different from Cathy in certain areas and in others they might be doing similar things. But I'm going to assume that Elaine will get to know my child well enough to know just what she can do and what she can't do and where to direct her and where not. I don't know that there's an age appropriateness for this type of school. I would say that this is the proper role of the school for any child at any age.

Mr. Mamis: I think this is true even in terms of rights. After our lawsuit the principal said, "Well, if you complained about the food in the lunchroom, I could understand that. Next thing you know, the kindergarten kids are going to be petitioning." He thinks as if there is an age distinction as to who is entitled to rights. The distinction is: if you can articulate what you want and what you feel you're entitled to, you're old enough to get it. If you recognize the problem, then you've got a right to that. So I think that that holds true to this kind of school too. If you come home in the fourth grade or fifth grade and say "I'm bored," you've recognized something that should be dealt with by the parent.

Will age differences influence individual reactions to the freedom in this school?

Mrs. Salit: Cathy is experiencing a kind of total freedom in the summer camp she's at now. And she was frustrated by this freedom that has with it the kind of responsibility she wasn't aware of. So last week she came home for a day to talk with me. She kept talking about needing authority. This really isn't what she meant. What she really meant was that she'd been given this banana split—everything she'd ever wanted—and she couldn't zero in on anything. She wanted her counsellor in a sense to say to her "Okay, it's time to go to weaving." At the same time she didn't want her counsellor to do that, because three days from now, she may not need that any more. So she was terribly conflicted with the experience of having genuine total freedom. We talked about it for a day and she couldn't wait to get back. Once she understood what was bothering her and once she understood that it might take her the whole summer to get used to it, she was all right.

You mentioned boredom. Will this school eliminate it?

Mrs. Salit: I seem to remember in an early discussion about the school, people mentioned that some students might just come in and sit around for weeks and weeks not doing anything. Will we be able to tell if this is "boredom" or something else?

Mr. Graham: I think we've overemphasized this boredom issue. I think that's one of the rights, and I don't think we're going to eliminate boredom by any means. That's one reason that I want my kid in this school—so he won't be bored. But I think boredom is an intellectual decision.

Mrs. Salit: Jerry, there's something though about boredom that frightens me. If a kid understands what's happening to him, that's one thing. But these kids are coming from a pretty rigid kind of experience. And that transition can be a frightening one for them if they don't understand where they're at.

Mr. Mamis: One of the things that happened to them in public or private schools was the sense that when they were bored, they felt themselves becoming disruptive.

Mr. Graham: And that they were failing.

Mr. Mamis: And they were failing. They felt like they were becoming troublemakers. Josh would come home and say, "I'm so bored, I can feel myself about to cause trouble in the class."

Mr. Graham: Being bored was causing trouble.

Mr. Mamis: So that at least in the area of being bored, in this school you can relax and—

Mrs. Salit: But there are all kinds of different kids in this situation. I don't think Cathy would react that way. I think that it would frighten her to think that she wasn't accomplishing something. That has been her only experience: you work, you achieve, you get a mark. And although it's the very thing she wants to escape, it is not a simple thing to unlearn. Some kids can go through a period of floundering and waiting to find themselves, some kids may not be able to.

Mr. Graham: All I was saying is that they have a right to do that. That's a right for those who have to do it that way.

Mrs. Salit: I think it's essential, however, to realize that there are children who will benefit through a period of floundering. But there are other children who will be worried by it. I hope the teachers will be sensitive to this and help these children through it.

Then does the parent have a right to go to the teacher and say, "My child is miserable and frightened about being bored, and you've got to do something about it."

Mrs. Salit: I would say it would be largely up to the parent. I guess I would have to grit my teeth for a while and wait.

The Storefront School:
A Vehicle for Change

WILLIAM C. NELSEN

The storefront school stands as a strong expression of
dissatisfaction with American public education. At the
same time it represents a belief that a better way of
educating youth can be demonstrated. Thus, along with
the writings of Charles Silberman, experiments in performance contracting, demands for accountability in teaching,
and cries for decentralization and community control, the
storefront school provides one mechanism for those
seeking educational change.

But is the storefront school—often called the street
academy—a useful and practical means of bringing about
educational change? The question is a crucial one, for all
the storefront schools that have sprung up throughout our
cities—including those that have failed—have touched only

Reprinted from "The Storefront School: A Vehicle for
Change" by William C. Nelsen, *The Journal of Negro Education*,
Vol. XXXX No. 3, Summer 1971. Copyright © 1971 *The Journal
of Negro Education*.

an extremely small percentage of the kids turned off or turned out by our public educational system. It is that system which will continue to attempt to educate our youth, and it is that system which must be changed if we are to enable especially our black and poor youth to be prepared to deal effectively with their social and physical environment. Without doubt, the vast majority of black youth and youth in general will remain dependent on the public system. As Fred M. Hechinger emphasizes in his recent assessment of "Education 1980":

. . . I am certain that an urban revival is still possible within the next decade, in which public education must play the key role. . . . I stress *public* education because I am convinced that there can be no effective substitute for it. I view as deceptive those currently fashionable schemes which would rely on private nongovernmental efforts to cure educational deficiencies. This is not to say that private schools and institutions of higher education cannot, indeed, must not, carry out experimental programs to help improve the educational process. On the contrary, such pioneering efforts as those illustrated by Harlem Prep, the street academies, and many other privately supported institutions and movements are imperative. They infuse new ideas into the public institutions. They give courage and inspiration to thousands of dedicated men and women in the public schools who are frustrated and disheartened by the lack of imagination in the school system. But the purpose of these private ventures remains to improve, not to circumvent public education.[1]

The terms "storefront school" and "street academy" have been used to describe a variety of alternative educational institutions, ideas and models. The best known is Harlem Prep and the system of street academies run by the New York Urban League, aimed at educating high school dropouts and getting many of them into a college or university.[2] But similar efforts have been organized in cities throughout the country—Boston, Philadelphia, Newark, Oakland, St. Louis, etc.—often using different educational styles and serving different age groups. Some are college preparatory schools like Harlem Prep or Sophia House in St. Louis; others aim at providing the General Equivalency Degree only. Some operate at the high school level, while others like the Mantua-Powelton Mini School in Philadelphia are elementary schools. (The storefront idea interestingly enough is now being tried at the higher educational level also. The University of Minnesota, for example, through its Storefront Program has discovered that higher education can become a meaningful experience to people who ordinarily view such education as irrelevant to their lives.)[3] Some street academies represent new schools for dropouts, but others serve as a supplement to the school experience by providing individualized tutoring or other special educational programs. (Some persons extend the definition of storefront schools to take in bold, comprehensive public-system-supported experiments like the Parkway School in Philadelphia or its new equivalent in Chicago or the perhaps more interesting Free School in Philadelphia—a cooperative program of the Philadelphia School District, the University of Pennsylvania, businessmen and local community residents.) Street academy leaders often vary widely in educational philosophy—holding differing ideas as to how much freedom to permit both teachers and students, what type of curriculum should be presented, and how much citizen-parent control should be exercised.

At the same time, however, the street academies have several important ideas in common. Each academy demonstrates a belief that there are a number of things radically wrong with the present public system in most cities, that education can and ought to be more relevant to the community and the individual and corporate problems of its residents, that children with the potential to do much better are being overlooked, that educational change is possible.

A brief examination of two examples with which the author is familiar in two different cities may be useful: the now extinct Mantua-Powelton Mini School in Philadelphia, operating at the elementary level; and Sophia House, a college prep academy in St. Louis.

In the western section of the city of Philadelphia are the communities of Mantua—almost entirely black and low-income—and Powelton Village—well integrated both racially and economically. The Mini School was a cooperative effort between several individuals in Powelton and a federation of neighborhood groups in Mantua known as the Mantua Community Planners. Almost all of the children in the Mini School (which extended from grades 5 through 8) came from Mantua, and predominantly from one of the East Coast's largest and most overcrowded elementary schools. In fact, the Mini School can be viewed as primarily a reaction against the large, impersonal structure of that urban school.

From the beginning the planners of the Mini School were in touch with the Philadelphia Board of Education, and after a good amount of discussion, it was decided that the School might serve as a model for a "scattered site" middle school. (The Board already had plans to build a more conventional middle school in the area in the early 1970s.) The idea was to build several small schools, spread throughout the community, instead of one large facility. The plan was aimed at permitting a more personalized and flexible structure and allowing each school to be a more integral part of the community. With cooperation—and money—from the Philadelphia Board and a grant from the Rockefeller Foundation, the Mini School got underway in the fall of 1968.

The school opened in an unused factory with approximately 150 students, a staff of approximately 12 (some educators with all the proper credentials, others not), and a curriculum emphasizing basic communicative skills and orientation of a child to his urban community. Its existence was short, unstable and problem-laden. The issue of community control had not been thought through carefully; a community Board was not set up, and when a teacher was fired, the unresolved question of who had administrative and policy-making authority created anger and dissension throughout the community. The School population was mostly problem children—much different from the original design of having a cross-section of children with varying educational abilities. Discipline remained a problem. A fire in the school in its second year led to its final demise.[4]

Yet, a number of positive things happened as a result of the Mini School. Although no scientific evaluative studies were done, the author witnessed what he considered to be positive changes in the attitudes and educational skills of a number of children. And the experiment was positive enough to encourage the Board to proceed with plans for a scattered-site Middle School in the area. In the words of the 1970 Rockefeller Foundation *Annual Report:* ". . . in Philadelphia an innovative demonstration mini-school has served as a model in the planning of a new school in the Mantua district."[5]

Sophia House in St. Louis offers a different model. Located in the inner city within several blocks of the infamous Pruitt-Igoe Public Housing Development, it is essentially a well-run, highly successful tutoring program for black high school males. Begun in 1966 by a then Jesuit seminarian, Sophia has grown to a point where there are now approximately seven full-time staff members and nearly 100 volunteer tutors serving approximately 130 students.

The Sophia program has emphasized the development of competence in the English language and in mathematics. Its record is highly successful as measured by high school completions, by college entrance test scores, and by the acceptance of Sophia-trained students into colleges and universities, including many of the Ivy League schools. In fact, the College Entrance Examination Board sent a representative to study the school because of the amount of improvement measured by its tests.

Sophia has been relatively successful also in gaining private individual, business and foundation support, although its ongoing financial situation has never been sound. It is assisted in fund raising by a fairly large interracial board, which includes a number of businessmen strongly committed to the Sophia program.

The Sophia story has not been completely smooth, however. A policy dispute between the original director and other staff and board members concerning educational philosophy and expansion of the program led to the director's leaving and establishing a separate day school for dropouts. Now under black staff leadership, the Sophia program continues to receive community support and to produce an excellent record of college admissions.

In one respect Sophia has been unsuccessful. It has not as yet been able to affect in any significant way the public school system. In 1969 it came close to obtaining a contract with the St. Louis Board of Education, but for financial and other reasons the Board could not complete the arrangement.

These two examples offer somewhat curious outcomes. By most standards a highly successful program has as yet been unable to gain public financial support. Yet, a relatively unsuccessful, short-lived experiment has provided a "model" for the public system. Obviously, there are many intangibles present. The Philadelphia system generally has seemed more responsive to innovative program ideas, and contacting the Board early in the game may have made a substantial difference. Also, the power exercised by community and street academy leaders may have been an important variable.

If the storefront school is to be an effective change agent in relation to the public system, experience gained from these examples, along with others around the country, suggests that academy leaders must pay attention to several important issues. Of particular importance are:

1. funding and survival of the storefront model school,
2. the relationship of the academy to the public school system,
3. the role of cooperative arrangements with other alternative school models,
4. program cost considerations,
5. evaluation and accountability, and
6. responsible community control arrangements.

FUNDING AND SURVIVAL

Most storefront schools begin with private foundation or business support. This situation is often quite useful in permitting a great deal of freedom and flexibility in establishing the school; but a serious question arises as to how long even the most successful storefront program will be able to count on private support. Harlem Prep and the New York Urban League's Street Academies, for example, lost major corporate and foundation financing this past year due to economic recession and disagreements over educational leadership and fiscal management. Moreover, most of the private financial supporters never envisioned that they would be asked to provide continuous assistance. In the long run, then, the storefront school must be able to reach into the public purse. This is possible if its performance is such that it can contract with the public system (or perhaps fit into the voucher system it it comes into being). Alternatively, it can work itself out of existence by presenting a model for the public system itself to undertake.

RELATIONSHIP TO THE PUBLIC SCHOOL SYSTEM

The philosophy and strategy of educational change is not very well formulated. Many wonder: Can change occur best from within or without? The answer seems to differ according to the situation. Witness the recent report on *Innovation in Education* produced by the Committee for Economic Development:

> If the schools are to make real progress in instruction, most of them must be jolted from their complacency by vigorous thrusts that will break through the old patterns and support experiment and innovation. Sometimes such thrusts can come from within the school system via the work of teachers and administrators possessing strong innovative talents, but sometimes they must come from without. . . . Change in school practices and organization can be both difficult and painful. . . .[6]

Often, productive changes can occur within the system. The Parkway Plan and the Free School in Philadelphia, and Project Stay (to prevent high school students from dropping out) in St. Louis are good examples. Strategists in New York recently have given more attention to what can be done within the system instead of using the private academy approach only. The New York Urban Coalition has assisted in the establishment of two mini-schools of roughly 125 students each in existing city high schools. A key concept is the use of streetworkers from the local community (trained by the Coalition) who help develop better relationships between students, teachers and school administrators. As stated by the Coalition: "The goal of the project is to convince city agencies to use the high school as the main channel for delivering existing municipal youth services, thus reinforcing with other elements of the project, the importance of school to the student."[7]

Change, however, is not always so easily brought about from within. Moreover, in the New York case just mentioned, one can quickly ask whether such public system experiments would be in operation had it not been for the example of the Street Academies which pioneered ideas such as the use of community streetworkers.

Perhaps some combination of "within-system" change and "without-system" change is the best route to take. Those involved with street academies ought to be conscious of creating those alternative models which can be translated into the public system. Thus, close contact between the storefront "challengers" and those key leaders of the system being challenged (although to some leaders on both sides this may be difficult, for they dislike communication with the "enemy") may produce significant change more quickly, and in the long run may result in the development of a better educational system for a greater number of youth.

COOPERATION AMONG ALTERNATIVE MODELS

In several cities—notably Boston, New York, Milwaukee and St. Louis—cooperative arrangements among storefront programs and similar alternative models are taking place or are in the process of being formed. For example, the Federation of Boston Community Schools (made up of the Highland Park Free School, the New School for Children, and the Roxbury Community School) came into being last year "in order to pool financial and personnel resources."[8] Other reasons for cooperating include the sharing of in-service training programs, joint purchasing of materials and other resources, sharing of educational philosophy and techniques of teaching and evaluation, developing common strategies for seeking funding and for communicating with and impacting upon the public system of education.

That latter item is vitally important if storefront schools are to be effective agents of change. A demonstration project of a confederation of alternative schools potentially could have much greater impact than a project run by one storefront operation alone. Some school systems might over time be willing to work out an arrangement with a federation or confederation of alternative schools in order to assist with the planning and development of joint demonstration programs.

COST CONSIDERATIONS

The street academy must give careful attention to the per-pupil costs involved in its alternative model. It must do so, not out of concern for its own normally uncertain security (although that is important), but primarily because it must demonstrate to the public system that it can produce better results at the same or even less cost. If a storefront school, for example, spends $2,000 per pupil in producing excellent academic results, leaders in a school system spending $600 per pupil can reply quickly, "So what! Give us $2,000 per pupil also, and we'll do just as well or better."

Keeping per-pupil costs low in a newly established school is not easy. Yet, at a time when public school systems are in financial difficulty and citizens are carefully eyeing educational costs, educational change will be next to impossible if per-pupil costs are too high.

EVALUATION AND ACCOUNTABILITY

In order to have some impact the storefront school must be able to perform better than the public system.

Accordingly, it must have a way of measuring or evaluating its results. In the example mentioned earlier, Sophia House could present the record of its students in terms of college acceptance, entrance exams and high school completion. Such traditional measuring devices may not always be possible in the storefront school. Certain tests may not accurately measure the performance or progress of disadvantaged children. Yet, few people will listen if the only evidence of achievement presented is the impression of the academy leaders that students seem "motivated" or "more interested."

Just as the public school system is being held accountable for the results obtained with the resources given it, so will the street academy be called to task. And if it is to be an effective change agent, the storefront school must be able to demonstrate clearly to the public its achievements.

COMMUNITY CONTROL

A major reason for the establishment of many storefront schools is to allow community residents and parents to exercise a significant degree of control over the education of their children. Such schools often represent decentralization from below rather than from above (in the public school system). It is surprising, then, that in spite of the fact that street academies are often established in the name of the "community" in many instances scant attention is given to key issues such as the representativeness of the governing body (recall that for a time the Mini School in Philadelphia actually had no such body), election procedures, and the relationship between directors, administration and teachers.

Decentralization and citizen participation will continue to be an important issue in large urban school systems. If storefront schools are to be change agents in relation not only to education policy but also to educational administration and governance, careful attention must be given to the polity of the storefront school itself.

One final warning must be given. What happens if a storefront school successfully impacts on the public system and has its "model" adopted? Something may be lost in the transition of the model from a small group of concerned teachers and parents to the bureaucracy. It is often difficult, if not impossible, to duplicate the experience of a fresh, unique operation.

Yet, impact on the public system must remain the major goal of the street academies. It does not seem possible to create a large new private system of education at a time when earlier private systems are losing funding sources and increasingly eyeing the public dollar.

The question remains, then: Is the storefront school a vehicle for educational change? Where change is possible within the system, resources for innovation ought to be concentrated there. Where such change is not possible or extremely slow the storefront school and similar alternative models must serve as challengers. But how effective an agent of change the storefront school is depends on how carefully its leaders attend to the key issues of ongoing funding, relationships with the public school system, cooperative arrangements with other alternative models, per-pupil costs, accountability and power control. The process of educational change is never simple, but with determination and a concern for strategy, leaders of storefront programs can play an important role in improving the education of our nation's youth.

NOTES

The author wishes to acknowledge the assistance of his colleague on the Danforth Foundation staff, Gene L. Schwilck, in the preparation and critique of this article.

1. Hechinger, F. M., "Education 1980" in *Conflicts in Urban Education*, Marcus, S. and Rivlin, H. N., eds. (New York: Basic Books, 1970) pp. 6-7.

2. See, for example, Black, J., "One Step Off the Sidewalk" in *Saturday Review* (November 15, 1969) pp. 88-9, 100.

3. Cooperman, D. "The Storefront Programs in the Twin Cities" in *Phi Delta Kappan* (January 1969) pp. 284-5.

4. For a critical review of the Mini-School demonstration, see Resnick, H. S., "The Education of Our Children is Through Power" in *Turning on the System: War in the Philadelphia Public Schools* (New York: Pantheon Books, 1970) pp. 160-87.

5. Rockefeller Foundation, *Annual Report* (1970) p. 106.

6. Committee for Economic Development, *Innovation in Education: New Directions for the American School* (New York: CED, 1968) p. 15.

7. The National Urban Coalition, *Third Annual Report* (1971) p. 27.

8. See the report of a Ford Foundation grant to the Federation in *Education Daily* (February 5, 1971) pp. 1-2.

Recurrent Education: An Alternative System

BRUNO STEIN and S. M. MILLER

Education traditionally takes place during an individual's early years, after which it stops for most people. Tradition, however, is a poor excuse for maintaining a system that is increasingly unable to cope with the needs of an urban and technologically oriented society, a society that requires flexibility from its members—ability to adapt to rapid change. Traditional education encourages rigidity with its once-and-for-all preparation for life. It has other undesirable social and economic consequences as well.

In the standard economic model of the life cycle, education is treated as an input that generally takes place during an individual's preproductive years. This may be called the front-end load model. Investment (education) decisions are made on the school child's behalf, out of funds provided by parents and by the taxpayers. When the

This is an edited version of a chapter in *Rethinking Urban Education* edited by Herbert Wahlberg and A. T. Kopan, to be published by Jossey-Bass Publishing Company in 1972.

child reaches his teens, full-time work becomes an alternative to school, and the cost of the investment expands to include the cost of the foregone work opportunity. At this stage, the model assumes that the child is an economic being who surveys his alternatives and "rationally" decides whether or not to continue school and, if he does, what kind of schooling to pursue. To be sure, his choices are made under a set of genetic, social and economic constraints. More to the point, they are made under the conditions of uncertainty, ignorance and emotional turmoil that characterize adolescence. Later in life, the dissatisfied individual can blame himself or his parents for a wrong decision. Each educational increment is "higher" and more specialized, and the cost of reversing erroneous choices rises exponentially. At some point, it approaches infinity. What's done can't be undone. The sum of a series of choices (whether or not to complete high school, whether or not to go to college, what to major in, whether or not to complete college and so forth) constitutes a lifetime commitment.

The economic reasoning underlying this model is popular with policymakers. It does not require reexamination of basic educational modes and institutions, which makes it easier to plan and to sell the plans to the body politic. Prejudice in favor of an economic model is confirmed by conclusions drawn from the usual popular and simplistic cost-benefit analysis, in which benefits are measured as the present value of the estimated earnings attributable to the added education. At any relevant rate of discount, benefits measured in this fashion are greater from a dollar added to early school programs than from a dollar added to adult education, since younger people have a longer remaining work life than those who are in midcareer. A better and broader measure of benefits—one that considers psychological and social factors—would probably yield different results, but no such measure has yet been developed. In

the meantime, hardnosed planners will have us believe that
a bad measure is better than no measure at all.

INEQUITIES AND INEFFICIENCIES

The standard front-end load model of education probably describes a reality that is unnecessarily grim. Furthermore, it is all too easy to overlook the fact that the model
operates in ways that are socially inequitable and economically inefficient.

The social inequity is both *vertical*—along the socioeconomic scale—and *horizontal*—among people of the
same socioeconomic status. The vertical inequity is obvious, and has been amply documented by data from a
large-scale study of high school students, which showed
that higher-ability students of lower socioeconomic status
are less likely to go to college than lower-ability students
of higher socioeconomic status.[1] The inequity is compounded by racial and ethnic discrimination. It would be a
mistake, however, to consider the inequity as principally a
race issue, for within racial and ethnic categories, it
operates along social-class lines.

Horizontal inequity, the unequal treatment of equals,
may seem to be a less pressing problem, but its magnitude
is really not well known. The labor market operates in
mysterious ways; so that three young men of roughly
equal social class, race, mechanical aptitude, intelligence
and education might take quite different kinds of work.
One might become a well-paid construction worker, the
second a medium-paid auto worker and the last an
unemployed coal miner. Fortuitous as well as economic
circumstances are likely to determine their occupational
paths. To call these circumstances "fate" is to leave more
to happenstance than is either necessary or desirable.

The economic inefficiency of the front-end load model
comes from its waste of human resources, which can be

manifested in rather sophisticated forms; in structural unemployment, for example, which occurs when a poorly trained labor force coexists with job vacancies. Or, stemming from this, in the existence of a poor trade-off between price stability and unemployment, so that inflation occurs while unemployment is relatively high. Since price stability has a high priority in the minds of fiscal and monetary policymakers, unemployment rates in the 5-to-6 percent range may easily become permanent minimum levels rather than temporary economic phenomena connected with recessions.

Although educational reforms are not offered as a panacea for our economic and social ills, it should be clear that the social and economic inequities built into the standard educational model make it a poor way to do business.

BEGINNING ALTERNATIVES

Alternatives to the front-end load model already exist. They are a response to private and social needs and are brought into being for political and economic reasons. Thus, high school equivalence exams can be taken by the ambitious dropout. Night schools offer collegiate education, some even as far as the Ph.D., although high-status schools *take pride* in their refusal to do this. Proprietory (profit-making) schools offer training in a large number of technical skills. Employers have training programs, both formal and informal, and some sponsor educational programs not only for executives but also for workers. Manpower training programs have become a major activity of the government in the past decade, and are widely touted as the remedy for poverty and the expanding welfare rolls. Clearly, alternative models of education are widely used (although exact information about the extent is imperfect). Despite this, alternative models suffer by invidious comparison with the front-end load. The exception rather than the rule, they evoke images of the *Education of H*Y*M*A*N *K*A*P*L*A*N* or of specialized, and often stigmatized, social programs for the needy.

Adult education and training is usually viewed as a one-shot corrective for some particular problem rather than as a process that can be repeated as someone develops and encounters new opportunities as well as new needs. This one-shot view is especially characteristic of publicly sponsored programs. For example, we have basic education courses for functional illiterates yet, where these exist, they do not provide the trainee with a next step. Similarly, we have retraining programs to meet various employment crises; clients are expected to enroll in whatever may be available, without reference to potential advancement or to the next technological change that may put them out of work. The retraining, often as not, is for another dead-end job to replace the one that just disappeared. As more and more people and their employers think in terms of career ladders, the need for educational ladders becomes greater. Change may be nearer than many might suspect.

The existing delivery system in adult education is hopelessly chaotic. The individual who has some need or yearning for more education finds the educational marketplace full of unconnected bits and pieces. The best he can hope for is a program here or a program there. Despite the vast amount of education that is available, there is little linkage.

The term "recurrent education" denotes a system that makes education and training available, in various doses, to individuals over their lifetimes. The concept, developed in Sweden and refined by the Center for Educational Reform and Innovation of the Organization for European Cooperational Development, presents an alternative to conventional education. On the one hand, it treats adult education as a system of services that provides a variety of educational choices. On the other hand, it differs from the usual concept of adult education in that it treats the education of an individual as a process that is not necessarily completed during youth but may *recur* during the person's life.

A system of recurrent education can provide the element of flexibility needed to overcome the inequity and inefficiency that are inherent in the dominant front-end load model. The beneficiaries would not merely be the system's clients, but also the entire community, whose stock of human resources would be enlarged and improved.

Recurrent education, the policy suggestion that we advocate, is not a projection for the distant future. In fact, it may already be emerging from the chaos of continuing education, peripheral education, and other aspects of alternative education. Only within the last few years have social policy analysts discovered this area of activity. Attempts to measure its extent have foundered, however, on the difficulty of formulating a commonly accepted definition.[2] Moreover, data are not easily available because most adult education activities are peripheral to the main purpose of the organizations engaged in this activity.[3] It is not surprising that estimates of the number of students in adult education range from 13 million[4] to 44 million[5], with an intermediate estimate of 25 million by the National Opinion Research Center.[6] A British scholar who surveyed university adult education in New York City commented with despair on the statistical confusion that marks the topic,[7] and her task was, after all, a relatively narrow one.

Nevertheless, it is useful to present a summary of existing measurements of adult education. One reason is to stimulate more exact research. Most studies merely count the number of students, and do this imperfectly. The most comprehensive of such studies, the Office of Education's

Participation Survey, has not been published yet. It is a household survey, attached to the May 1969 Current Population Survey (to be repeated in 1972). Preliminary information indicates that it may have undercounted students by a very serious margin of error. There is no complete survey of educational establishments from which to get information on the delivery system itself, its costs and other data needed for planning purposes.

A second more important objective is to show that the basis for a vast recurrent education system already exists. It would not have to be built from scratch, but could make use of ongoing activities. In effect, a third-tier educational program is already evolving. It differs from the first tier of locally-run, local- and state-financed public education (with recent increases in federal funds) and the second tier of private and parochial education. These two tiers constitute "the core educational institutions." The third tier with many components but few connections is built of longstanding activities and new programs like the federally sponsored manpower programs. Because of the diversity of the components, their similarities in purpose and their numbers have gone unrecognized. Consequently the contemporary significance of a third tier has not been recognized and progress toward a system of recurrent education has been hampered.

PUTTING THE NUMBERS IN

We have adapted the categories developed by Stanley Moses[8] in order to group data on numbers of students on some consistent basis. Our categories are: organizational; proprietory; manpower and antipoverty; correspondence; television; continuing education at the college level; adult education below the college level; and "other."

Organizational. This category includes programs conducted by private business, labor unions, government and the military, to train and upgrade their employees and members. Moses estimates that in 1965 approximately 14.5 million adults were involved in organizational education programs in the United States. Yet at best, this is a minimum estimate, and the data are, of course, dated now. In the case of business, the relevant figures may be subsumed under categories other than education and cannot easily be abstracted from company reports and similar sources. In labor unions, one cannot even hazard a guess as to the size of the educational sector, since not even the AFL-CIO keeps statistics on labor activity in this area.

Governments engage in considerable education and training of employees. In the fiscal year ending June 1969, the federal government spent at least $104 million to train slightly more than one million civil servants.[9] No aggregate figures are available for state and local governments.

"Join the Army and learn a trade" is an old slogan. Excluding the professional schools, service academies and ROTC programs, the Department of Defense reports 367,858 servicemen students registered with the United States Armed Forces Institute, where general education at the high school and college levels is made available to servicemen in their off-duty hours through correspondence courses.[10] Another 240,875 servicemen are registered in other off-duty educational programs.[11] Here, the reader will note the definitional problem and its data-gathering consequences. The Armed Forces Institute spans four of our categories: organizational, correspondence, continuing education at the college level and adult education below college level. This kind of overlapping plagues the subject, and considerable disaggregation is needed to untangle the figures and avoid double counting.

Technical training programs in the Armed Forces are significant, but we were able to locate figures only for the Army. These show that in Fiscal Year 1971 380,000 soldiers received technical noncombat training in programs ranging from 6 to 8 weeks to more than a year, depending on the complexity of the skill involved.[12] If the rest of the Armed Forces were included, the real figure would probably be over half a million.

A general problem in locating appropriate figures is that data on numbers of servicemen receiving training are derived from cost figures. The Department of Defense accounting system does not, by and large, break down costs by combat and noncombat skills. Accordingly, ordinary published data from the Department of Defense must be used with care by those who are not interested in adult education for combat.

Proprietory Schools. These are private schools, usually run for profit, which administer programs outside of the educational "core." The magnitude of this activity is indicated by the table below, derived from a study conducted by Harvey Belitsky of the Upjohn Institute for Employment Research.

Estimated Attendance at Proprietory Schools, 1966[13]

Type of School	No. of Schools	No. of Students
Trade and Technical	3,000	835,710
Business	1,300	439,500
Cosmetology	2,477	272,470
Barber	294	15,876
Total	7,071	1,563,556

The preceding numbers may be an understatement. Contact with relevant trade associations leads us to believe that the number of trade and technical schools alone is closer to 7,000, with enrollments of about two million per year.[14] Similarly, 600,000 may be a more accurate estimate of business-school attendance.[15] Moses estimates the number in proprietory schools as about three times the 2.6 million indicated in the table—7.8 million in 1965.[16]

Economically, proprietory schools constitute a lively

industry. These enterprises have met the test of the marketplace; in some fashion, good or ill, they satisfy demand at prices above the cost of production, often competing with university-based continuing education programs. The industry's profitability has attracted investment from corporations such as Bell & Howell, RCA, ITT, Time-Life and Control Data Corporation. Consumers' willingness to pay shows that their need for the services rendered by these schools is strong enough to survive the charlatans who constantly plague the industry.

Manpower and Antipoverty Programs. A range of federal programs is operated or sponsored by the Department of Labor and Health, Education and Welfare. Most of these were developed during the Kennedy-Johnson years, and operate on the assumption that manpower training is a proper antidote to unemployment, poverty and welfare dependency. In 1969, some 8 million people took part in these programs, at a cost of $1.7 billion.[17] In practice, some of the programs are merely disguised forms of income-transfer payments. In many cases this is unintended: their operators hope that the clients will become employed upon graduation. Sometimes welfare departments put relief clients into the program in order to shift the relief payment from a federal-state account to an all-federal one. The Neighborhood Youth Corps' summer program is clearly designed to "cool" hot temperature rioting; expenditures display a seasonality that is unrelated to any conceivable educational or training need.

Considering their size and cost, antipoverty manpower programs have been disappointing. Confusion of purpose may be a factor, but the problem also lies in the very nature of the programs: they are short-term, narrowly vocational, constructed to deal with immediate crises and, in the case of the poverty population, aimed at students with more than usual difficulty with study. A manpower training program aimed at a broader clientele would do a better job for its entire student body. A broader clientele would include workers, both employed and unemployed, above and below the poverty line; their reasons for participation would include desire for advancement, higher income and more satisfying work.

Correspondence Schools. Learning-by-mail programs are conducted by a great variety of organizations, such as universities, government, and business and industry. Accordingly, data on correspondence education overlap with data on other types of education. The interested researcher must take care to factor them out in order to avoid double counting.

The best source of data is the National Home Study Council. A 1969 survey by that organization estimated a total student body of 4.9 million, half of which consisted of students in federal and military schools.[18] Members of the National Home Study Council accounted for 1.6 million students, and nonmember private schools reported another 161,000. The remainder consisted of students in correspondence courses given by universities, religious groups, businesses and miscellaneous organizations. Students taking courses in more than one school are counted twice in some cases, so that these data, like others, need a closer look before they can be added to other educational statistics.

Television. Moses estimates that approximately 5 million adults were involved in televised "programs of instruction which are presented in a systematic manner and which allow for formal contact between the learner and the program."[19] This does not include documentary or other special educational programs. Television has, of course, great potential in the form of the Open University and other approaches to schools without walls. For example, in California, a group of engineers are pursuing further studies in their employer's quarters through television lectures provided by a university which is a considerable distance away.

Continuing Education at the College Level. A bewildering

variety of courses and activities ranging from courses in "Art Styles through the Ages" to "Sales Brokerage Practices and Techniques" to degree programs that compete with community colleges[20] are included in this category. In 1969, an estimated 3.5 million adults were enrolled in continuing education programs.[21] Many were taking the classic types of extension courses, foreign languages, art appreciation and modern literature. (Indeed, it is possible for individuals to put together programs that are remarkably rich in scope and content.) Others were in packaged programs that lead to specific skills and certificates, such as in practical nursing, secretarial skills, bookkeeping, factory supervision techniques and industrial relations. Similar programs are found in the proprietory schools. Still others were involved in courses for credit, many leading to college degrees.

Degree study for adults is available at community colleges, where the associate degree is offered, as well as at many regular colleges and universities (particularly urban ones), where degree possibilities include the associate, bachelor's, master's and even doctorates. The availability of part-time study at any given school may be an historical accident, often having arisen from a need to fill empty buildings in the evening. Similar economics of overhead cost led to the creation of many university extension divisions. Elite universities do not as a rule engage in such activity. Thus, no one can work his way through Yale Law School at night; the adult businessmen who attend Harvard Business School are on leave—usually paid leave—from their firms. This sometimes leads to futile imitative behavior on the part of universities and their subdivisions, which seek to improve their public images by abolishing their night schools. Unfortunately, the simple act of excluding students in and of itself is not likely to improve either the quality or the reputation of a school, except in the eyes of its president and trustees.

Adult Education below the College Level. Four million

adults,[22] including a half million who are learning adult basic education,[23] are involved in precollege education. We have not estimated the number of credentials and diplomas that result from all these efforts. We know, however, that some employers are beginning to look upon the night school diploma more favorably. This reflects both appreciation of the students' energies and enterprise and realization that the standard high school diploma proves little about the ability and even literacy of a graduate.

The distribution of night-school opportunities is only partly related to the demand and need for them. The tradition was established in central cities at a time when secondary education was not assumed to be universal. Suburban and other outer-city conurbations are less likely to provide such services, even at cost. The lower the level of education, the lower the income of the actual or potential students. Local governments have little or no commitment to educate adults and the private sector does not find low-level adult education profitable. Adult basic education is commonly associated with welfare programs, and thus enjoys federal subsidies along with the stigma of public assistance.

Other. Inevitably, we wind up with a category called "other." This includes the education activities of libraries, museums, YMCAs, religious groups and various community organizations. If some of this activity seems trivial, much of it is not. And in all cases, the students are people who are making an effort to grow, to develop, to do something with themselves and their lives. They operate in a chaotic educational market and usually without information about alternatives. Rarely does one find even a complete directory of available courses. The cost of collecting information is great in time and effort. Impulse buying, therefore, replaces informed choice; it is as wasteful in education as it is in consumer goods.

WHO ARE THE STUDENTS?

Obviously, it would be useful to parallel the previous section on the institutional sponsorship of continuing education programs with an analysis of the students (age, sex, previous education and work experience) in each of these programs. At this point, the best that we can do is to try to characterize broadly the kinds of students involved. The four overlapping categories we employ are the disadvantaged, college dropouts, reentrants, and job shifters and upgraders. It is important to realize that just as education has become noncontinuous, so have work patterns, thereby requiring education, training and readjustment aid at many points.

The Disadvantaged. The poor and the black (the educationally deprived) have had particular trouble with schools, and as a result, their occupational and income potentials have been severely blunted. In the sixties, many had entered programs, whether labelled educational or not, by which they sought to improve their competitive position in the labor market. The strong emphasis on equality of opportunity and social mobility and the schools' continuing difficulties in working effectively with the disadvantaged have created a large body of clients for recurrent education.

The College Dropout. Many youths are dropping out of college; four continuous years is not the only model for a degree; many start but never finish college. Continuing education programs provide later opportunities to get a degree or to move into more specialized training without a degree but with the chance for higher income. A 24-year-old or a 34-year-old completing college or getting specialized training is different from an 18-year-old in a similar position. New institutions are developing in response to these new needs.

Reentrants. A surprising number of people do not work

continuously from school leaving to retirement. When they reenter the labor market, they frequently need to be "refreshed" or "retooled." Obviously, this situation applies to a growing number of women who reenter the labor market after their children are three or six or 18. Less obviously, many people in institutions (prisons, hospitals) reenter the work sphere and need training, in the institution or later, to facilitate their employment. And perhaps counterculture youth who return to the "straight" world will be occupationally disadvantaged if they do not have training and education available to them.

Shifters and Upgraders. Technological changes and unemployment may lead many to learn new skills. Many employed blue-collar as well as white-collar workers engage in additional training in order to be upgraded into better paid jobs. Indeed, it may well be that the upgrading of blue-collar workers will be one of the most important uses of recurrent education in the next years. (France now has extensive plans for the retraining of blue-collar workers.) The notion is spreading that people should not be dead-ended, that better paid, more interesting jobs should be available to all rather than restricted to those who received higher education when young and chose the job-promotion ladder instead of the low-ceiling route. In the future, a new group is likely to become important: people who want to shift jobs just for variety. Thus, desires for horizontal mobility as well as vertical mobility may engender considerable retraining for the older generation.

It is clear that a wide spectrum of individuals are involved or may be involved in recurrent education. There will be need not only for a broad range of programs but for interconnected activities that facilitate shifting from one type of education to another.

We have been discussing the educational needs of the United States but we suspect that recurrent education may be even more important for developing societies. Frequently these countries train a select few in skills that are inappropriate to technical needs and provide no means for later education; some nations overproduce persons with particular skills, again with no opportunity for retraining. Social mobility is increasingly considered an important element of social justice, but the front-end load model serves to limit opportunities for mobility. There is considerable waste from the narrow view of investment in (unutilized and unutilizable) human capital and from the broader view of developing individuals. Flexible, adaptive recurrent education would seem much more useful in developing countries than standard, fixed curriculum, traditional, front-end models.

CONSTRUCTING AN ALTERNATIVE

Alternatives to the front-end load model exist as correctives to deficiencies in the core schools. These correctives developed because of individuals' demands for different schooling arrangements and governmental and employers' responses to special economic and social needs. There is ample evidence of the shortcomings of the standard system; but alternative systems also have shortcomings. A brief review is, therefore, in order.

Education is a long-term continuous process. Any working professional knows that he cannot afford to stop learning. It is true, if less obviously, of others. To concentrate the learning process into a few years of life is to engage in the absurd: much of what happens in school does not constitute learning and much learning takes place outside the schools.

The in-school, front-end learning process has many functions aside from the transmission of knowledge. It is an aging vat for young people prior to their entry into the labor market. It allocates educational capital, and therefore income, in a way that largely preserves the existing distribution of income. It gives youngsters a tolerance for tedium that is useful for boring jobs. It provides credentials that do not necessarily reflect the possession of a set of abilities for any particular job.

Some of the learning that takes place outside of school is directly valuable. Anyone on a new job spends time in learning, often formal instruction, dignified with the title "on-the-job-training" and at times even credentialed. However, the worker who has learned all he needs to know about a job is in a dead-end job. There is little point or interest in paying him more, and many jobs dead-end at an early stage and at low wages.

Alternative education, as presently structured, suffers from a variety of faults: promises that will not be kept ("train at home to earn $10,000 in your spare time"), foolish demands for educational credentials,[24] and far too often, tragically low-caliber training. Anyone connected with manpower programs or continuing education can tell anecdotes about "Mickey Mouse" courses. Why then do we believe that these diverse activities have promise only if viewed as one system?

1. The absence of a notion of a full system encourages a *low degree of comprehensiveness* in programming. The individual may not be able to find in his or her locale all he needs for development.

2. An emphasis on training by particular employers is likely to lead to the development of skills with *low transferability*. Where the program is oriented to the trainee's employer or prospective employer, the skills developed are likely to be narrow and specific, with limited usefulness in other employment situations. What is needed are useful, highly transferable skills which at the same time meet a specific employer's needs.

3. An atomistic system limits the development of a long-run program for the individual; what is required is meshing educational and training facilities with the needs of individuals as they emerge over time.

4. The absence of a unified system makes it difficult to impose quality controls over programs and to connect them effectively with each other.

5. When programs are discrete, disconnected activities, they may become narrowly vocational so that broader considerations of developing the citizen and social competence of individuals receive little attention.

PROBLEMS OF RECURRENT EDUCATION

What are some principal issues then, in the development of a system of recurrent education?

1. Can we achieve systematization without stifling the innovative energies that are now inherent in the unorganized adult educational system? Its very haphazard quality may, as some argue, be a source of strength rather than weakness.

2. How would the rigidities and faddism of public education be overcome? After Sputnik we spent billions to expand higher education for the young—the front-end load. Now we have sent men to the moon and we have a surplus of college graduates and Ph.D.s (but not of nurses or MDs). Are we prepared to allocate education expenditures differently with less emphasis on the front-end and more on continuing education? We are close to guaranteeing all children 14 to 16 years of education. Need it be confined to children and must it be all at once? How should funds be allocated between front-end and continuing education?

3. Won't the possibility of regaining educational opportunities later in life encourage young people to be even less interested in school and lower their ability to utilize later educational possibilities? At the same time, won't the pressure be lifted from the core-school institutions to change and improve if those in difficulty with these institutions quietly depart with everyone's confidence that somehow they will manage in the future to

compensate for their present educational deprivation? Could a general result be that credentialism would be even more emphasized since education would still play an important role and would be seemingly available to all persons at some point?

4. Recurrent education is expensive because of the lost time from work (opportunity costs) for adults going full time and is burdensome for those working full time and also going to school. Are there special adaptations like work sabbaticals (secured by the United Steelworkers' Union in collective bargaining) which can overcome these difficulties?

5. What is a desirable administrative arrangement for recurrent education? To what extent should there be state-local control and finance as there is in much public education today? Should federal financing and thereby influence be more important than they are in contemporary public education? Since the students are adults and the emphasis is less on a set curriculum, should not students be involved in decisions?

These are difficult questions. They make us aware that recurrent education is not an easy panacea and that it will be difficult to build on a systematic basis. On the other hand, they do not shake our confidence that recurrent education should play a significant role. One evidence of its vitality is the variety of activity occurring.

New proposals for organizing and financing the continuing education of those in the labor market are emerging with increased frequency: the open university for nonresidential, part-time students; a federally financed training allowance that individuals can offer employers; collective-bargaining provisions for educational subsidies to workers; redesigning job ladders and training to promote greater mobility; upgrading programs, including the utilization of the fifth day as an education training segment in firms with a four-day week. These proposals reflect an understanding and occasionally an explicit assumption that training and education need not be a once-in-a-lifetime activity.

But there are threats in this very vitality. While innovation and experiment are desirable, we fear that there is a great danger that the nation will proliferate the interesting small demonstration project and substitute it for a comprehensive, easily accessible, quality recurrent-education system. Instead of serving as the foundation for a full-recurrent education system useful to all, demonstration projects may prevent its emergence by implying more than they deliver.

It is time to develop a national vision about a *system*, not bits and pieces, of recurrent education which operates as a realistic alternative for the education of many different kinds of Americans.

NOTES

1. Flanagan, J. and Cooley, W., *Project Talent: One Year Follow-up Studies* Technical Report to the U.S. Office of Education, Cooperative Research Project 233 (University of Pittsburgh, Project Talent Office, 1966) p. 93.

2. Moses, S., *The Learning Force: An Approach to the Politics of Education* (Syracuse, New York: Syracuse University Research Corporation, 1970) p. 22. The concept of the "learning force" was developed by Bert M. Gross.

3. U. S. Office of Education, *Noncredit Activities in Institutions of Higher Education, 1967-8* (Washington, D.C.: U. S. Govt. Printing Office, 1970) p. iii.

4. Cortright, R. W., Asst. Director, Division of Adult Education of the National Education Association. Letter from him dated April 9, 1971, in our files.

5. Moses, *loc. cit.*

6. Johnstone, J. W. C., and Rivera, R. J., *Volunteers in Learning* (Chicago: Aldine, 1965) pp. 1-2.

7. Ellwood, C., *Survey of University Adult Education in the Metropolitan Area of New York* (New York: New York University, School of Continuing Education, 1967) p. 2.

8. Moses, *loc. cit.* We have expanded Moses' categories from six to eight.

9. U. S. Civil Service Commission, Bureau of Training,

Employee Training in the Federal Service (Washington, D.C.: U.S. Govt. Printing Office, 1970) pp. 95, 124-6.

10. Ducey, C. A., Capt. U.S. Navy, Office of Asst. to the Secretary of Defense for Education. Telephone conversation on April 13, 1971. We are indebted to Catherine Manning for obtaining this and other information.

11. *Ibid.*

12. Quigley, D. B., U.S. Navy, Deputy Director for Enlisted Manpower Management Systems, Office of the Asst. Secretary of Defense. Letter from him dated April 21, 1971, in our files.

13. Belitsky, A. H., *Private Vocational Schools and Their Students* (Cambridge: Schenkman, 1969) p. 9.

14. Taylor, P., National Association of Trade and Technical Schools. Telephone conversation on April 13, 1971.

15. Telephone conversation on April 13, 1971, with representative of the United Business Schools Association.

16. Moses, *op. cit.*, p. 22.

17. Manpower Information Service, *Reference File* (Washington, D.C.: Bureau of National Affairs, 1970), pp. 21: 1006-9.

18. Taylor, R., National Home Study Council. Telephone conversation on April 13, 1971.

19. Moses, *op. cit.*, p. 24.

20. New York University, School of Continuing Education and Extension Services, Bulletin (Spring 1971).

21. Report issued jointly by the Association of University Evening Colleges and the National University Extension Association for its members in 1969, pp. 27-31. This is based on a survey and involves some double counting of students. The National Center for Educational Statistics shows 6.5 million registrations in continuing education programs of colleges and universities of which 5.6 million were in noncredit programs (U.S. Office of Education, *Noncredit Activities in Institutions of Higher Education, 1967-68*, Washington, D.C.: U.S. Govt. Printing Office, 1970 Table A-1). The reader is warned not to confuse registrations with the number of students.

22. Cortright, R. W., Asst. Director, Division of Adult Education of the National Education Association. Letter from him dated April 9, 1971, in our files.

23. U. S. Office of Education, *Adult Basic Education Program Statistics* (Washington, D.C.: U. S. Govt. Printing Office, 1970) p. 1.

24. Miller, S. M., "Breaking the Credentials Barrier," in Miller, S. M., and Riessman, F., *Social Class and Social Policy* (New York: Basic Books, 1968) and Berg, I., *Education and Jobs: The Great Training Robbery* (New York: Praeger, 1970).

The Alternative
to Schooling

IVAN ILLICH

For generations we have tried to make the world a better place by providing more and more schooling, but so far the endeavor has failed. What we have learned instead is that forcing all children to climb an open-ended education ladder cannot enhance equality but must favor the individual who starts out earlier, healthier or better prepared; that enforced instruction deadens for most people the will for independent learning; and that knowledge treated as a commodity, delivered in packages, and accepted as private property once it is acquired, must always be scarce.

In response, critics of the educational system are now proposing strong and unorthodox remedies that range from the voucher plan, which would enable each person to buy the education of his choice on an open market, to shifting the responsibility for education from the school to

Reprinted from "The Alternative to Schooling" by Ivan Illich in *Saturday Review,* June 19, 1971. Copyright ©1971 Saturday Review, Inc.

the media and to apprenticeship on the job. Some individuals foresee that the school will have to be disestablished just as the church was disestablished all over the world during the last two centuries. Other reformers propose to replace the universal school with various new systems that would, they claim, better prepare everybody for life in modern society. These proposals for new educational institutions fall into three broad categories: the reformation of the classroom within the school system; the dispersal of free schools throughout society; and the transformation of all society into one huge classroom. But these three approaches—the reformed classroom, the free school and the worldwide classroom—represent three stages in a proposed escalation of education in which each step threatens more subtle and more pervasive social control than the one it replaces.

I believe that the disestablishment of the school has become inevitable and that this end of an illusion should fill us with hope. But I also believe that the end of the "age of schooling" could usher in the epoch of the global schoolhouse that would be distinguishable only in name from a global madhouse or global prison in which education, correction and adjustment become synonymous. I therefore believe that the breakdown of the school forces us to look beyond its imminent demise and to face fundamental alternatives in education. Either we can work for fearsome and potent new educational devices that teach about a world which progressively becomes more opaque and forbidding for man, or we can set the conditions for a new era in which technology would be used to make society more simple and transparent, so that all men can once again know the facts and use the tools that shape their lives. In short, we can disestablish schools or we can deschool culture.

In order to see clearly the alternatives we face, we must first distinguish education from schooling, which means separating the humanistic intent of the teacher from the impact of the invariant structure of the school. This hidden structure constitutes a course of instruction that stays forever beyond the control of the teacher or of his school board. It conveys indelibly the message that only through schooling can an individual prepare himself for adulthood in society, that what is not taught in school is of little value and that what is learned outside of school is not worth knowing. I call it the hidden curriculum of schooling, because it constitutes the unalterable framework of the system, within which all changes in the curriculum are made.

The hidden curriculum is always the same regardless of school or place. It requires all children of a certain age to assemble in groups of about 30, under the authority of a certified teacher, for some 500 to 1,000 or more hours each year. It doesn't matter whether the curriculum is designed to teach the principles of fascism, liberalism, Catholicism or socialism; or whether the purpose of the school is to produce Soviet or United States citizens, mechanics or doctors. It makes no difference whether the teacher is authoritarian or permissive, whether he imposes his own creed or teaches students to think for themselves. What is important is that students learn that education is valuable when it is acquired in the school through a graded process of consumption; that the degree of success the individual will enjoy in society depends on the amount of learning he consumes; and that learning *about* the world is more valuable than learning *from* the world.

It must be clearly understood that the hidden curriculum translates learning from an activity into a commodity—for which the school monopolizes the market. In all countries knowledge is regarded as the first necessity for survival, but also as a form of currency more liquid than rubles or dollars. We have become accustomed, through Karl Marx's writings, to speak about the alienation of the worker from his work in a class society. We must now recognize the estrangement of man from his learning when it becomes the product of a service profession and he becomes the consumer.

The more learning an individual consumes, the more "knowledge stock" he acquires. The hidden curriculum therefore defines a new class structure for society within which the large consumers of knowledge—those who have acquired large quantities of knowledge stock—enjoy special privileges, high income and access to more powerful tools of production. This kind of knowledge-capitalism has been accepted in all industrialized societies and establishes a rationale for the distribution of jobs and income. (This point is especially important in the light of the lack of correspondence between schooling and occupational competence established in studies such as Ivar Berg's *Education and Jobs: The Great Training Robbery.*)

The endeavor to put all men through successive stages of enlightenment is rooted deeply in alchemy, the Great Art of the waning Middle Ages. John Amos Comenius, a Moravian bishop, self-styled Pansophist and pedagogue, is rightly considered one of the founders of the modern schools. He was among the first to propose seven or 12 grades of compulsory learning. In his *Magna Didactica,* he described schools as devices to "teach everybody everything" and outlined a blueprint for the assembly-line production of knowledge, which according to his method would make education cheaper and better and make growth into full humanity possible for all. But Comenius was not only an early efficiency expert, he was an alchemist who adopted the technical language of his craft to describe the art of rearing children. The alchemist sought to refine base elements by leading their distilled spirits through 12 stages of successive enlightenment, so that for their own and all the world's benefit they might be transmuted into gold. Of course, alchemists failed no matter how often they tried, but each time their "science" yielded new reasons for their failure, and they tried again.

Pedagogy opened a new chapter in the history of Ars Magna. Education became the search for an alchemic process that would bring forth a new type of man, who would fit into an environment created by scientific magic. But, no matter how much each generation spent on its schools, it always turned out that the majority of people were unfit for enlightenment by this process and had to be discarded as unprepared for life in a man-made world.

Educational reformers who accept the idea that schools have failed fall into three groups. The most respectable are certainly the great masters of alchemy who promise better schools. The most seductive are popular magicians, who promise to make every kitchen into an alchemic lab. The most sinister are the new Masons of the Universe, who want to transform the entire world into one huge temple of learning. Notable among today's masters of alchemy are certain research directors employed or sponsored by the large foundations who believe that schools, if they could somehow be improved, could also become economically more feasible than those that are now in trouble, and simultaneously could sell a larger package of services. Those who are concerned primarily with the curriculum claim that it is outdated or irrelevant. So the curriculum is filled with new packaged courses on African Culture, North American Imperialism, Women's Lib, Pollution, or the Consumer Society. Passive learning is wrong—it is indeed—so we graciously allow students to decide what and how they want to be taught. Schools are prison houses. Therefore, principals are authorized to approve teach-outs, moving the school desks to a roped-off Harlem street. Sensitivity training becomes fashionable. So, we import group therapy into the classroom. School, which was supposed to teach everybody everything, now becomes all things to all children.

Other critics emphasize that schools make inefficient use of modern science. Some would administer drugs to make it easier for the instructor to change the child's behavior. Others would transform school into a stadium for educational gaming. Still others would electrify the classroom. If they are simplistic disciples of McLuhan, they replace blackboards and textbooks with multimedia happenings; if they follow Skinner, they claim to be able to modify behavior more efficiently than old-fashioned classroom practitioners can.

Most of these changes have, of course, some good effects. The experimental schools have fewer truants. Parents do have a greater feeling of participation in a decentralized district. Pupils, assigned by their teacher to an apprenticeship, do often turn out more competent than those who stay in the classroom. Some children do improve their knowledge of Spanish in the language lab because they prefer playing with the knobs of the tape recorder to conversations with their Puerto Rican peers. Yet all these improvements operate within predictably narrow limits, since they leave the hidden curriculum of school intact.

Some reformers would like to shake loose from the hidden curriculum, but they rarely succeed. Free schools that lead to further free schools produce a mirage of freedom, even though the chain of attendance is frequently interrupted by long stretches of loafing. Attendance through seduction inculcates the need for educational treatment more persuasively than the reluctant attendance enforced by a truant officer. Permissive teachers in a padded classroom can easily render their pupils impotent to survive once they leave.

Learning in these schools often remains nothing more than the acquisition of socially valued skills defined, in this instance, by the consensus of a commune rather than by the decree of a school board. New presbyter is but old priest writ large.

Free schools, to be truly free, must meet two conditions: First, they must be run in a way to prevent the reintroduction of the hidden curriculum of graded attendance and certified students studying at the feet of certified teachers. And, more importantly, they must provide a framework in which all participants—staff and pupils—can free themselves from the hidden foundations of a schooled society. The first condition is frequently incorporated in the stated aims of a free school. The second condition is only rarely recognized, and is difficult to state as the goal of a free school.

It is useful to distinguish between the hidden curriculum, which I have described, and the occult foundations of schooling. The hidden curriculum is a ritual that can be considered the official initiation into modern society, institutionally established through the school. It is the purpose of this ritual to hide from its participants the contradictions between the myth of an egalitarian society and the class-conscious reality it certifies. Once they are recognized as such, rituals lose their power, and this is what is now beginning to happen to schooling. But there are certain fundamental assumptions about growing up—the occult foundations—which now find their expression in the ceremonial of schooling, and which could easily be reinforced by what free schools do.

Among these assumptions is what Peter Schrag calls the "immigration syndrome," which impels us to treat all people as if they were newcomers who must go through a naturalization process. Only certified consumers of knowledge are admitted to citizenship. Men are not born equal, but are made equal through gestation by Alma Mater.

The rhetoric of all schools states that they form a man for the future, but they do not release him for his task before he has developed a high level of tolerance to the ways of his elders: education *for* life rather than *in* everyday life. Few free schools can avoid doing precisely this. Nevertheless they are among the most important centers from which a new life style radiates, not because of the effect their graduates will have but, rather, because elders who choose to bring up their children without the benefit of properly ordained teachers frequently belong to a radical minority and because their preoccupation with the rearing of their children sustains them in their new style.

The most dangerous category of educational reformer is one who argues that knowledge can be produced and sold much more effectively on an open market than on one controlled by school. These people argue that most skills can be easily acquired from skill-models if the learner is truly interested in their acquisition; that individual entitlements can provide a more equal purchasing power for education. They demand a careful separation of the process by which knowledge is acquired from the process by which it is measured and certified. These seem to me obvious statements. But it would be a fallacy to believe that the establishment of a free market for knowledge would constitute a radical alternative in education.

The establishment of a free market would indeed abolish what I have previously called the hidden curriculum of present schooling—its age-specific attendance at a graded curriculum. Equally, a free market would at first give the appearance of counteracting what I have called the occult foundations of a schooled society: the "immigration syndrome," the institutional monopoly of teaching, and the ritual of linear initiation. But at the same time a free market in education would provide the alchemist with innumerable hidden hands to fit each man into the multiple, tight little niches a more complex technocracy can provide.

Many decades of reliance on schooling has turned knowledge into a commodity, a marketable staple of a special kind. Knowledge is now regarded simultaneously as a first necessity and also as society's most precious currency. (The transformation of knowledge into a commodity is reflected in a corresponding transformation of language. Words that formerly functioned as verbs are becoming nouns that designate possessions. Until recently dwelling and learning and even healing designated activities. They are now usually conceived as commodities or services to be delivered. We talk about the manufacture of housing or the delivery of medical care. Men are no longer regarded fit to house or heal themselves. In such a society people come to believe that professional services are more valuable than personal care. Instead of learning how to nurse grandmother, the teenager learns to picket the hospital that does not admit her.) This attitude could easily survive the disestablishment of school, just as affiliation with a church remained a condition for office long after the adoption of the First Amendment. It is even more evident that test batteries measuring complex knowledge-packages could easily survive the disestablishment of school—and with this would go the compulsion to obligate everybody to acquire a minimum package in the knowledge stock. The scientific measurement of each man's worth and the alchemic dream of each man's "educability to his full humanity" would finally coincide. Under the appearance of a "free" market, the global village would turn into an environmental womb where pedagogic therapists control the complex navel by which each man is nourished.

At present schools limit the teacher's competence to the classroom. They prevent him from claiming man's whole life as his domain. The demise of school will remove this restriction and give a semblance of legitimacy to the life-long pedagogical invasion of everybody's privacy. It will open the way for a scramble for "knowledge" on a free market, which would lead us toward the paradox of a vulgar, albeit seemingly egalitarian, meritocracy. Unless the

concept of knowledge is transformed, the disestablishment
of school will lead to a wedding between a growing
meritocratic system that separates learning from certification and a society committed to provide therapy for each
man until he is ripe for the gilded age.

For those who subscribe to the technocratic ethos,
whatever is technically possible must be made available at
least to a few whether they want it or not. Neither the
privation nor the frustration of the majority counts. If
cobalt treatment is possible, then the city of Tegucigalpa
needs one apparatus in each of its two major hospitals, at a
cost that would free an important part of the population
of Honduras from parasites. If supersonic speeds are
possible, then it must speed the travel of some. If the flight
to Mars can be conceived, then a rationale must be found
to make it appear a necessity. In the technocratic ethos
poverty is modernized: Not only are old alternatives closed
off by new monopolies, but the lack of necessities is also
compounded by a growing spread between those services
that are technologically feasible and those that are in fact
available to the majority.

A teacher turns "educator" when he adopts this
technocratic ethos. He then acts as if education were a
technological enterprise designed to make man fit into
whatever environment the "progress" of science creates.
He seems blind to the evidence that constant obsolescence
of all commodities comes at a high price: the mounting
cost of training people to know about them. He seems to
forget that the rising cost of tools is purchased at a high
price in education: They decrease the labor intensity of
the economy, make learning on the job impossible or, at
best, a privilege for a few. All over the world the cost of
educating men for society rises faster than the productivity
of the entire economy, and fewer people have a sense of
intelligent participation in the commonweal.

A revolution against those forms of privilege and power,

which are based on claims to professional knowledge, must start with a transformation of consciousness about the nature of learning. This means, above all, a shift of responsibility for teaching and learning. Knowledge can be defined as a commodity only as long as it is viewed as the result of institutional enterprise or as the fulfillment of institutional objectives. Only when a man recovers the sense of personal responsibility for what he learns and teaches can this spell be broken and the alienation of learning from living be overcome.

The recovery of the power to learn or to teach means that the teacher who takes the risk of interfering in somebody else's private affairs also assumes responsibility for the results. Similarly, the student who exposes himself to the influence of a teacher must take responsibility for his own education. For such purposes educational institutions—if they are at all needed—ideally take the form of facility centers where one can get a roof of the right size over his head, access to a piano or a kiln, and to records, books or slides. Schools, TV stations, theaters and the like are designed primarily for use by professionals. Deschooling society means above all the denial of professional status for the second-oldest profession, namely teaching. The certification of teachers now constitutes an undue restriction of the right to free speech: the corporate structure and professional pretensions of journalism an undue restriction on the right to free press. Compulsory attendance rules interfere with free assembly. The deschooling of society is nothing less than a cultural mutation by which a people recovers the effective use of its Constitutional freedoms: learning and teaching by men who know that they are born free rather than treated to freedom. Most people learn most of the time when they do whatever they enjoy; most people are curious and want to give meaning to whatever they come in contact with; and most people are capable of personal intimate intercourse with others unless they are stupefied by inhuman work or turned off by schooling.

The fact that people in rich countries do not learn much on their own constitutes no proof to the contrary. Rather it is a consequence of life in an environment from which, paradoxically, they cannot learn much, precisely because it is so highly programed. They are constantly frustrated by the structure of contemporary society in which the facts on which decisions can be made have become elusive. They live in an environment in which tools that can be used for creative purposes have become luxuries, an environment in which channels of communication serve a few to talk to many.

A modern myth would make us believe that the sense of impotence with which most men live today is a consequence of technology that cannot but create huge systems. But it is not technology that makes systems huge, tools immensely powerful, channels of communication one-directional. Quite the contrary: Properly controlled, technology could provide each man with the ability to understand his environment better, to shape it powerfully with his own hands, and to permit him full intercommunication to a degree never before possible. Such an alternative use of technology constitutes the central alternative in education.

If a person is to grow up he needs, first of all, access to things, to places and to processes, to events and to records. He needs to see, to touch, to tinker with, to grasp whatever there is in a meaningful setting. This access is now largely denied. When knowledge became a commodity, it acquired the protections of private property, and thus a principle designed to guard personal intimacy became a rationale for declaring facts off limits for people without the proper credentials. In schools teachers keep knowledge to themselves unless it fits into the day's program. The media inform, but exclude those things they regard as unfit to print. Information is locked into special languages, and specialized teachers live off its retranslation. Patents are protected by corporations, secrets are guarded by bureaucracies, and the power to keep others out of private preserves—be they cockpits, law offices, junkyards or clinics—is jealously guarded by professions, institutions and nations. Neither the political nor the professional structure of our societies, East and West, could withstand the elimination of the power to keep entire classes of people from facts that could serve them. The access to facts that I advocate goes far beyond truth in labeling. Access must be built into reality, while all we ask from advertising is a guarantee that it does not mislead. Access to reality constitutes a fundamental alternative in education to a system that only purports to teach *about* it.

Abolishing the right to corporate secrecy—even when professional opinion holds that this secrecy serves the common good—is, as shall presently appear, a much more radical political goal than the traditional demand for public ownership or control of the tools of production. The socialization of tools without the effective socialization of know-how in their use tends to put the knowledge-capitalist into the position formerly held by the financier. The technocrat's only claim to power is the stock he holds in some class of scarce and secret knowledge, and the best means to protect its value is a large and capital-intensive organization that renders access to know-how formidable and forbidding.

It does not take much time for the interested learner to acquire almost any skill that he wants to use. We tend to forget this in a society where professional teachers monopolize entrance into all fields, and thereby stamp teaching by uncertified individuals as quackery. There are few mechanical skills used in industry or research that are as demanding, complex and dangerous as driving cars, a skill that most people quickly acquire from a peer. Not all people are suited for advanced logic, yet those who are make rapid progress if they are challenged to play mathematical games at an early age. One out of 20 kids in Cuernavaca can beat me at Wiff 'n' Proof after a couple of weeks' training. In four months all but a small percentage of motivated adults at our CIDOC center learn Spanish well enough to conduct academic business in the new language.

A first step toward opening up access to skills would be to provide various incentives for skilled individuals to share their knowledge. Inevitably, this would run counter to the interest of guilds and professions and unions. Yet, multiple apprenticeship is attractive: It provides everybody with an opportunity to learn something about almost anything. There is no reason why a person should not combine the ability to drive a car, repair telephones and toilets, act as a midwife and function as an architectural draftsman. Special-interest groups and their disciplined consumers would, of course, claim that the public needs the protection of a professional guarantee. But this argument is now steadily being challenged by consumer protection associations. We have to take much more seriously the objection that economists raise to the radical socialization of skills: that "progress" will be impeded if knowledge— patents, skills and all the rest—is democratized. Their argument can be faced only if we demonstrate to them the growth rate of futile diseconomies generated by any existing educational system.

Access to people willing to share their skills is no guarantee of learning. Such access is restricted not only by the monopoly of educational programs over learning and of unions over licensing but also by a technology of scarcity. The skills that count today are know-how in the use of highly specialized tools that were designed to be scarce. These tools produce goods or render services that everybody wants but only a few can enjoy, and which only a limited number of people know how to use. Only a few privileged individuals out of the total number of people who have a given disease ever benefit from the results of sophisticated medical technology, and even fewer doctors develop the skill to use it.

The same results of medical research have, however, also been employed to create a basic medical tool kit that permits Army and Navy medics, with only a few months of training, to obtain results, under battlefield conditions, that would have been beyond the expectations of full-fledged doctors during World War II. On an even simpler level any peasant girl could learn how to diagnose and treat most infections if medical scientists prepared dosages and instructions specifically for a given geographic area.

All these examples illustrate the fact that educational considerations alone suffice to demand a radical reduction of the professional structure that now impedes the mutual relationship between the scientist and the majority of people who want access to science. If this demand were heeded, all men could learn to use yesterday's tools, rendered more effective and durable by modern science, to create tomorrow's world.

Unfortunately, precisely the contrary trend prevails at present. I know a coastal area in South America where most people support themselves by fishing from small boats. The outboard motor is certainly the tool that has changed most dramatically the lives of these coastal fishermen. But in the area I have surveyed, half of all outboard motors that were purchased between 1945 and 1950 are still kept running by constant tinkering, while half the motors purchased in 1965 no longer run because they were not built to be repaired. Technological progress provides the majority of people with gadgets they cannot afford and deprives them of the simpler tools they need.

Metals, plastics and ferro cement used in building have greatly improved since the 1940s and ought to provide more people the opportunity to create their own homes. But while in the United States, in 1948, more than 30 percent of all one-family homes were owner-built, by the end of the 1960s the percentage of those who acted as their own contractors had dropped to less than 20 percent. The lowering of the skill level through so-called economic development becomes even more visible in Latin America. Here most people still build their own homes from floor to roof. Often they use mud, in the form of adobe, and thatchwork of unsurpassed utility in the moist, hot and windy climate. In other places they make their dwellings out of cardboard, oil drums and other industrial refuse. Instead of providing people with simple tools and highly standardized, durable and easily repaired components, all governments have gone in for the mass production of low-cost buildings. It is clear that not one single country can afford to provide satisfactory modern dwelling units for the majority of its people. Yet, everywhere this policy makes it progressively more difficult for the majority to acquire the knowledge and skills they need to build better houses for themselves.

Educational considerations permit us to formulate a second fundamental characteristic that any post-industrial society must possess: a basic tool kit that by its very nature counteracts technocratic control. For educational reasons we must work toward a society in which scientific knowledge is incorporated in tools and components that can be used meaningfully in units small enough to be within the reach of all. Only such tools can socialize access to skills. Only such tools favor temporary associations among those who want to use them for a specific occasion. Only such tools allow specific goals to emerge in the process of their use, as any tinkerer knows. Only the combination of guaranteed access to facts and of limited power in most tools renders it possible to envisage a subsistence economy capable of incorporating the fruits of modern science.

The development of such a scientific subsistence economy is unquestionably to the advantage of the overwhelming majority of all people in poor countries. It is also the only alternative to progressive pollution, exploitation and opaqueness in rich countries. But, as we have seen, the dethroning of the GNP cannot be achieved without simultaneously subverting GNE (Gross National Education—usually conceived as manpower capitalization). An egalitarian economy cannot exist in a society in which the right to produce is conferred by schools.

The feasibility of modern subsistence economy does not depend on new scientific inventions. It depends primarily on the ability of a society to agree on fundamental self-chosen antibureaucratic and antitechnocratic restraints.

These restraints can take many forms, but they will not work unless they touch the basic dimensions of life. (The decision of Congress against development of the supersonic transport plane is one of the most encouraging steps in the right direction.) The substance of these voluntary social restraints would be very simple matters that can be fully understood and judged by any prudent man. The issues at stake in the SST controversy provide a good example. All such restraints would be chosen to promote stable and equal enjoyment of scientific know-how. The French say that it takes a thousand years to educate a peasant to deal with a cow. It would not take two generations to help all people in Latin America or Africa to use and repair outboard motors, simple cars, pumps, medicine kits and ferro cement machines if their design does not change every few years. And since a joyful life is one of constant meaningful intercourse with others in a meaningful environment, equal enjoyment does translate into equal education.

At present a consensus on austerity is difficult to imagine. The reason usually given for the impotence of the majority is stated in terms of political or economic class.

What is not usually understood is that the new class structure of a schooled society is even more powerfully controlled by vested interests. No doubt an imperialist and capitalist organization of society provides the social structure within which a minority can have disproportionate influence over the effective opinion of the majority. But in a technocratic society the power of a minority of knowledge capitalists can prevent the formation of true public opinion through control of scientific know-how and the media of communication. Constitutional guarantees of free speech, free press and free assembly were meant to ensure government by the people. Modern electronics, photo-offset presses, time-sharing computers and telephones have in principle provided the hardware that could give an entirely new meaning to these freedoms. Unfortunately, these things are used in modern media to increase the power of knowledge-bankers to funnel their program-packages through international chains to more people, instead of being used to increase true networks that provide equal opportunity for encounter among the members of the majority.

Deschooling the culture and social structure requires the use of technology to make participatory politics possible. Only on the basis of a majority coalition can limits to secrecy and growing power be determined without dictatorship. We need a new environment in which growing up can be classless, or we will get a brave new world in which Big Brother educates us all.

Contributors

Judith Areen is a fellow at the Center for the Study of Public Policy in Cambridge and instructor at Boston College School of Law.

Norman K. Denzin is associate professor of sociology at the University of Illinois, Urbana. He has conducted extensive partici-pant-observation studies of young children and is preparing a book on the subject entitled *Children, Society and Social Relationships*. He is author of *The Research Act* and editor of *The Values of Social Science*.

Mario D. Fantini is an urban education specialist with the Ford Foundation and co-author of *The Disadvantaged: Challenge to Education, Toward a Contact Curriculum*, and *Community Control and the Urban School*.

Paul Goodman is an author and critic of various facets of American society. He has written numerous books and articles on a variety of topics including education, poetry, fiction, literature, gestalt therapy and youth.

Charles V. Hamilton is professor of political science at Columbia

275

University. He is co-author of *Black Power* and has contributed articles to a number of journals including *Harvard Educational Review, Phylon* and *Journal of Negro Education.*

Ivan Illich is co-founder of the Center for Intercultural Documentation (CIDOC) in Cuernavaca, Mexico, and author of books and articles on education and Latin American Development. His most recent book is *Deschooling Society.*

Christopher Jencks is associate professor of education at Harvard Graduate School of Education, co-author of *The Academic Revolution* and contributor of numerous articles on education. He is also on the board of editors of *Education and Urban Society.*

S.M. Miller is a professor of urban studies (education and sociology), a director of the Urban Center and a senior fellow at the Center for International Studies—all at New York University. He is author or co-author of *The Future of Inequality, Social Class and Social Policy* and *Comparative Social Mobility.*

William C. Nelsen is program executive at the Danforth Foundation with a special interest in urban education and educational innovation.

Frank Riessman is professor of educational sociology and a director of the New Careers Development Center at New York University. Among his numerous books on education and poverty are *The Culturally Deprived Child, New Careers for the Poor, Up From Poverty* and *Strategies Against Poverty.*

Ray C. Rist is associate professor of sociology at Portland State University. He is editor of *Pornography in America* and author of articles on urban politics, urban education and Black Studies programs. His articles have appeared in such journals as the *Harvard Educational Review, Journal of Higher Education* and the *Journal of Reading.*

Norman E. Silberberg is director of research at Kenny Rehabilitation Institute in Minneapolis. He has been a school psychologist and conducted research in the areas of remedial reading, reading readiness and bookless programs.

Margaret C. Silberberg is psychological consultant with the Family Health Project at Lutheran Deaconness Hospital in Minneapolis. She has done research in the areas of reading readiness and reading abilities and directed the development of a bookless program in eleventh-grade humanities.

Bruno Stein is professor of economics and the associate director of the Institute of Labor Relations at New York University. He is author of *On Relief: The Economics of Poverty and Public Welfare* and a forthcoming book on wage controls.

Name and Title Index

adult education, role for, *see* recurrent education, need for

Barker, Roger G., 42, 44
Bennett, Lerone Jr., 159
bidialectalism in schools, need for, *see* schools, bidialectalism in
bilingualism in schools, *see* schools, bilingualism in
Black American English, use of in schools, *see* schools, bidialectalism in
black nationalist schools, role for, *see* racial separatism, role for in education
    See also private schools for black children

Coleman, James, 3, 145, 170
community control, *see* schools, community control of
compensatory education, 39, 52, 169-70
    See also Head Start
comprehensive community schools, need for, 163-5
compulsory attendance, *see* schools, compulsory attendance in
"culturally deprived," teaching the, 30-1, 51-2, 54, 102, 113, 117-8, 160
    See also low income child, teaching the